# DAY HIKES AROUND
# Los Angeles

## 135 GREAT HIKES

### Robert Stone

5th EDITION

**Day Hike Books, Inc.**
RED LODGE, MONTANA

Published by Day Hike Books, Inc.
P.O. Box 865
Red Lodge, Montana 59068
www.dayhikebooks.com

Distributed by The Globe Pequot Press
246 Goose Lane
P.O. Box 480
Guilford, CT 06437-0480
800-243-0495 (direct order) · 800-820-2329 (fax order)
www.globe-pequot.com

Front cover photograph by
Gary Valle: PhotographyontheRun.com

Back cover photograph by Roy Mata

Design by Paula Doherty

The author has made every attempt to provide accurate information in this book. However, trail routes and features may change—please use common sense and forethought, and be mindful of your own capabilities. Let this book guide you, but be aware that each hiker assumes responsibility for their own safety. The author and publisher do not assume any responsibility for loss, damage, or injury caused through the use of this book.

Cover photo:
Eagle Rock, Hike 58

Back cover photo:
Point Dume Natural Preserve, Hike 18

## ALSO BY ROBERT STONE

*Day Hikes On the California Central Coast*

*Day Hikes On the California Southern Coast*

*Day Hikes Around Sonoma County*

*Day Hikes Around Napa Valley*

*Day Hikes Around Big Sur*

*Day Hikes Around Monterey and Carmel*

*Day Hikes In San Luis Obispo County, California*

*Day Hikes Around Santa Barbara*

*Day Hikes Around Ventura County*

*Day Hikes Around Los Angeles*

*Day Hikes Around Orange County*

*Day Hikes In Sedona, Arizona*

*Day Hikes In Yosemite National Park*

*Day Hikes In Sequoia & Kings Canyon Nat'l. Parks*

*Day Hikes In Yellowstone National Park*

*Day Hikes In Grand Teton National Park*

*Day Hikes In the Beartooth Mountains*

*Day Hikes Around Bozeman, Montana*

*Day Hikes Around Missoula, Montana*

*Day Hikes On Oahu*

*Day Hikes On Maui*

*Day Hikes On Kauai*

*Day Hikes In Hawaii*

LINDA STONE

Hiking partner, Kofax

# Table of Contents

Hiking the Los Angeles Area. . . . . . . . . . . . . . . . . . . . . . . . . . . . . . . . . . . . . . . . . 11

Map of the Hikes . . . . . . . . . . . . . . . . . . . . . . . . . . . . . . . . . . . . . . . . . . . . . . . 14

## THE HIKES

### Santa Monica Mountains
### Point Mugu to Malibu Canyon

POINT MUGU to MALIBU CANYON MAP (Hikes 1—48). . . . . . . . . . . . . . . . . 16

POINT MUGU to DECKER ROAD (Hikes 1—15) . . . . . . . . . . . . . . . . . . . . . . . . 18

1. Chumash Trail—Mugu Peak Loop: Point Mugu State Park. . . . . . . . . . . . 20

2. La Jolla Valley Loop from La Jolla Canyon
   Point Mugu State Park. . . . . . . . . . . . . . . . . . . . . . . . . . . . . . . . . . . . . . . . 23

3. Scenic and Overlook Trails Loop: Point Mugu State Park . . . . . . . . . . . . 25

4. Old Boney Trail to Danielson Monument
   Boney Mountain State Wilderness • Point Mugu State Park. . . . . . . . . . . 27

5. Big Sycamore Canyon Trail: Point Mugu State Park . . . . . . . . . . . . . . . . . 30

6. Grotto Trail: Circle X Ranch. . . . . . . . . . . . . . . . . . . . . . . . . . . . . . . . . . . . . 33

7. Canyon View—Yerba Buena Road Loop: Circle X Ranch. . . . . . . . . . . . . 35

8. Sandstone Peak: Mishe Mokwa—Backbone Loop
   Circle X Ranch. . . . . . . . . . . . . . . . . . . . . . . . . . . . . . . . . . . . . . . . . . . . . . . . 36

9. White Horse Canyon Trail: Los Robles Trail System. . . . . . . . . . . . . . . . . 40

10. Triunfo Canyon Trail: Los Robles Trail System. . . . . . . . . . . . . . . . . . . . . .41

11. Yellow Hill Trail: Leo Carrillo State Park . . . . . . . . . . . . . . . . . . . . . . . . . . 44

12. Lower Arroyo Sequit Trail and Sequit Point
    Leo Carrillo State Park. . . . . . . . . . . . . . . . . . . . . . . . . . . . . . . . . . . . . . . . . 46

13. Nicholas Flat and Willow Creek Loop: Leo Carrillo State Park. . . . . . . . 48

14. Nicholas Flat : Leo Carrillo State Park. . . . . . . . . . . . . . . . . . . . . . . . . . . . . 50

15. Arroyo Sequit Park . . . . . . . . . . . . . . . . . . . . . . . . . . . . . . . . . . . . . . . . . . . . 52

16. Charmlee County Park. . . . . . . . . . . . . . . . . . . . . . . . . . . . . . . . . . . . . . . . . 54

17. El Matador, La Piedra and El Pescador State Beaches
    Robert H. Meyer Memorial State Beach. . . . . . . . . . . . . . . . . . . . . . . . . . . 56

18.  Point Dume Natural Preserve........................................ 59

ZUMA/TRANCAS CANYONS MAP (Hikes 19—22)........................ .61

19.  Zuma Loop Trail
     Zuma/Trancas Canyons: Lower Zuma Canyon...................... 62

20.  Ocean View—Canyon View Loop
     Zuma/Trancas Canyons: Lower Zuma Canyon...................... 64

21.  Newton Canyon Falls
     Zuma/Trancas Canyons: Upper Zuma Canyon..................... 66

22.  Newton Canyon: Zuma/Trancas Canyons · Castro Crest N.P.S......... 68

23.  Rocky Oaks Park...................................................... 70

24.  China Flat Trail: Cheeseboro/Palo Comado Canyons................. 72

25.  Palo Comado—Cheeseboro Canyons Loop
     Cheeseboro/Palo Comado Canyons ............................. 74

26.  Cheeseboro Canyon to Shepherds' Flat
     Cheeseboro/Palo Comado Canyons ............................. 76

27.  Canyon View—Cheesseboro Canyon Loop
     Cheeseboro/Palo Comado Canyons ............................. 78

28.  Cheeseboro Ridge—Cheeseboro Canyon Loop
     Cheeseboro/Palo Comado Canyons ............................. 80

29.  Chumash Trail: Rocky Peak Park ................................... 82

30.  Hummingbird Trail: Rocky Peak Park .............................. 84

31.  Rocky Peak Trail: Rocky Peak Park ............................... 86

32.  Corriganville Park.................................................. 88

SIMI VALLEY AREA MAP (Hikes 29—35) ............................... 90

33.  Old Stagecoach Trail............................................... .91

34.  Sage Ranch Park ................................................... 94

35.  Orcutt Ranch Horticulture Center ................................ 96

36.  Escondido Falls.................................................... 98

37.  Rising Sun—Solstice Canyon Loop: Solstice Canyon............... 100

38.  Sostomo—Deer Valley Loop: Solstice Canyon.................... 102

39.  Dry Canyon Trail to waterfall: Solstice Canyon.................... 104

40.  Corral Canyon Loop ............................................. 106

41.  Malibu Bluffs Recreation Area and Community Park............... 108

42.  Malibu Lagoon State Beach: Malibu Point........................ 110

43.  Peter Strauss Ranch .............................................. .112

MALIBU CREEK STATE PARK MAP (Hikes 44—48) . . . . . . . . . . . . . . . . . . . . . . . . 114

44. Paramount Ranch . . . . . . . . . . . . . . . . . . . . . . . . . . . . . . . . . . . . . . . . . . . . . . 116

45. Reagan Ranch: Malibu Creek State Park . . . . . . . . . . . . . . . . . . . . . . . . . .118

46. Rock Pool and Century Lake: Malibu Creek State Park . . . . . . . . . . . . . . 120

47. Liberty Canyon Natural Preserve
    Malibu Creek Natural Preserve . . . . . . . . . . . . . . . . . . . . . . . . . . . . . . . . . . . 122

48. Talepop Trail—Las Virgenes Loop: Malibu Creek State Park . . . . . . . . . 124

## Malibu Canyon to Beverly Hills

MALIBU CANYON to BEVERLY HILLS MAP (Hikes 49—75) . . . . . . . . . . . . . . . . . 126

49. Calabasas Peak . . . . . . . . . . . . . . . . . . . . . . . . . . . . . . . . . . . . . . . . . . . . . . . . 128

50. Red Rock Canyon . . . . . . . . . . . . . . . . . . . . . . . . . . . . . . . . . . . . . . . . . . . . . . 129

51. Cold Creek Trail: Cold Creek Preserve . . . . . . . . . . . . . . . . . . . . . . . . . . . . 132

52. Cold Creek Canyon Preserve . . . . . . . . . . . . . . . . . . . . . . . . . . . . . . . . . . . . 134

53. Topanga Fire Lookout
    Cold Creek Canyon Preserve . . . . . . . . . . . . . . . . . . . . . . . . . . . . . . . . . . . . 136

54. Summit Valley Trail: Edmund D. Edelman Park . . . . . . . . . . . . . . . . . . . . . 138

55. Woodland Ridge Trail: Serrania Park to Dirt Mulholland . . . . . . . . . . . . . 140

56. Caballero Canyon Loop
    Marvin Braude Mulholland Gateway Park . . . . . . . . . . . . . . . . . . . . . . . . . . 142

57. Dead Horse Trail: Topanga State Park . . . . . . . . . . . . . . . . . . . . . . . . . . . . . 144

58. Eagle Rock Loop: Topanga State Park . . . . . . . . . . . . . . . . . . . . . . . . . . . . . 145

59. Parker Mesa Overlook from Topanga State Park
    Topanga State Park . . . . . . . . . . . . . . . . . . . . . . . . . . . . . . . . . . . . . . . . . . . . . 148

60. Parker Mesa Overlook from Paseo Miramar
    Topanga State Park . . . . . . . . . . . . . . . . . . . . . . . . . . . . . . . . . . . . . . . . . . . . . 150

61. Santa Ynez Canyon Trail to Santa Ynez Waterfall
    Topanga State Park . . . . . . . . . . . . . . . . . . . . . . . . . . . . . . . . . . . . . . . . . . . . . 152

62. Temescal Canyon Loop: Topanga State Park . . . . . . . . . . . . . . . . . . . . . . . 154

TOPANGA STATE PARK MAP (Hikes 57—62) . . . . . . . . . . . . . . . . . . . . . . . . . . . 156

63. Inspiration Point
    Will Rogers State Historic Park . . . . . . . . . . . . . . . . . . . . . . . . . . . . . . . . . . . .157

64. Rustic Canyon Loop
    Will Rogers State Historic Park · Topanga State Park . . . . . . . . . . . . . . . . 159

65. Sullivan Canyon . . . . . . . . . . . . . . . . . . . . . . . . . . . . . . . . . . . . . . . . . . . . . . . 160

66. Sullivan Canyon—Westridge Fire Road Loop . . . . . . . . . . . . . . . . . . . . . . 162

67. San Vicente Mountain from Mulholland Scenic Overlook . . . . . . . . . . . 166

68. Getty View Trail. . . . . . . . . . . . . . . . . . . . . . . . . . . . . . . . . . . . . . . . . 168

69. Dixie Canyon Park: Barbara Asa—Dorian Trail. . . . . . . . . . . . . . . . . . . 170

70. Hastian—Discovery Loop: Lower Franklin Canyon Park . . . . . . . . . . . . 172

71. Franklin Canyon Lake Loop
    Upper Franklin Canyon Park. . . . . . . . . . . . . . . . . . . . . . . . . . . . . . . . . . 175

72. Blinderman Trail: Upper Franklin Canyon Park. . . . . . . . . . . . . . . . . . . 176

73. Coldwater Canyon Park—Wilacre Park Loop . . . . . . . . . . . . . . . . . . . . 180

74. Dearing Mountain Trail
    Fryman Canyon Park to TreePeople Park . . . . . . . . . . . . . . . . . . . . . . . 183

75. Fryman Canyon Loop
    Fryman Canyon Park • Cross Mountain Park System. . . . . . . . . . . . . . . . 184

## Hollywood Hills and Griffith Park

HOLLYWOOD HILLS and GRIFFITH PARK MAP (Hikes 76—87). . . . . . . . . . . . . . 188

76. Runyan Canyon Park. . . . . . . . . . . . . . . . . . . . . . . . . . . . . . . . . . . . . . . 190

77. Hollywood Reservoir . . . . . . . . . . . . . . . . . . . . . . . . . . . . . . . . . . . . . . . 192

GRIFFITH PARK TRAILS MAP (Hikes 78—87) . . . . . . . . . . . . . . . . . . . . . . . . . 194

78. Mount Lee and the "Hollywood" sign: Griffith Park. . . . . . . . . . . . . . . . 196

79. Bronson Caves: Griffith Park. . . . . . . . . . . . . . . . . . . . . . . . . . . . . . . . . . 198

80. Brush Canyon to Mount Bell: Griffith Park. . . . . . . . . . . . . . . . . . . . . . .200

81. Griffith Park Observatory to Ferndell Park: Griffith Park . . . . . . . . . . .202

82. Mount Hollywood and Dante's View: Griffith Park . . . . . . . . . . . . . . . .204

83. Bird Sanctuary Nature Trail: Griffith Park. . . . . . . . . . . . . . . . . . . . . . .206

84. Beacon Hill: Griffith Park . . . . . . . . . . . . . . . . . . . . . . . . . . . . . . . . . . . .208

85. Fern Canyon Nature Trail: Griffith Park. . . . . . . . . . . . . . . . . . . . . . . . . 210

86. Bee Rock and Old Zoo Park: Griffith Park . . . . . . . . . . . . . . . . . . . . . . . 212

87. Amir's Garden: Griffith Park . . . . . . . . . . . . . . . . . . . . . . . . . . . . . . . . . . 214

## San Gabriel Mountains and Verdugo Mountains

SAN GABRIEL MOUNTAINS MAP (Hikes 88—115) . . . . . . . . . . . . . . . . . . . . . . 216

88. East Canyon and Rice Canyon
    Santa Clarita Woodlands Park. . . . . . . . . . . . . . . . . . . . . . . . . . . . . . . . . 218

89. Placerita Canyon Trail
    Placerita Canyon State Park and Natural Area. . . . . . . . . . . . . . . . . . . . 221

90. Placerita Waterfall Trail
Placerita Canyon State Park and Natural Area. . . . . . . . . . . . . . . . . . . . . . 222

91. Los Pinetos Trail
Placerita Canyon State Park and Natural Area. . . . . . . . . . . . . . . . . . . . . 226

92. Stough Canyon Loop: Verdugo Mountains. . . . . . . . . . . . . . . . . . . . . . 230

93. Wildwood Canyon Trail to Wardens Grove
Verdugo Mountains: Wildwood Canyon Park . . . . . . . . . . . . . . . . . . . . 232

94. La Tuna Canyon Trail: Verdugo Mountains. . . . . . . . . . . . . . . . . . . . . 235

95. Trail Canyon Falls . . . . . . . . . . . . . . . . . . . . . . . . . . . . . . . . . . . . . . . . . 237

96. Haines Canyon . . . . . . . . . . . . . . . . . . . . . . . . . . . . . . . . . . . . . . . . . . . 240

97. Rim of the Valley Trail: Deukmejian Wilderness Park. . . . . . . . . . . . . . .241

98. Dunsmore Canyon—Le Mesnager Loop
Deukmejian Wilderness Park . . . . . . . . . . . . . . . . . . . . . . . . . . . . . . . . . 245

99. Cerro Negro (Black Hill): San Rafael Hills . . . . . . . . . . . . . . . . . . . . . . 248

100. Fall Creek Falls. . . . . . . . . . . . . . . . . . . . . . . . . . . . . . . . . . . . . . . . . . . . 250

101. Vetter Mountain Fire Lookout . . . . . . . . . . . . . . . . . . . . . . . . . . . . . . . . 252

102. Cooper Canyon Falls via Burkhart Trail . . . . . . . . . . . . . . . . . . . . . . . . 254

ARROYO SECO to MOUNT LOWE MAP (Hikes 103–109). . . . . . . . . . . . . . . . 256

103. Switzer Falls: Gabrielino National Recreation Trail . . . . . . . . . . . . . . . . 258

104. Mount Lowe Summit from Eaton Saddle. . . . . . . . . . . . . . . . . . . . . . . 261

105. Arroyo Seco Trail to Gould Mesa Campground
Gabrielino National Recreation Trail . . . . . . . . . . . . . . . . . . . . . . . . . . . 264

106. Echo Mountain via the Sam Merrill Trail . . . . . . . . . . . . . . . . . . . . . . . 267

107. Sunset Ridge Loop. . . . . . . . . . . . . . . . . . . . . . . . . . . . . . . . . . . . . . . . . 270

108. Brink of Millard Falls. . . . . . . . . . . . . . . . . . . . . . . . . . . . . . . . . . . . . . . .271

109. Base of Millard Falls. . . . . . . . . . . . . . . . . . . . . . . . . . . . . . . . . . . . . . . . 276

110. Eaton Canyon Falls
Eaton Canyon County Park and Natural Area . . . . . . . . . . . . . . . . . . . . 278

111. Mount Wilson Toll Road: Eaton Canyon to Henninger Flats
Eaton Canyon County Park and Natural Area . . . . . . . . . . . . . . . . . . . . 281

112. Sturtevant Falls: Santa Anita Canyon . . . . . . . . . . . . . . . . . . . . . . . . . . 284

113. Winter Creek Canyon to Hoegees Camp
Santa Anita Canyon · Winter Creek Canyon. . . . . . . . . . . . . . . . . . . . . . 288

114. Hermit Falls: Santa Anita Canyon. . . . . . . . . . . . . . . . . . . . . . . . . . . . . 291

115. Monrovia Canyon Falls: Monrovia Canyon Park . . . . . . . . . . . . . . . . . . 293

## Los Angeles Basin Coastline
### Santa Monica to Marina Del Rey

SANTA MONICA TO MARINA DEL REY MAP (Hikes 116–121) . . . . . . . . . . . . . 296

116. Palisades Park and Santa Monica Pier . . . . . . . . . . . . . . . . . . . . . . . . . . . . 298

117. Santa Monica Pier to Venice Beach. . . . . . . . . . . . . . . . . . . . . . . . . . . . . .300

118. Venice Beach. . . . . . . . . . . . . . . . . . . . . . . . . . . . . . . . . . . . . . . . . . . . . .302

119. The Venice Canals . . . . . . . . . . . . . . . . . . . . . . . . . . . . . . . . . . . . . . . . . . 303

120. Ballona Lagoon Marine Preserve
     Grand Canal to Marina Del Rey Harbor Channel. . . . . . . . . . . . . . . . . . . .306

121. Del Rey Lagoon and Ballona Creek. . . . . . . . . . . . . . . . . . . . . . . . . . . . . . 307

### Palos Verdes Peninsula
### Torrance to Long Beach

PALOS VERDES PENINSULA to LONG BEACH MAP (Hikes 122–135) . . . . . . . . 310

122. The Strand: Manhattan, Hermosa and Redondo Beaches . . . . . . . . . . . . 312

123. Malaga Cove and Flat Rock Point . . . . . . . . . . . . . . . . . . . . . . . . . . . . . . . 314

124. Bluff Cove to Lunada Bay. . . . . . . . . . . . . . . . . . . . . . . . . . . . . . . . . . . . . 316

125. Paseo Del Mar Bluffs
     Palos Verdes Estates Shoreline Preserve. . . . . . . . . . . . . . . . . . . . . . . . . 318

126. Point Vicente Fishing Access Trail
     to Point Vicente and Long Point. . . . . . . . . . . . . . . . . . . . . . . . . . . . . . . .320

127. Long Point (Marineland). . . . . . . . . . . . . . . . . . . . . . . . . . . . . . . . . . . . . . 322

128. Abalone Cove and Portuguese Point . . . . . . . . . . . . . . . . . . . . . . . . . . . . 324

129. Crenshaw Extension Trail and Portuguese Bend Overlook . . . . . . . . . . 326

130. South Coast Botanic Garden. . . . . . . . . . . . . . . . . . . . . . . . . . . . . . . . . . . 328

131. White Point and Point Fermin Park . . . . . . . . . . . . . . . . . . . . . . . . . . . . . 330

132. Sunken City . . . . . . . . . . . . . . . . . . . . . . . . . . . . . . . . . . . . . . . . . . . . . . . . 332

133. Long Beach Oceanfront Trail: Long Beach City Beach . . . . . . . . . . . . . . 334

134. Belmont Pier to Alamitos Bay Channel: Long Beach City Beach . . . . . . . 337

135. El Dorado Nature Center: El Dorado Park . . . . . . . . . . . . . . . . . . . . . . . . .340

Companion Guides . . . . . . . . . . . . . . . . . . . . . . . . . . . . . . . . . . . . . . . . . . . . . . 344

Index. . . . . . . . . . . . . . . . . . . . . . . . . . . . . . . . . . . . . . . . . . . . . . . . . . . . . . . . . . 347

# Hiking the Los Angeles area

Despite the imminent presence of the Los Angeles metropolis, there are thousands of acres of natural, undeveloped land with countless out-of-the-way hiking trails. *Day Hikes Around Los Angeles* includes 135 day hikes within a 50-mile radius of the city, providing access to the area's cherished green space. Most hikes are found on local, state, and national land; wilderness areas; in the expansive Santa Monica Mountains National Recreation Area; and within the San Gabriel Mountain Range. The large number of trails provide an excellent cross section of scenery and difficulty levels, ranging from coastal beach walks to steep canyon climbs with far-reaching views.

All of these hikes can be completed within a day. A quick glance at the hikes' summaries will allow you to choose a hike that is appropriate to your ability and intentions. An overall map on page 14 identifies the general locations of the hikes and major roads. Several other regional maps (underlined in the table of contents), as well as maps for each hike, provide the essential details. The Thomas Guide, or other comparable street guide, is essential for navigating through the urban areas. Other relevant maps are listed under the hikes' statistics if you wish to explore more of the area.

A few basic necessities will make your hike more pleasurable. Wear supportive, comfortable hiking shoes and layered clothing. Take along hats, sunscreen, sunglasses, drinking water, snacks, and appropriate outerwear. Bring swimwear and outdoor gear if heading to the beaches. Ticks may be prolific and poison oak flourishes in the canyons and shady moist areas. Exercise caution by using insect repellent and staying on the trails.

Use good judgement about your capabilities—reference the hiking statistics for an approximation of difficulty and allow extra time for exploration.

---

The National Forest Adventure Pass is a parking permit issued and required by the U.S. Forest Service for a fee. Adventure Passes are required in the Angeles National Forest, Los Padres National Forest, Cleveland National Forest, and San Bernardino National Forest. Nearly all of the hikes in the San Gabriel Mountains section of this book will require the pass, which needs to be displayed in the vehicles. The daily or annual Adventure Passes can either be purchased online, at any Forest Service facility, or at various local outdoor shops and sporting goods stores.

## Coastal Region of the Santa Monica Mountains
## Point Mugu to Santa Monica

Hikes 1—75 are found along the Pacific Coast and among the foot-hills, canyons, and peaks of the Santa Monica Mountains. This range extends roughly 50 miles east and west parallel to the coast, from downtown Los Angeles to Point Mugu. The mountains are 8—12 miles wide and lie along the San Andreas Fault. Elevations range from sea level to 3,111 feet at Sandstone Peak.

The trails meander along the coastal foothills, traverse peaks and ridges, and drop down across the northern side of the range facing into the rolling landscape of interior California. Highlights of the hikes include panoramic views from the ocean to the city, unusual geo-logical formations and rock outcroppings, waterfalls, cliff overlooks, ridge walks, canyons, old ranch roads (including Ronald Reagan's ranch), filming locations, and shady retreats. Many state parks have been established in this region, including the expansive Point Mugu, Malibu Creek, and Topanga State Parks. Beaches and coastal communi-ties are scattered along the Pacific Coast Highway (Highway 1), the access road to most of these hikes.

The mountain's best known trail is the Backbone Trail. It extends approximately 64 miles across ridges and canyons on a nearly con-tinuous trail, linking the Santa Monica Mountains from east to west. Several hikes include segments of this trail.

### Hollywood Hills and Griffith Park

Hollywood Hills and Griffith Park sit at the east end of the Santa Monica Mountain Range. Twelve hikes (76—87) are located in this area, just minutes from downtown Los Angeles. Griffith Park, the largest munici-pal park in the United States, has both tourist attractions and solitary retreats within its 4,100 acres. The rugged urban wilderness contains a 53-mile network of hiking and equestrian trails through semi-arid foothills, oak groves, and wooded glens. The mountains and steep interior canyons of the Hollywood Hills are largely undeveloped and offer a haven for humans and animals in the midst of Los Angeles.

Highlights of these hikes include overlooks of the city, secluded canyons, gardens, the Hollywood Reservoir, Griffith Park Observatory and Planetarium, a 1926 merry-go-round, and a hike up to the famous "HOLLYWOOD" sign. Several other local attractions are within easy access, such as the Los Angeles Zoo, Gene Autry Western Heritage Museum, Travel Town Museum, and five golf courses.

## San Gabriel Mountains and Verdugo Mountains

The San Gabriel Mountains are at the northern end of Los Angeles County. The range lies between the Los Angeles basin to the south and the Mojave Desert to the north. The highest peak is over 10,000 feet in elevation. The Verdugo Mountains are a small off-shoot range along the western end of the San Gabriels. Hikes 88—115 are located in these surprisingly remote and rugged mountains. Many of the hikes lead up stream-fed, wooded canyons to waterfalls. Fire roads and old wagon routes are often utilized to access overlooks with magnificent vistas of the greater Los Angeles area and coastline.

## Los Angeles Basin Coastline:
## Santa Monica to Marina Del Rey

Hikes 116—121 explore the metropolitan oceanfront and its interesting culture along Santa Monica Bay. A continuous series of oceanside paths and boardwalks connect the beaches, from Santa Monica to Marina Del Rey. Well-known Venice Beach and the Venice Canals are located here.

## Palos Verdes Peninsula: Torrance to Long Beach

Hikes 122—135 are scattered along the coast of the Palos Verdes Peninsula and San Pedro Bay at the southernmost point of Los Angeles County. This geographically interesting area includes ocean-side cliffs, beaches, coves, grassy bluffs, actively slipping landslides, and some of the best tidepools in the area. A beautiful lighthouse sits at the tip of Point Fermin. Sunken City, also at Point Fermin, is a surreal uninhabited landscape of house foundations and chimneys that continue to slide closer to the ocean.

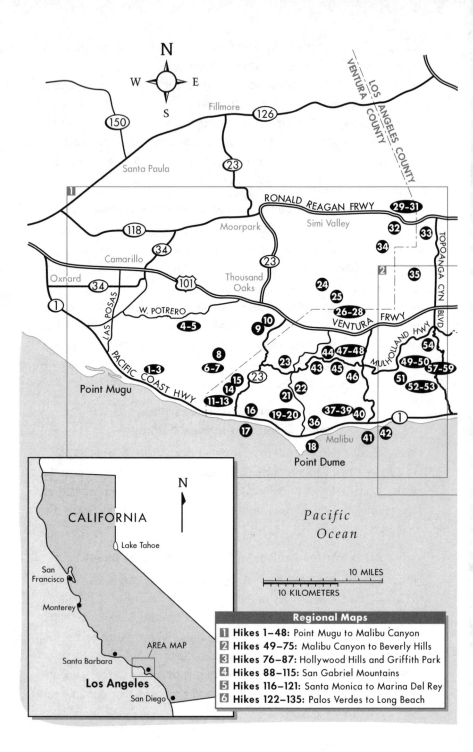

N
W E
S

Fillmore
150
126

Santa Paula

23

LOS ANGELES COUNTY
VENTURA COUNTY

118
Moorpark
RONALD REAGAN FRWY
Simi Valley
29-31
32
33
34
34
Camarillo
Oxnard
34
101
Thousand
Oaks
2
35
1
LAS POSAS
W. POTRERO
24
25
26-28
VENTURA FRWY
TOPOANGA CYN BLVD
MULHOLLAND HWY
54
PACIFIC COAST HWY
4-5
9 10
49-50
57-59
8
6-7
44 47-48
51
52-53
1-3
23
43 45
46
Point Mugu
15
14
23
22
11-13
21
16
19-20
37-39
40
17
36
1
18
Malibu
41 42
Point Dume

Pacific
Ocean

CALIFORNIA
N

Lake Tahoe

San
Francisco

Monterey

AREA MAP

Santa Barbara

Los Angeles

San Diego

10 MILES
10 KILOMETERS

### Regional Maps

1 **Hikes 1–48:** Point Mugu to Malibu Canyon
2 **Hikes 49–75:** Malibu Canyon to Beverly Hills
3 **Hikes 76–87:** Hollywood Hills and Griffith Park
4 **Hikes 88–115:** San Gabriel Mountains
5 **Hikes 116–121:** Santa Monica to Marina Del Rey
6 **Hikes 122–135:** Palos Verdes to Long Beach

# MAP of the HIKES
## LOS ANGELES and VICINITY

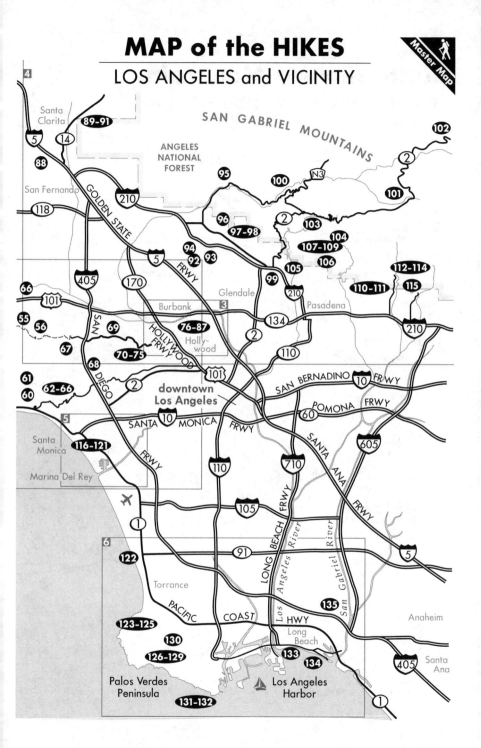

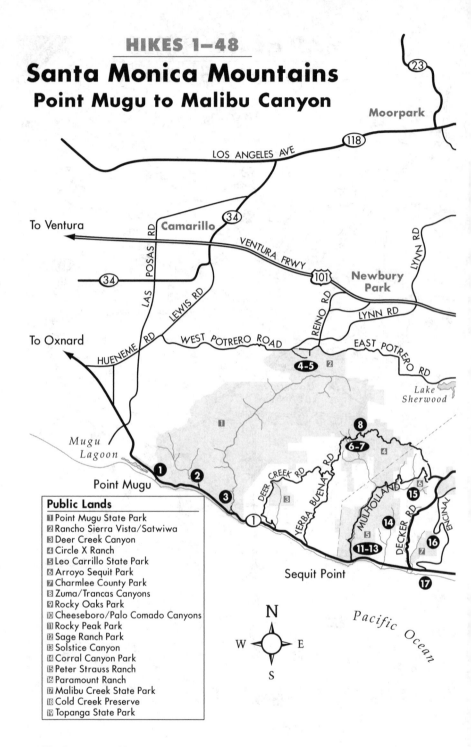

# HIKES 1–48
# Santa Monica Mountains
## Point Mugu to Malibu Canyon

Moorpark

23

LOS ANGELES AVE

118

To Ventura

LAS POSAS RD

Camarillo

34

VENTURA FRWY

101

Newbury Park

LYNN RD

34

LEWIS RD

REINO RD

LYNN RD

To Oxnard

HUENEME RD

WEST POTRERO ROAD

EAST POTRERO RD

Lake Sherwood

4-5    2

Mugu Lagoon

1

Point Mugu

1    2

3

DEER CREEK RD

YERBA BUENA RD

3

8

6-7    4

MULHOLLAND

15

14

DECKER RD

ENCINAL

5

11-13

16

7

Sequit Point

17

**Public Lands**
1 Point Mugu State Park
2 Rancho Sierra Vista/Satwiwa
3 Deer Creek Canyon
4 Circle X Ranch
5 Leo Carrillo State Park
6 Arroyo Sequit Park
7 Charmlee County Park
8 Zuma/Trancas Canyons
9 Rocky Oaks Park
10 Cheeseboro/Palo Comado Canyons
11 Rocky Peak Park
12 Sage Ranch Park
13 Solstice Canyon
14 Corral Canyon Park
15 Peter Strauss Ranch
16 Paramount Ranch
17 Malibu Creek State Park
18 Cold Creek Preserve
19 Topanga State Park

N
W    E
S

Pacific Ocean

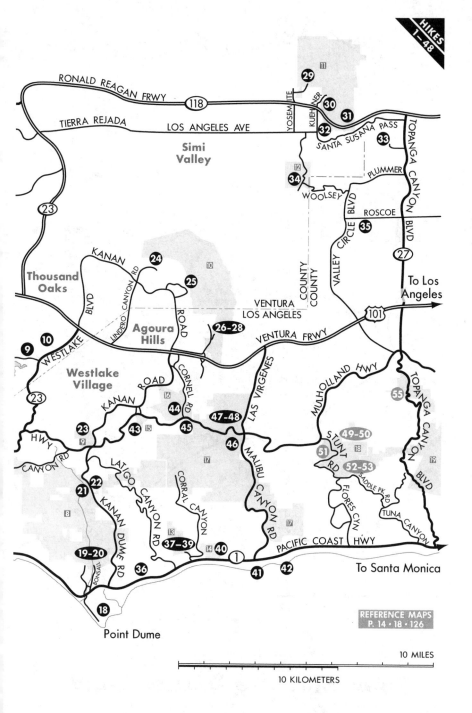

RONALD REAGAN FRWY

118

TIERRA REJADA

LOS ANGELES AVE

Simi
Valley

YOSEMITE

KUEHNER

29

11

30

31

32

SANTA SUSANA PASS

33

TOPANGA CANYON BLVD

12

34

WOOLSEY

PLUMMER

VALLEY CIRCLE BLVD

ROSCOE

35

23

KANAN BLVD

24

10

25

LINDERO CANYON RD

VENTURA
LOS ANGELES

COUNTY
COUNTY

27

To Los
Angeles

Thousand
Oaks

ROAD

Agoura
Hills

26-28

VENTURA FRWY

101

10

9

23

WESTLAKE

Westlake
Village

ROAD

KANAN

CORNEL RD

16

44

45

47-48

LAS VIRGENES

MULHOLLAND HWY

55

TOPANGA CANYON BLVD

HWY

23

CANYON RD

9

43

15

46

STUNT RD

49-50

18

51

52-53

19

22

21

LATIGO CANYON RD

KANAN DUME RD

17

CORRAL CANYON RD

MALIBU CANYON RD

FLORES CYN

SADDLE PK RD

TUNA CANYON

8

13

37-39

14

40

17

PACIFIC COAST HWY

19-20

TINSONG

36

1

41

42

To Santa Monica

18

Point Dume

10 MILES

10 KILOMETERS

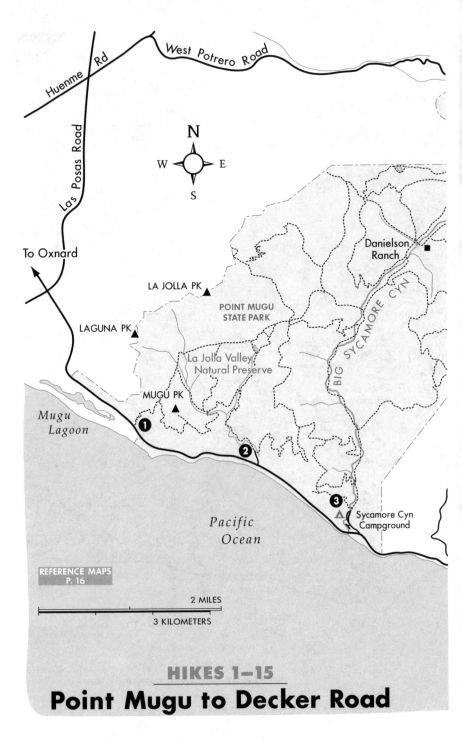

**HIKES 1–15**

# Point Mugu to Decker Road

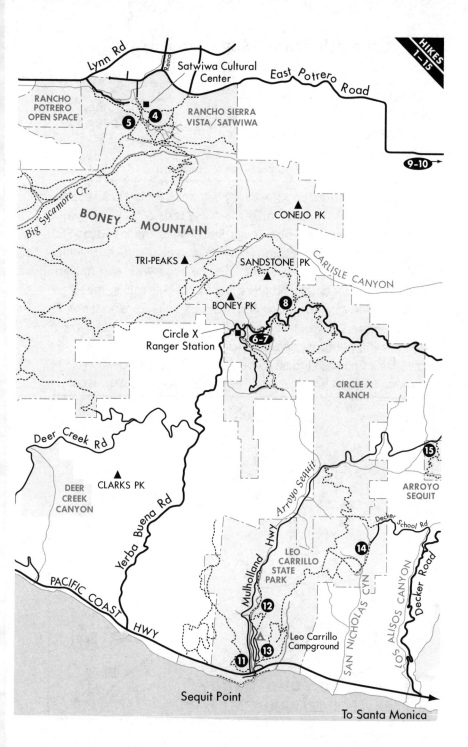

Lynn Rd

Reino

Satwiwa Cultural
Center

East Potrero Road

**RANCHO
POTRERO
OPEN SPACE**

**5**

**4**

**RANCHO SIERRA
VISTA/SATWIWA**

**9-10**

*Big Sycamore Cr.*

**BONEY** **MOUNTAIN**

▲ **CONEJO PK**

CARLISLE CANYON

**TRI-PEAKS** ▲

**SANDSTONE PK**
▲

▲
**BONEY PK**

**8**

Circle X
Ranger Station

**6-7**

**CIRCLE X
RANCH**

Deer Creek Rd

▲ **CLARKS PK**

**DEER
CREEK
CANYON**

**15**

**ARROYO
SEQUIT**

*Arroyo Sequit*

Decker School Rd

Yerba Buena Rd

Mulholland Hwy

**14**

**LEO
CARRILLO
STATE
PARK**

SAN NICHOLAS CYN

LOS ALISOS CANYON

Decker Road

**PACIFIC COAST**

**12**

**13**

Leo Carrillo
Campground

**HWY**

**11**

Sequit Point

To Santa Monica

# 1. Chumash Trail—Mugu Peak Loop
## POINT MUGU STATE PARK

**Hiking distance:** 4.5-mile loop
**Hiking time:** 2.5 hours
**Elevation gain:** 1,100 feet
**Maps:** U.S.G.S. Point Mugu
      Santa Monica Mountains West Trail Map

map
page 22

**Summary of hike:** La Jolla Valley Natural Preserve is an expansive high-mountain valley at the far western end of the Santa Monica Mountains in Point Mugu State Park. The oak-studded grassland rests 800 feet above the ocean at the foot of Mugu Peak. The high ridges of Laguna Peak, La Jolla Peak, and the serrated Boney Mountain ridgeline surround the rolling meadow. La Jolla Valley can be accessed from La Jolla Canyon (Hike 2), Big Sycamore Canyon (Hike 5), and the Chumash Trail (this hike), which is the steepest and most direct route. For centuries, this trail was a Chumash Indian route connecting their coastal village at Mugu Lagoon with La Jolla Valley. This hike steeply ascends

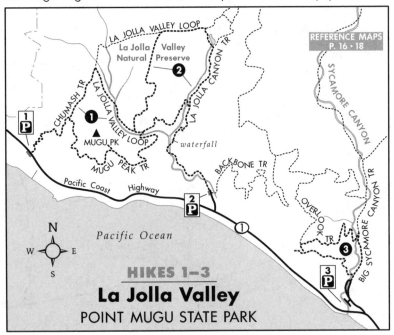

the coastal slope on the west flank of Mugu Peak. The elevated Mugu Peak Trail circles the mountain slope below the twin peaks, offering sweeping mountain-to-coast vistas. A side path leads to the grassy summit

**Driving directions:** From Santa Monica, drive 35 miles northbound on the Pacific Coast Highway/Highway 1 to the large parking pullout on the right, across from the Navy Rifle Range and Mugu Lagoon. (The trailhead parking area is 16.8 miles past Kanan Dume Road in Malibu and 3.5 miles west of the well-marked Sycamore Canyon.)

Heading southbound on the Pacific Coast Highway/Highway 1 from Las Posas Road in southeast Oxnard, drive 2.3 miles to the parking area on the left by the posted trailhead.

**Hiking directions:** Begin climbing up the hillside covered in chaparral and cactus, gaining elevation with every step. At a half mile, the trail temporarily levels out on a plateau with sweeping coastal views that include the Channel Islands. The steadily ascending trail gains 900 feet in 0.7 miles to a T-junction on a saddle. Begin the loop to the left, crossing over the saddle into the vast La Jolla Valley. The valley is surrounded by rounded mountain peaks, the jagged Boney Mountain ridge, and the surrealistic Navy radar towers by Laguna Peak. Cross the open expanse to a posted junction with the La Jolla Valley Loop Trail at 1.2 miles. Take the right fork and head southeast across the meadow on a slight downward slope. Drop into an oak woodland and cross a stream. Parallel the stream through a small draw to another junction. Take the right fork 100 yards to a path on the right by an old circular metal tank. Bear right on the Mugu Peak Trail and cross the creek. Traverse the hillside to the west edge of La Jolla Canyon. Follow the ridge south on the oceanfront cliffs. Wind along the south flank of Mugu Peak, following the contours of the mountain to a trail split on a saddle between the mountain's double peaks. The right fork ascends the rounded grassy summit. Veer left, hiking along the steep hillside to the west side of the peak. Cross another saddle and complete the loop. Return down the mountain to the trailhead. ■

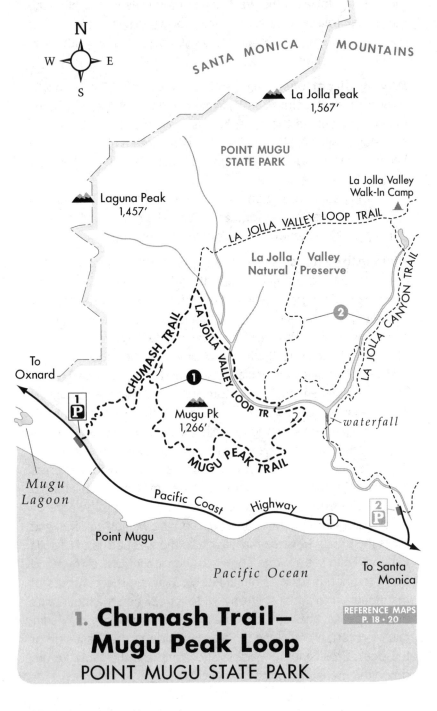

N
W · E
S

SANTA MONICA MOUNTAINS

La Jolla Peak
1,567'

POINT MUGU
STATE PARK

La Jolla Valley
Walk-In Camp

Laguna Peak
1,457'

LA JOLLA VALLEY LOOP TRAIL

La Jolla Valley
Natural Preserve

CHUMASH TRAIL

LA JOLLA VALLEY LOOP TR

LA JOLLA CANYON TRAIL

To
Oxnard

**1**

Mugu Pk
1,266'

**2**

*waterfall*

MUGU PEAK TRAIL

*Mugu
Lagoon*

Pacific Coast Highway ①

**1 P**

**2 P**

Point Mugu

To Santa
Monica

*Pacific Ocean*

## 1. **Chumash Trail–
Mugu Peak Loop**
### POINT MUGU STATE PARK

REFERENCE MAPS
P. 18 · 20

# 2. La Jolla Valley Loop from La Jolla Canyon

## POINT MUGU STATE PARK

**Hiking distance:** 6-mile loop
**Hiking time:** 3 hours
**Elevation gain:** 750 feet
**Maps:** U.S.G.S. Point Mugu
       Tom Harrison Maps: Point Mugu State Park Trail Map
       Santa Monica Mountains West Trail Map

**map page 24**

**Summary of hike:** La Jolla Canyon is a narrow, steep gorge with a perennial stream and a 15-foot waterfall. The canyon leads up to La Jolla Valley Natural Preserve in Point Mugu State Park. The preserve sits at an 800-foot elevation in a broad valley with rolling grasslands at the west end of the Santa Monica Mountains. Mugu Peak, La Jolla Peak, and Laguna Peak surround the oak-dotted meadow. This hike climbs through the rock-walled canyon and loops around the meadow to a coastal overlook and a pond with a picnic area.

**Driving directions:** From Santa Monica, drive 33 miles northbound on the Pacific Coast Highway/ Highway 1 to the posted La Jolla Canyon entrance on the right. (The trailhead entrance is 15 miles past Kanan Dume Road in Malibu and 1.6 miles west of the well-marked Sycamore Canyon.)

Heading southbound on the Pacific Coast Highway/ Highway 1 from Las Posas Road in southeast Oxnard, drive 4.2 miles to the entrance on the left.

**Hiking directions:** From the north end of the parking lot, at the Ray Miller Trailhead, take the La Jolla Canyon Trail north. Follow the wide path up the canyon, crossing the stream several times. The third crossing is just below a beautiful 15-foot waterfall and a pool surrounded by large boulders. Natural rock steps lead up to the top of the falls. Continue along the east side of the canyon, passing large sandstone rocks and caves. At a gorge, the trail sharply doubles back to the right, leading up the side of the canyon. At 1.2 miles, take the left fork towards Mugu Peak. Cross the stream and head southwest to a ridge above La Jolla Canyon and the ocean. The trail levels out and passes two trail junctions with the Hike 1 loop. Stay to the right both times, heading north across the rolling grassland. At 2.7 miles the trail joins the wide La Jolla Valley Loop Trail—head to the right. As you near the mountains of La Jolla Canyon, take the first cutoff trail to the right, leading past the pond and rejoining the La Jolla Canyon Trail. Head to the right, and go two miles down canyon, returning to the trailhead. ■

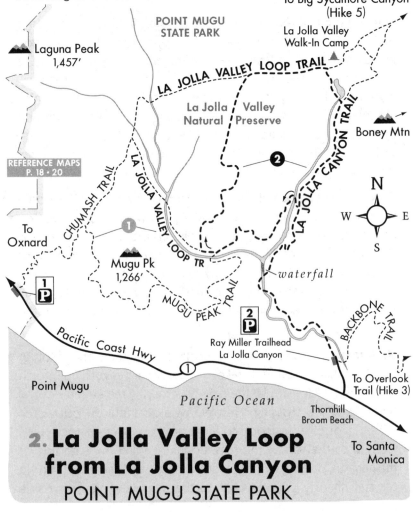

## 2. La Jolla Valley Loop from La Jolla Canyon
### POINT MUGU STATE PARK

# 3. Scenic and Overlook Trails Loop

## POINT MUGU STATE PARK

**Hiking distance:** 2-mile loop
**Hiking time:** 1 hour
**Elevation gain:** 900 feet
**Maps:** U.S.G.S. Point Mugu
       Tom Harrison Maps: Point Mugu State Park Trail Map
       Santa Monica Mountains West Trail Map

map
page 26

**Summary of hike:** The Scenic and Overlook Trails are located along the coastal frontage of Point Mugu State Park. The trail follows the ridge separating Big Sycamore Canyon from La Jolla Canyon. This short but beautiful hike climbs up the chaparral-covered ridge to several panoramic overlooks of the Pacific Ocean.

**Driving directions:** From Santa Monica, drive 31 miles northbound on the Pacific Coast Highway/Highway 1 to the posted Big Sycamore Canyon entrance on the right. (The trailhead entrance is 13.3 miles past Kanan Dume Road in Malibu and 5.3 miles west of the well-marked Leo Carrillo State Beach.) Turn right and park in the day-use pay parking lot 0.1 mile ahead on the left. (Parking is free in the pullouts along the PCH.)

Heading southbound on the Pacific Coast Highway/ Highway 1 from Las Posas Road in southeast Oxnard, drive 5.8 miles to the Point Mugu State Park entrance on the left.

**Hiking directions:** From the parking area, walk up the road past the campground to the Big Sycamore Canyon trailhead gate. Continue up the unpaved road about 50 yards to the signed junction with the Scenic Trail. Take the trail to the left (west) across Big Sycamore Creek, and head up the wooden steps. The trail steadily gains elevation up an open, grassy hillside with views of Big Sycamore Canyon. At the saddle near the top of the hill is a trail split. The left fork leads a short distance to an ocean overlook. Continue up to several more viewpoints. Return back to the junction, and head north to a junction with the Overlook Trail. Take this service road downhill to the right, winding 0.9

miles back to the Big Sycamore Canyon floor. Near the bottom, five gentle switchbacks lead to the junction across the creek. Take the canyon trail to the right, leading 0.4 miles back to the trailhead gate. ■

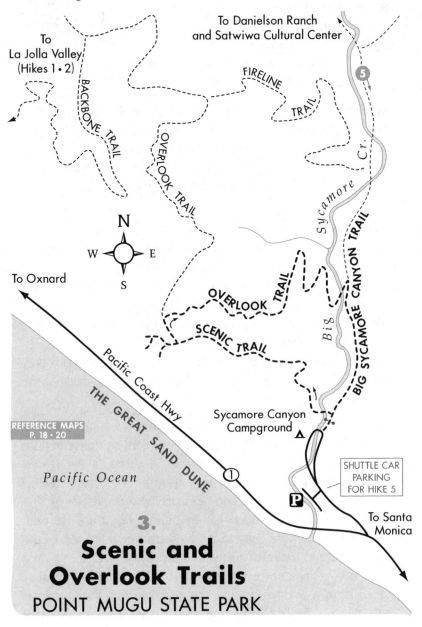

# 3.
# **Scenic and Overlook Trails**
## POINT MUGU STATE PARK

# 4. Old Boney Trail to Danielson Monument

## BONEY MOUNTAIN STATE WILDERNESS and POINT MUGU STATE PARK

**Hiking distance:** 7.8-mile loop
**Hiking time:** 4 hours
**Elevation gain:** 1,000 feet
**Maps:** U.S.G.S. Newbury Park
　　　Tom Harrison Maps: Point Mugu State Park Trail Map
　　　N.P.S. Rancho Sierra Vista/Satwiwa map

*map page 29*

**Summary of hike:** The Boney Mountain State Wilderness area occupies the eastern portion of Point Mugu State Park. The centerpiece of the preserved area is Boney Mountain, a rocky, jagged formation that rises 1,500 feet above Sycamore Canyon. The scenic mountain contains four of the highest peaks in the coastal Santa Monica Range, including well-known Sandstone Peak (Hike 8). This hike follows the Old Boney Trail in Upper Sycamore Canyon to Danielson Monument, a stone monument with a metal arch honoring Richard Danielson. Danielson donated the ranch to the National Park Service for preservation as an open space. Near the monument is the old cabin site of Richard Danielson Jr., where the rock fireplace still remains. En route to the monument, the trail passes Sycamore Canyon Falls, a 70-foot cascade in a lush box canyon along the riparian corridor of Big Sycamore Creek. The hike weaves through open grassland, wooded forests, a stream-fed canyon, and mountain overlooks with close-up views of the sheer rock face of Boney Mountain.

**Driving directions:** From Highway 101 (Ventura Freeway) in Newbury Park, exit on Wendy Drive. Drive 2 miles south to Lynn Road. Turn right and continue 1.7 miles to Via Goleta, the park entrance road. Turn left and drive 0.7 miles to the main parking lot at the end of the road.

**Hiking directions:** Take the posted trail past the restrooms a quarter mile to the service road at the Satwiwa Native American

Indian Cultural Center. Bear right on the road, entering Point Mugu State Park. As you approach the ridge overlooking Big Sycamore Canyon, take the Boney Mountain Trail to the left along the brink of the canyon. Climb a short hill, passing the Satwiwa Loop Trail on the left, and continue around to a ridge to a trail split. Take the right fork, descending down to the forested canyon floor and a junction with the Upper Sycamore Canyon Trail at 1.3 miles, our return route.

Begin the loop straight ahead under a canopy of oaks, sycamores, and bay laurel to a U-shaped right bend. Detour 100 yards to the left to seasonal Sycamore Canyon Falls in a rock-walled box canyon. Return to the Old Boney Trail, and continue up the hillside on the north flank of Boney Mountain to an overlook of Sycamore Canyon, the Oxnard Plain, and the Channel Islands. Inland views extend to the Los Padres National Forest. Steadily climb to a posted junction and views of the rounded rock formations of upper Boney Mountain. Detour 0.3 miles on the left fork, dropping down and crossing a seasonal drainage to the Danielson Monument at the end of the trail. To the right is the old cabin site with the remaining rock chimney and fireplace.

Return to the Old Boney Trail, and walk through the tall brush, gaining elevation while passing occasional overlooks of Point Mugu State Park to the Pacific Ocean. Gradually descend to a signed junction with the Fossil Trail at 4.4 miles. Straight ahead, the Old Boney Trail leads 2.1 miles to the Blue Canyon Trail, part of the Backbone Trail. (To the west, the Backbone Trail connects to the Danielson Ranch in Big Sycamore Canyon—Hike 5. To the east, the trail leads to Sandstone Peak—Hike 6.)

For this hike go to the right on the Fossil Trail, and descend into the stream-fed canyon. Follow the east canyon wall downstream, passing dozens of shell fossils embedded in the rock along the path. Near the bottom, enter an oak grove to a T-junction with the Upper Sycamore Canyon Trail. The left fork leads 0.1 mile to the Big Sycamore Canyon Fire Road/Trail. Bear right and head east, following the canyon floor. Complete the loop at 6.5 miles, 0.2 miles shy of Sycamore Canyon Falls. Bear left and retrace your steps 1.3 miles back to the trailhead. ■

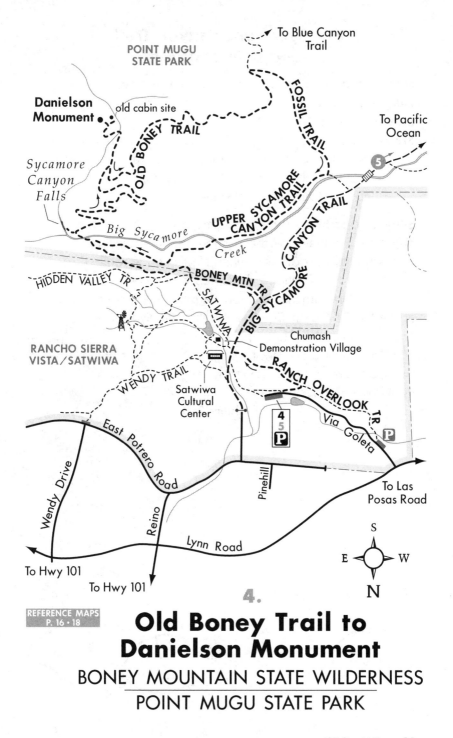

POINT MUGU
STATE PARK

To Blue Canyon
Trail

**Danielson
Monument** • old cabin site

*Sycamore
Canyon
Falls*

OLD BONEY TRAIL

FOSSIL TRAIL

To Pacific
Ocean

5

*Big Sycamore*

*Creek*

**UPPER SYCAMORE
CANYON TRAIL**

CANYON TRAIL

HIDDEN VALLEY TR

**BONEY MTN TR**

SATWIWA

BIG SYCAMORE

Chumash
Demonstration Village

**RANCHO SIERRA
VISTA/SATWIWA**

WENDY TRAIL

Satwiwa
Cultural
Center

**RANCH OVERLOOK TR**

4
5
P

*Via Goleta*

P

East Potrero Road

Wendy Drive

Reino

Pinehill

To Las
Posas Road

*Lynn* Road

To Hwy 101

To Hwy 101

S
E ⊕ W
N

REFERENCE MAPS
P. 16 · 18

4.
# Old Boney Trail to
# Danielson Monument
## BONEY MOUNTAIN STATE WILDERNESS
## POINT MUGU STATE PARK

# 5. Big Sycamore Canyon Trail
## POINT MUGU STATE PARK

**Hiking distance:** 8.4 miles one way (car shuttle)
**Hiking time:** 3 hours
**Elevation loss:** 900 feet
**Maps:** U.S.G.S. Newbury Park, Camarillo and Point Mugu
Tom Harrison Maps: Point Mugu State Park Trail Map
Santa Monica Mountains West Trail Map
N.P.S. Rancho Sierra Vista/Satwiwa map

**Summary of hike:** The Big Sycamore Canyon Trail is a one-way, mountains-to-the-sea journey. The Canyon was originally part of the Chumash Indian trade route. The trail, now an unpaved service road, connects Newbury Park with the Sycamore Canyon Campground at the Pacific Ocean. The hike parallels Big Sycamore Creek through the heart of 15,000-acre Point Mugu State Park in a deep, wooded canyon under towering sycamores and oaks.

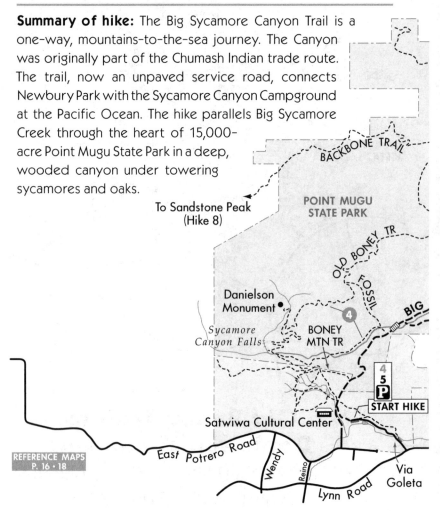

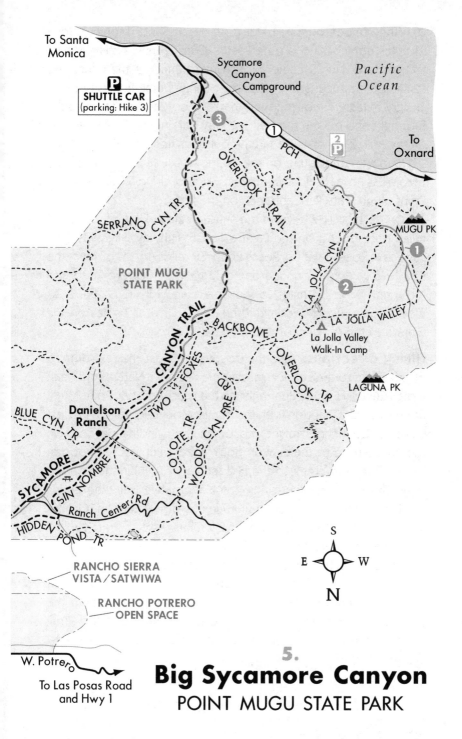

To Santa Monica

**SHUTTLE CAR**
(parking: Hike 3)

Sycamore Canyon Campground

*Pacific Ocean*

PCH

To Oxnard

MUGU PK

OVERLOOK TRAIL

SERRANO CYN TR

POINT MUGU STATE PARK

LA JOLLA CYN

LA JOLLA VALLEY

La Jolla Valley Walk-In Camp

CANYON TRAIL

BACKBONE

OVERLOOK TR

LAGUNA PK

TWO FOXES

COYOTE TR

WOODS CYN FIRE RD

Danielson Ranch

BLUE CYN TR

SYCAMORE

SIN NOMBRE

Ranch Center Rd

HIDDEN POND TR

RANCHO SIERRA VISTA/SATWIWA

RANCHO POTRERO OPEN SPACE

W. Potrero

To Las Posas Road and Hwy 1

S

E — W

N

**5.**
# Big Sycamore Canyon
## POINT MUGU STATE PARK

**Driving directions:** SHUTTLE CAR: From Santa Monica, drive 31 miles northbound on the Pacific Coast Highway/Highway 1 to the posted Big Sycamore Canyon entrance on the right. (The trailhead entrance is 13.3 miles past Kanan Dume Road in Malibu and 5.3 miles west of the well-marked Leo Carrillo State Beach.) Turn right and park in the day-use pay parking lot 0.1 mile ahead on the left. (Parking is free in the pullouts along the PCH.)

Heading southbound on the Pacific Coast Highway/ Highway 1 from Las Posas Road in southeast Oxnard, drive 5.8 miles to the Point Mugu State Park entrance on the left.

TO THE TRAILHEAD: From the shuttle car parking lot, drive 5.8 miles northbound on the Pacific Coast Highway/Highway 1 to Las Posas Road. Take Las Posas Road 2.9 miles north to Hueneme Road—turn right. Continue one mile to West Potrero Road and turn right. Drive 5.4 miles to Via Goleta and turn right (En route, West Potrero Road becomes Lynn Road). Drive 0.7 miles on Via Goleta to the parking lot at the end of the road.

**Hiking directions:** Take the posted trail past the restrooms a quarter mile to the service road at the Satwiwa Native American Indian Cultural Center. Bear right on the road, entering Point Mugu State Park, to a junction with the Boney Mountain Trail on the left (Hike 4). Continue straight and begin the winding descent on the paved road to the canyon floor. The trail crosses a wooden bridge over the creek to the Hidden Pond Trail junction on the right. This is an excellent single track alternative trail that rejoins the Big Sycamore Canyon Trail 1.7 miles down canyon. On the alternative trail, there is a split at 2.2 miles. Take the left fork to the Sycamore Camping and Picnic Area. At 3 miles is a signed "beach" path on the right. This is where the alternative trail rejoins the service road. Just past the junction is the Danielson Ranch. Past the ranch, the trail is unpaved. Continue south down the forested canyon, past the Backbone Trail and the Overlook Trail (Hike 3) to the gate. From the gate, a paved road leads back to the shuttle car. ■

# 6. Grotto Trail
## CIRCLE X RANCH

**Hiking distance:** 3.5 miles round trip
**Hiking time:** 2 hours
**Elevation gain:** 650 feet
**Maps:** U.S.G.S. Triunfo Pass

map
page 34

Tom Harrison Maps: Point Mugu State Park Trail Map
Santa Monica Mountains West Trail Map
N.P.S. Circle X Ranch Site

**Summary of hike:** The Grotto Trail is located in the 1,655-acre Circle X Ranch bordering Point Mugu State Park. Once a Boy Scout wilderness retreat, the Circle X Ranch is now a national park and recreation area. At the end of this trail is The Grotto, a maze of large, volcanic boulders in a sheer, narrow gorge formed from landslides. The West Fork of the Arroyo Sequit flows through the caves and caverns of The Grotto, creating cascades and pools.

**Driving directions:** From the Pacific Coast Highway/ Highway 1 in Santa Monica, drive 38 miles northbound to Yerba Buena Road and turn right. (Yerba Buena Road is 10.1 miles past Kanan Dume Road and 2 miles past Leo Carrillo State Beach.) Continue 5.3 miles up the winding road to the Circle X Ranger Station on the right. Park by the ranger station, or continue 0.2 miles downhill to the day-use parking area, located just past the posted Grotto Trailhead.

From the Pacific Coast Highway/Highway 1 and Las Posas Road in southeast Oxnard, drive 9 miles southbound to Yerba Buena Road (3.3 miles past Big Sycamore Canyon) and turn left. Continue up Yerba Buena Road, following the directions above.

**Hiking directions:** From the ranger station, walk 0.2 miles down the unpaved road to the posted Grotto Trailhead, just before reaching the lower parking area. Continue downhill, crossing the West Fork of Arroyo Sequit. At 0.4 miles, the trail passes the Canyon View Trail (Hike 7) and recrosses the creek at a 30-foot waterfall. After crossing, curve left, traversing a grassy ridge. Descend to the canyon floor where the trail joins the Happy

Hollow Campground Road at 1.2 miles. Follow the road to the left into a primitive campground and cross the creek, picking up the posted Grotto Trail again. Head downstream to a bridge that crosses the creek into the Happy Hollow Campground. Instead of crossing the bridge, continue straight ahead and cross the creek by a pumphouse. Follow the creek a few hundred feet to The Grotto.

After exploring The Grotto, return to the bridge that accesses the campground. Walk through the campground to the road and bear to the right. Follow the winding road and rejoin the Grotto Trail on the left. Retrace your steps to the parking lot. ■

6
7
**P**

Yerba Buena Rd

Circle X
Ranger
Station **P**

*waterfall*

West Fork Arroyo Sequit

CANYON VIEW TRAIL

7

GROTTO TRAIL

BACKBONE TRAIL

8

8
**P**

N
W E
S

REFERENCE MAPS
P. 16 · 18

CIRCLE X
RANCH

To Hwy 1

The Grotto

△
Happy Hollow
Campground

## 6. **Grotto Trail**
### CIRCLE X RANCH

# 7. Canyon View—
## Yerba Buena Road Loop
### CIRCLE X RANCH

**Hiking distance:** 3.2-mile loop
**Hiking time:** 1.5 hours
**Elevation gain:** 500 feet

map
page 37

**Maps:** U.S.G.S. Triunfo Pass
Tom Harrison Maps: Point Mugu State Park Trail Map
Santa Monica Mountains West Trail Map
N.P.S. Circle X Ranch Site

**Summary of hike:** Circle X Ranch, a former Boy Scout camp, sits below majestic Boney Mountain in the upper canyons of Arroyo Sequit. The Canyon View Trail traverses the brushy hillside of the deep, east-facing canyon. The panoramic views extend down the canyon to the Pacific Ocean. The northern views reach the jagged Boney Mountain ridge and the 3,111-foot Sandstone Peak, the highest peak in the Santa Monica Mountains. The trail connects the Grotto Trail (Hike 6) with the Backbone Trail (Hike 8).

**Driving directions:** From the Pacific Coast Highway/ Highway 1 in Santa Monica, drive 38 miles northbound to Yerba Buena Road and turn right. (Yerba Buena Road is 10.1 miles past Kanan Dume Road and 2 miles past Leo Carrillo State Beach.) Continue 5.3 miles up the winding road to the Circle X Ranger Station on the right. Park by the ranger station, or continue 0.2 miles downhill to the day-use parking area, located just past the posted Grotto Trailhead.

From the Pacific Coast Highway/Highway 1 and Las Posas Road in southeast Oxnard, drive 9 miles southbound to Yerba Buena Road (3.3 miles past Big Sycamore Canyon) and turn left. Continue up Yerba Buena Road, following the directions above.

**Hiking directions:** From the ranger station, walk 0.2 miles down the unpaved road to the posted Grotto Trailhead, just before reaching the lower parking area. Pass the trail gate and follow the dirt road past a picnic area to another trail sign. Take the footpath downhill and cross the West Fork Arroyo Sequit. Parallel the east side of the creek to a signed junction. (Twenty yards to the right is a waterfall. Hike 6 continues down the trail to The Grotto.) Bear left on the Canyon View Trail, and traverse the canyon wall, following the contours of the mountain. Climb two switchbacks to a junction. For a shorter 1.5-mile loop, take the Connector Trail 100 yards to the left to Yerba Buena Road, and return 0.35 miles to the ranger station.

For this longer hike, stay to the right and cross a rocky wash. Head up the hillside to a south view that spans down canyon to the ocean and the Channel Islands and a north view of the Boney Mountain ridge. Continue to Yerba Buena Road, across from the Backbone Trail (Hike 8). For a loop hike, return to the left on Yerba Buena Road, and walk 1.1 mile back to the trailhead at the Circle X Ranger Station. ■

# 8. Sandstone Peak
## Mishe Mokwa—Backbone Loop
### CIRCLE X RANCH

**Hiking distance:** 6-mile loop
**Hiking time:** 3 hours
**Elevation gain:** 1,100 feet
**Maps:** U.S.G.S. Triunfo Pass and Newbury Park
      Tom Harrison Maps: Point Mugu State Park Trail Map
      Santa Monica Mountains West Trail Map
      N.P.S. Circle X Ranch Site

map
page 39

**Summary of hike:** The Mishe Mokwa Trail in Circle X Ranch follows Carlisle Canyon along Boney Mountain past weathered red volcanic formations. There are views of the sculpted caves and crevices of Echo Cliffs and a forested streamside picnic area by a huge, split boulder known as Split Rock. The return route on the Backbone Trail leads to Inspiration Point and Sandstone Peak, the highest point in the Santa Monica Mountains. Both points overlook the Pacific Ocean, the Channel Islands, and the surrounding mountains.

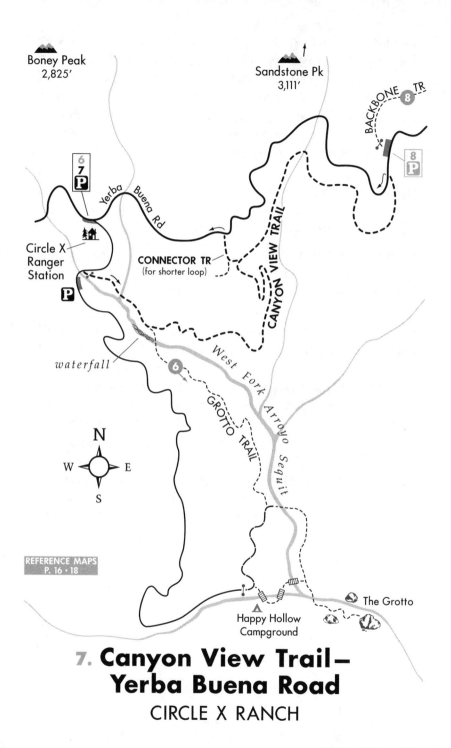

Boney Peak
2,825'

Sandstone Pk
3,111'

BACKBONE TR

8

6
7
P

Yerba Buena Rd

8
P

Circle X
Ranger
Station

P

CONNECTOR TR
(for shorter loop)

CANYON VIEW TRAIL

waterfall

West Fork Arroyo Sequit

6

GROTTO TRAIL

N
W  E
S

REFERENCE MAPS
P. 16 · 18

The Grotto

Happy Hollow
Campground

# 7. **Canyon View Trail–**
# **Yerba Buena Road**
## CIRCLE X RANCH

**Driving directions:** From the Pacific Coast Highway/ Highway 1 in Santa Monica, drive 38 miles northbound to Yerba Buena Road and turn right. (Yerba Buena Road is 10.1 miles past Kanan Dume Road and 2 miles past Leo Carrillo State Beach.) Continue 5.3 miles up the winding road to the Circle X Ranger Station on the right. From the ranger station, continue one mile to the Backbone Trailhead parking lot on the left.

From the Pacific Coast Highway/Highway 1 and Las Posas Road in southeast Oxnard, drive 9 miles southbound to Yerba Buena Road (3.3 miles past Big Sycamore Canyon) and turn left. Continue up Yerba Buena Road, following the directions above.

**Hiking directions:** Take the Backbone Trail (a fire road) uphill to the north. At 0.3 miles, leave the road and take the signed Mishe Mokwa Connector Trail straight ahead. Continue 0.2 miles to a junction with the Mishe Mokwa Trail and take the left fork. The trail contours along Boney Mountain on the western edge of Carlisle Canyon. At 1.4 miles, Balanced Rock can be seen on the opposite side of the canyon. Descend into the canyon shaded by oaks, laurel, and sycamores to Split Rock and the picnic area. Take the trail across the stream, heading out of the canyon to another stream crossing by sculptured volcanic rocks. Parallel the stream to a signed junction. Take the left fork—the Backbone Trail—curving uphill towards Inspiration Point. A short side path leads up to the overlook. Continue east on the Backbone Trail to another junction. This side trail switchbacks up to the 360-degree views at Sandstone Peak. From the junction, it is 0.8 miles downhill back to the Mishe Mokwa Connector Trail, completing the loop. ■

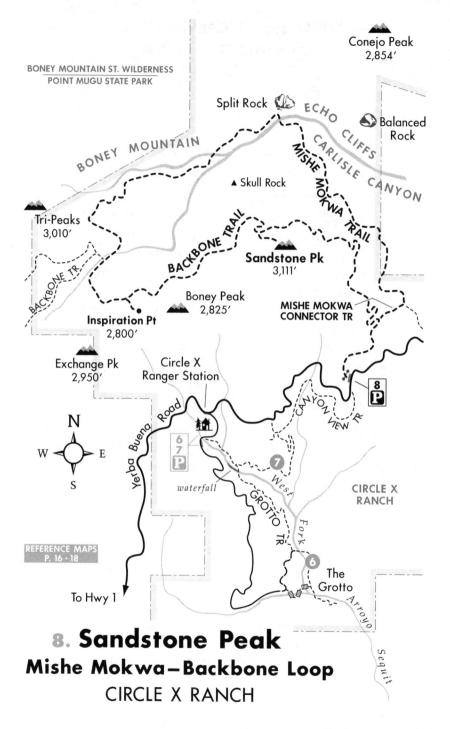

# 8. Sandstone Peak
## Mishe Mokwa–Backbone Loop
### CIRCLE X RANCH

# 9. White Horse Canyon Trail
## LOS ROBLES TRAIL SYSTEM

**Hiking distance:** 3.5-mile loop
**Hiking time:** 1.5 hours
**Elevation gain:** 500 feet
**Maps:** U.S.G.S. Thousand Oaks
       Santa Monica Mountains West Trail Map
       Los Robles Trail to Lake Sherwood map

map
page 42

**Summary of hike:** The Los Robles Trail System is a well-planned network of trails weaving through the growing residential communities of Westlake Village, Thousand Oaks, and Newbury Park. The multi-use trails link the open spaces of the inland valley with the oceanfront Santa Monica Mountains at Point Mugu State Park. This is an important wildlife corridor between the Santa Monica Mountains and the Simi Hills. The White Horse Canyon Trail, near the east end of the trail system, loops around the rolling, chaparral-covered foothills to a ridge overlooking Westlake Village and Thousand Oaks. There is an additional overlook with a panoramic view of Lake Sherwood, the cliffs above Hidden Valley, and the Santa Monica Mountains.

**Driving directions:** From Ventura Freeway/Highway 101 in Thousand Oaks, exit on Westlake Boulevard. Drive 1.8 miles south to East Potrero Road and turn right. Continue 0.5 miles and park on the right across from the Foxfield Riding Club, just beyond the bridge over Potrero Valley Creek.

**Hiking directions:** From the parking area, the trailhead and kiosk are across the creekbed to the north. Head up the hill, past the homes on the right, to a fire road. The fire road leads to a junction. The left fork is a short side trip to a scenic overlook of Lake Sherwood. Back at the junction, take the north fork 0.5 miles to another junction with the White Horse Canyon Trail on the left. This footpath loops around the back side of the canyon before rejoining the fire road. Take the road to the right uphill a short distance to a junction with the Conejo Crest Trail on the left. Head left along the ridge as it descends back down to Potrero Valley Creek. Cross the creekbed into the park. Take the park path to the right, leading back to the parking area. ■

## 10. Triunfo Canyon Trail
### LOS ROBLES TRAIL SYSTEM

**Hiking distance:** 2.5-mile loop
**Hiking time:** 1 hour
**Elevation gain:** 400 feet
**Maps:** U.S.G.S. Thousand Oaks
      Santa Monica Mountains West Trail Map
      Los Robles Trail to Lake Sherwood map

map
page 42

**Summary of hike:** The Los Robles Trail System is a network of paths linking the Conejo and Russell Valleys by Westlake Village, Thousand Oaks, and Newbury Park with the Santa Monica Mountains at Point Mugu State Park. The multi-use trails connect numerous open spaces, thoughtfully blended with the encroaching residential areas. The Triunfo Canyon Trail is part of an open space near Westlake Village. The hike follows Triunfo Canyon to rolling grasslands on the ridge, where it connects with the Los Robles Trail. Atop the ridge are sweeping vistas of Westlake Village, the Conejo Valley, Lake Sherwood, and the Santa Monica Mountains.

**Driving directions:** From Ventura Freeway/Highway 101 in Thousand Oaks, exit on Hampshire Road. Drive 0.6 miles south to Triunfo Canyon Road and turn right. Continue 0.5 miles to Tamarack Street and turn right. The trailhead is 0.2 miles ahead in the parking lot at the north end of Triunfo Community Park.

**Hiking directions:** From the parking lot, head northwest on the signed trail past the kiosk. The trail gradually climbs along the contours of Triunfo Canyon to the ridgeline. Near the top, a short series of steep switchbacks lead to a bench. From the bench are great views of the valley below. The trail then levels out to a junction with the Los Robles Trail—go to the left. Thirty feet ahead is a ridge with views of the mountains and another junction. Take the signed Los Robles Trail South to the left to a

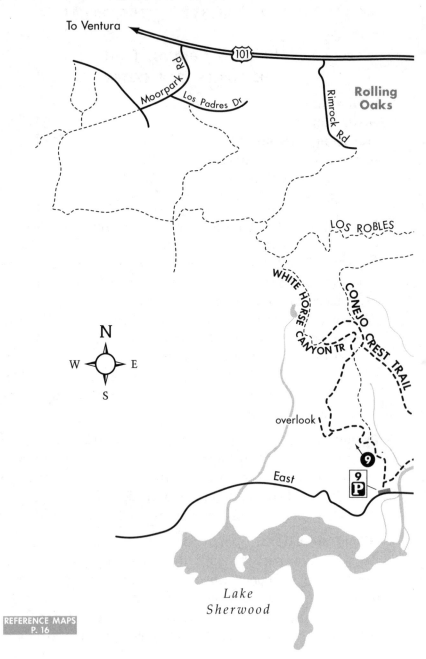

To Ventura

101

Moorpark Rd

Los Padres Dr

Rimrock Rd

Rolling Oaks

LOS ROBLES

WHITE HORSE CANYON TR

CONEJO CREST TRAIL

N
W · E
S

overlook

9

9
P

East

Lake
Sherwood

REFERENCE MAPS
P. 16

third trail split. Proceed downhill on the left fork. The trail ends at Brookview Avenue. Walk through the neighborhood one block to Stonesgate Street. Go to the left and proceed one block to Aranmoor Avenue. Go left again, returning to the park. The park path heads left, leading back to the parking lot. ■

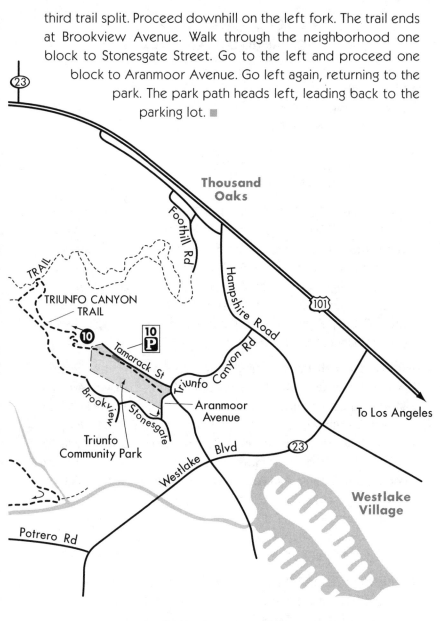

# Los Robles Trail System

## 9: White Horse Canyon Trail
## 10: Triunfo Canyon Trail

# 11. Yellow Hill Trail
## LEO CARRILLO STATE PARK

**Hiking distance:** 5 miles round trip
**Hiking time:** 2.5 hours
**Elevation gain:** 1,300 feet
**Maps:** U.S.G.S. Triunfo Pass
Tom Harrison Maps: Point Mugu State Park Trail Map
Santa Monica Mountains West Trail Map
Leo Carrillo State Beach map

**Summary of hike:** The Yellow Hill Trail is within Leo Carrillo State Park, a 3,000-acre park at the western tip of Los Angeles County. The trail steadily climbs a fire road up Sequit Ridge in the backcountry hills. The trailhead begins on the west side of Mulholland Highway in Los Angeles County and follows the mountain ridge, leaving the west side of the state park into Ventura County. En route are outstanding ocean views, including the four Channel Islands.

**Driving directions:** Heading northbound on the Pacific Coast Highway (Highway 1) from Santa Monica, drive 14 miles past Malibu Canyon Road and 8 miles past Kanan Dume Road to Mulholland Highway. The highway is located 0.2 miles past the Leo Carrillo State Beach entrance. Turn right and go 100 yards to the gated fire road on the left. Park along the side of the road. Parking is also available in Leo Carrillo State Park off the PCH.

From the Pacific Coast Highway (Highway 1) and Las Posas Road in southeast Oxnard, drive 10.8 miles southbound on the PCH to Mulholland Highway, just before the posted Leo Carrillo State Beach entrance. Proceed with the directions above.

**Hiking directions:** Walk around the trailhead gate, and follow the old dirt road, passing prickly pear cactus. Coastal views quickly expand, from Point Dume to Point Mugu and across the ocean to the Channel Islands. The trail parallels the coast for 0.3 miles, then curves inland. Climb steadily up the ridge. Cross over a minor side canyon to a view of the sculptured land forms in the interior of Leo Carrillo State Park and the Arroyo Sequit drainage. At 1.4 miles, the encroaching vegetation narrows the winding road to a single track trail. Cross the county line and walk around a gate, continuing 300 yards ahead to a Y-fork. The left fork descends to the PCH. Stay to the right, below a water tank on the right. At 2 miles the road/trail makes a left bend. On the bend is a footpath veering up the knoll to the right, our return route. Continue on the main trail, curving around the west flank of the knoll. Near the ridge, the uphill grade eases, reaching a trail sign. Continue to the ridge 150 yards ahead, with an outstanding view of the Boney Mountain ridgeline. Leave the road and return on the trail to the right, climbing up the north face of the knoll. Cross over the 1,366-foot summit, and descend along the ridge to the junction with the road at the water tank. Return along the same route. ■

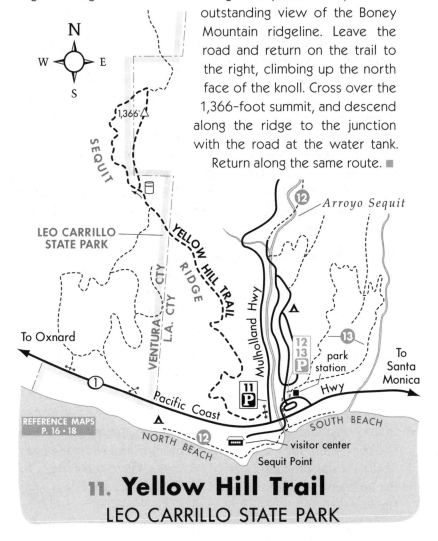

# 11. Yellow Hill Trail
## LEO CARRILLO STATE PARK

# 12. Lower Arroyo Sequit Trail and Sequit Point

## LEO CARRILLO STATE PARK

**Hiking distance:** 3 miles round trip
**Hiking time:** 1.5 hours
**Elevation gain:** 200 feet
**Maps:** U.S.G.S. Triunfo Pass
Tom Harrison Maps: Point Mugu State Park Trail Map
Leo Carrillo State Beach map

**Summary of hike:** Leo Carrillo State Park is a 2,000-acre haven with a 1.5-mile stretch of coastline, mountain canyons, and steep chaparral-covered hillsides. The area was once inhabited by the Chumash Indians. The Lower Arroyo Sequit Trail leads into a cool, stream-fed canyon shaded with willow, sycamore, oak and bay trees. The path ends in the deep-walled canyon by large multi-colored boulders and the trickling stream. At the oceanfront, Sequit Point, a rocky bluff, juts out from the shoreline, dividing North Beach from South Beach. The weather-carved point has sea caves and coves, ocean-sculpted arches, tidepools, and pocket beaches.

**Driving directions:** From Santa Monica, drive 26 miles northbound on the Pacific Coast Highway/Highway 1 to the posted Leo Carrillo State Beach entrance and turn right. (The state park is 14 miles past Malibu Canyon Road and 8 miles past Kanan Dume Road.) Park in the day-use parking lot. A parking fee is required.

**Hiking directions:** LOWER ARROYO SEQUIT TRAIL: Hike north through the campground on the road past mature sycamores and oaks. Pass the amphitheater on the right to a gated road. Continue past the gate, crossing over the seasonal Arroyo Sequit to the end of the paved road. Take the footpath a hundred yards, and rock hop over the creek by a small grotto. Follow the path upstream along the east side of the creek. Recross the creek to the trail's end in a steep-walled box canyon with pools and large boulders.

Retrace your steps to the amphitheater, and now bear left on the footpath. Cross to the east side of the creek and head through the forest canopy. Switchbacks and two sets of wooden steps lead to a flat above the canyon. Descend back to the campground road.

SEQUIT POINT: To reach Sequit Point, take the paved path under Highway 1 to the sandy beach. To the right (west), by the lifeguard station, are sandstone rock formations with caves, tunnels, a rock arch, tidepools, and a series of beach coves. ■

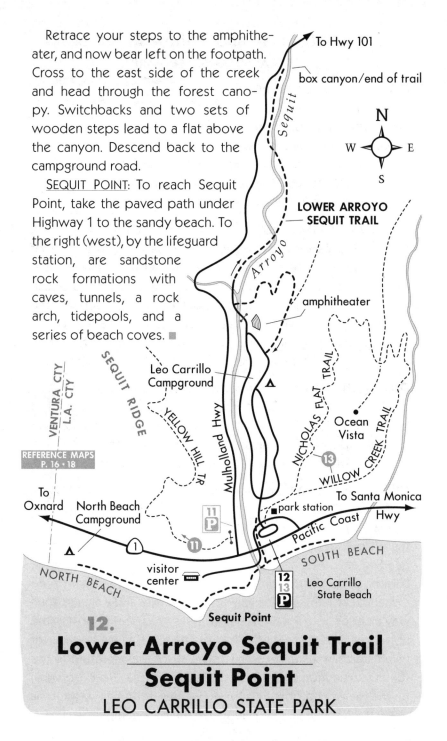

# 12.
# Lower Arroyo Sequit Trail
## Sequit Point
### LEO CARRILLO STATE PARK

# 13. Nicholas Flat and Willow Creek Loop
## LEO CARRILLO STATE PARK

**Hiking distance:** 2.5-mile loop
**Hiking time:** 1.3 hours
**Elevation gain:** 612 feet
**Maps:** U.S.G.S. Triunfo Pass
Tom Harrison Maps: Point Mugu State Park Trail Map
Santa Monica Mountains West Trail Map
Leo Carrillo State Beach map

**Summary of hike:** This loop hike in Leo Carrillo State Park leads to Ocean Vista, a 612-foot bald knoll with great views of the Malibu coastline and Point Dume. The Willow Creek Trail traverses the east-facing hillside up Willow Creek Canyon to Ocean Vista at the north end of the loop. En route to the overlook, the trail leads through native grasslands and coastal sage scrub. The hike returns along the Nicholas Flat Trail, one of the few trails connecting the Santa Monica Mountains to the Pacific Ocean.

**Driving directions:** From Santa Monica, drive 26 miles northbound on the Pacific Coast Highway/Highway 1 to the posted Leo Carrillo State Beach entrance and turn right. (The state park is 14 miles past Malibu Canyon Road and 8 miles past Kanan Dume Road.) Park in the day-use parking lot. A parking fee is required.

**Hiking directions:** The trailhead is 50 yards outside the park entrance station. Take the signed trail 100 yards northeast to a trail split. The loop begins at this junction. Take the right fork—the Willow Creek Trail—up the hillside and parallel to the ocean, heading east. At a half mile the trail curves north, traversing the hillside while overlooking the arroyo and Willow Creek. Three switchbacks lead aggressively up to a saddle and a signed four-way junction with the Nicholas Flat Trail, which leads north to the upper reaches of the park (Hike 14). The left fork leads a quarter mile to Ocean Vista. After marveling at the views, return to the four-way junction and take the left (west) fork. Head downhill on the lower end of the Nicholas Flat Trail, returning to the trailhead along the grassy slopes above the park campground. ■

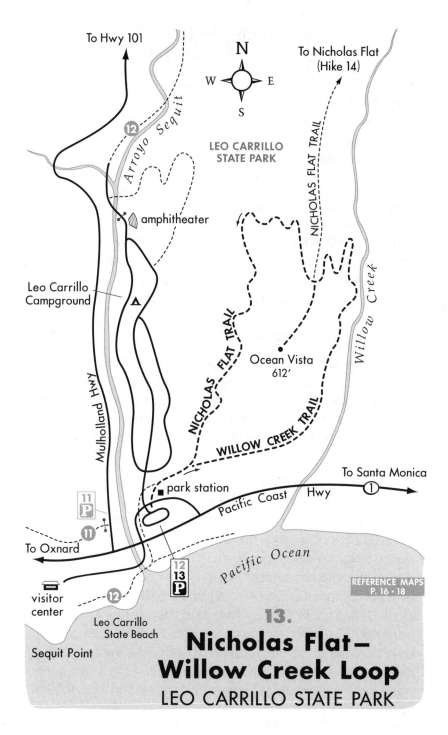

To Hwy 101

**N**
W   E
S

To Nicholas Flat
(Hike 14)

LEO CARRILLO
STATE PARK

NICHOLAS FLAT TRAIL

Arroyo Sequit

amphitheater

Leo Carrillo
Campground

NICHOLAS FLAT TRAIL

Ocean Vista
612'

Willow Creek

WILLOW CREEK TRAIL

Mulholland Hwy

park station

To Santa Monica

Pacific Coast Hwy

To Oxnard

Pacific Ocean

REFERENCE MAPS
P. 16 · 18

visitor
center

Leo Carrillo
State Beach

Sequit Point

**13.**
# Nicholas Flat—
# Willow Creek Loop
## LEO CARRILLO STATE PARK

# 14. Nicholas Flat
## LEO CARRILLO STATE PARK

**Hiking distance:** 2.5-mile double loop
**Hiking time:** 1.3 hours
**Elevation gain:** 100 feet
**Maps:** U.S.G.S. Triunfo Pass
Tom Harrison Maps: Point Mugu State Park Trail Map
Santa Monica Mountains West Trail Map
Leo Carrillo State Beach map

**Summary of hike:** Nicholas Flat, in the upper reaches of Leo Carrillo State Park, is a grassy highland meadow with large oak trees, an old cattle pond, and sandstone outcroppings that lie 1,700 feet above the sea. This hike skirts around Nicholas Flat, with spectacular views of the ocean, San Nicholas Canyon, and the surrounding mountains. The Nicholas Flat Trail may be hiked 3.5 miles downhill to the Pacific Ocean, connecting to Hike 13.

**Driving directions:** From Santa Monica, drive 23.8 miles northbound on the Pacific Coast Highway/Highway 1 to Decker Road and turn right. (Decker Road is 11.8 miles past Malibu Canyon Road.) Continue 2.4 miles north to Decker School Road and turn left. Drive 1.5 miles to the road's end and park alongside the road.

**Hiking directions:** Hike south past the gate and kiosk. Stay on the wide, oak-lined trail to a junction at 0.3 miles. Take the right fork, beginning the first loop. At 0.6 miles is another junction. Again take the right fork—the Meadows Trail. Continue past the Malibu Springs Trail on the right to Vista Point, where there are great views into the canyons. The trail curves south to a junction with the Nicholas Flat Trail, leading to the coastline at the southern end of Leo Carrillo State Park. Take the left fork around the perimeter of the flat. A trail on the right leads to another vista point. Complete the first loop at 1.8 miles. Take the trail to the right at two successive junctions to a pond. Follow along the pond through the meadow, completing the second loop. Return to the trailhead. ∎

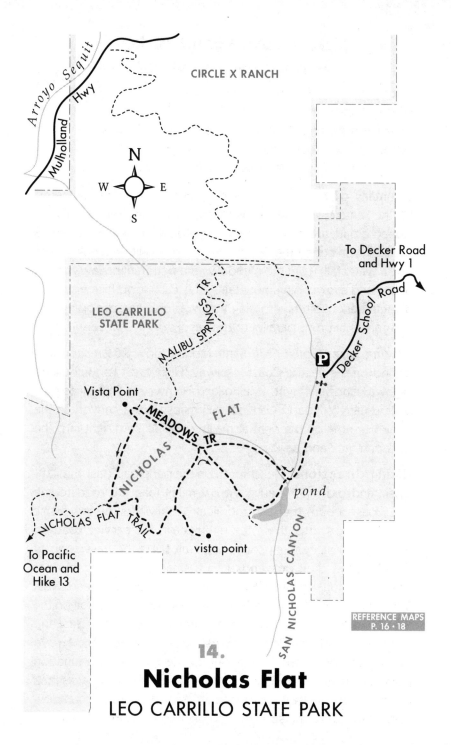

CIRCLE X RANCH

Arroyo Sequit

Mulholland Hwy

N
W E
S

To Decker Road
and Hwy 1

Decker School Road

LEO CARRILLO
STATE PARK

MALIBU SPRINGS TR

P

Vista Point

MEADOWS TR

FLAT

NICHOLAS

pond

NICHOLAS FLAT TRAIL

SAN NICHOLAS CANYON

vista point

To Pacific
Ocean and
Hike 13

REFERENCE MAPS
P. 16 · 18

**14.**
# Nicholas Flat
## LEO CARRILLO STATE PARK

# 15. Arroyo Sequit Park

34138 Mulholland Highway · Malibu

**Hiking distance:** 2-mile loop
**Hiking time:** 1 hour
**Elevation gain:** 250 feet
**Maps:** U.S.G.S. Triunfo Pass
       Santa Monica Mountains West Trail Map

**Summary of hike:** Arroyo Sequit Park was a ranch purchased by the Santa Monica Mountains Conservancy in 1985. Within the 155-acre park are open grassland meadows, picnic areas, and a small canyon cut by the East Fork Arroyo Sequit with oak groves and a waterfall. From the meadows are panoramic views of the ocean and surrounding mountains. This easy loop hike visits the diverse park habitats, crossing the meadows and dropping into the gorge that runs parallel to the East Fork Arroyo Sequit.

**Driving directions:** From Santa Monica, drive 26.2 miles north-bound on the Pacific Coast Highway/Highway 1 to Mulholland Highway and turn right. (Mulholland Highway is 14.2 miles past Malibu Canyon Road.) Continue 5.5 miles up the canyon to the signed turnoff on the right at mailbox 34138. Turn right into the park entrance and park.

**Hiking directions:** Head south on the park road past the gate, kiosk, and old ranch house. At 0.2 miles take the road to the left—past a barn, the astronomical observing site, and picnic area—to the footpath on the right. Leave the service road on the nature trail, heading south. The trail skirts the east edge of the meadow, then descends into a small canyon and crosses several seasonal tributaries of the Arroyo Sequit. Head west along the southern wall of the canyon, passing a waterfall on the left. Cross a wooden footbridge over the stream, and descend to the canyon floor. Continue west, cross the East Fork Arroyo Sequit, and begin the ascent out of the canyon to a junction. Continue straight ahead up the hill. A series of switchbacks lead up the short but steep hill. Once at the top, cross the meadow to the road. Take the service road back to the parking area. ▪

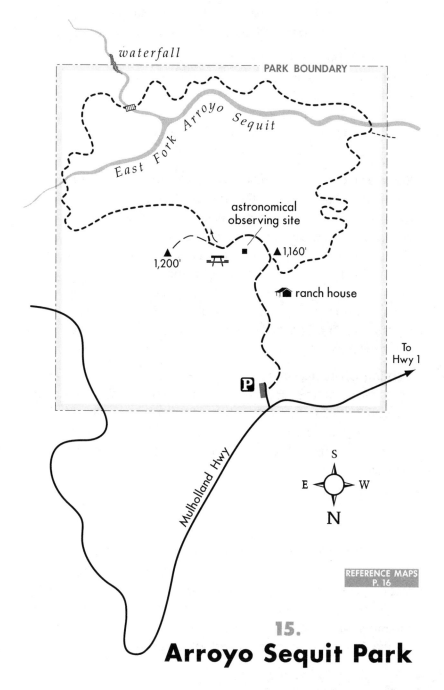

waterfall

PARK BOUNDARY

East Fork Arroyo Sequit

astronomical
observing site

▲ 1,200'

▲ 1,160'

🏠 ranch house

To
Hwy 1

P

Mulholland Hwy

S
E ✦ W
N

REFERENCE MAPS
P. 16

## 15.
# Arroyo Sequit Park

# 16. Charmlee County Park

2577 S. Encinal Canyon Road · Malibu
Open 8:00 a.m. to sunset daily

**Hiking distance:** 3-mile loop
**Hiking time:** 1.5 hours
**Elevation gain:** 600 feet
**Maps:** U.S.G.S. Triunfo Pass
    Santa Monica Mountains West Trail Map
    City of Malibu—Charmlee Natural Area map

**Summary of hike:** Perched on oceanfront cliffs 1,300 feet above the sea, Charmlee County Park has a magnificent bird's-eye view of the Malibu coastline. The 460-acre wilderness park was once a cattle ranch. It was purchased by Los Angeles County in 1968 and opened as a county park in 1981. Eight miles of interconnecting footpaths and old ranch roads weave through expansive grassy meadows, oak and eucalyptus woodlands, mountain slopes, rocky ridges, and 1,250-foot bluffs overlooking the sea. The park has picnic areas and a nature center with plant exhibits.

**Driving directions:** From Santa Monica, drive 23.2 miles northbound on the Pacific Coast Highway/Highway 1 to Encinal Canyon Road and turn right/north. (Encinal Canyon Road is 11.2 miles past Malibu Canyon Road.) Continue 3.7 miles to the park entrance on the left. Drive 0.2 miles on the park road to the parking lot.

**Hiking directions:** Hike past the information board and picnic area on the wide trail. Pass a second picnic area on the left in an oak grove, and continue uphill to a three-way trail split. The middle trail is a short detour leading to an overlook set among rock formations and an old house foundation. Take the main trail to the left into the large grassy meadow. Two trails cross the meadow and rejoin at the south end—the main trail heads through the meadow while the right fork skirts the meadow's western edge. At the far end is an ocean overlook and a trail fork. Bear left past an old ranch reservoir, and pass two junctions to a 1,200-foot overlook on the right. Continue downhill, curving north through an oak grove to the unsigned Botany Trail, a narrow footpath on the right. The Botany Trail winds back to the picnic area and the trailhead. ■

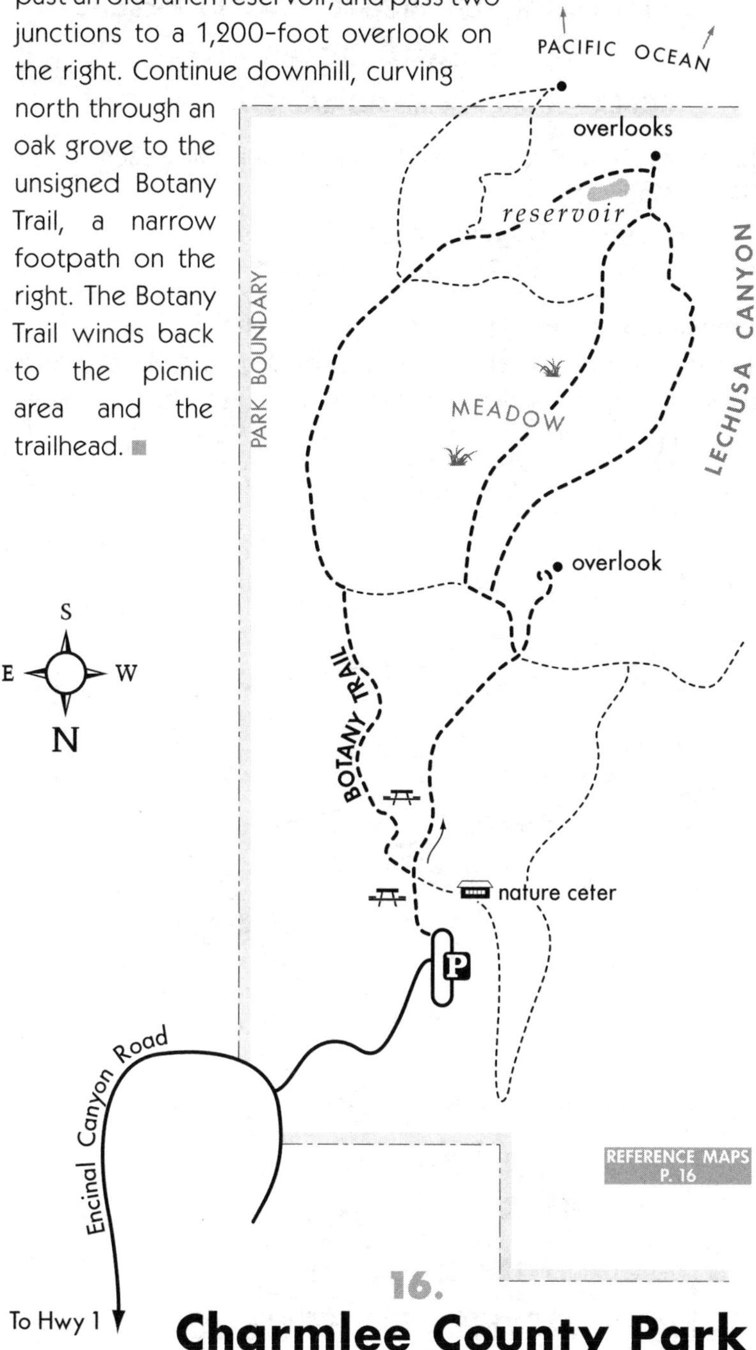

PACIFIC OCEAN

overlooks

*reservoir*

LECHUSA CANYON

PARK BOUNDARY

MEADOW

overlook

BOTANY TRAIL

S

E ⟡ W

N

nature ceter

P

Encinal Canyon Road

REFERENCE MAPS
P. 16

To Hwy 1

**16.**
**Charmlee County Park**

# 17. El Matador, La Piedra and El Pescador State Beaches

## ROBERT H. MEYER MEMORIAL STATE BEACH

**Hiking distance:** 2 miles round trip (total for all beaches)
**Hiking time:** 2 hours
**Elevation gain:** 100 feet for each hike
**Maps:** U.S.G.S. Triunfo Pass and Point Dume

**Summary of hike:** El Matador, La Piedra, and El Pescador State Beaches are three small oceanfront parks on the Malibu bluffs. Together they comprise the Robert H. Meyer Memorial State

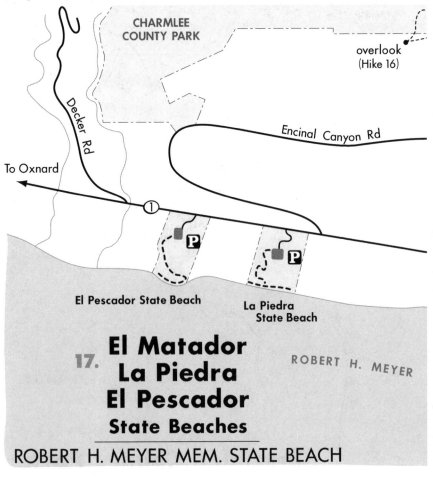

Beach. The three pocket beaches are within a one-mile stretch, bounded by rocky points. Each park contains a blufftop parking lot, a picnic area with overlooks, a pretty beach strand, and a trail down the 100-foot eroded cliffs to the shoreline. Of the three, El Matador Beach is the largest and most scenic, with large rock formations, arches, and caves.

**Driving directions:** EL PESCADOR STATE BEACH: 32860 Pacific Coast Highway in Malibu. Heading northbound on the Pacific Coast Highway (Highway 1) from Santa Monica, drive 20 miles past Malibu Canyon Road and 6 miles past Kanan Dume Road to the posted turnoff on the left (oceanside).

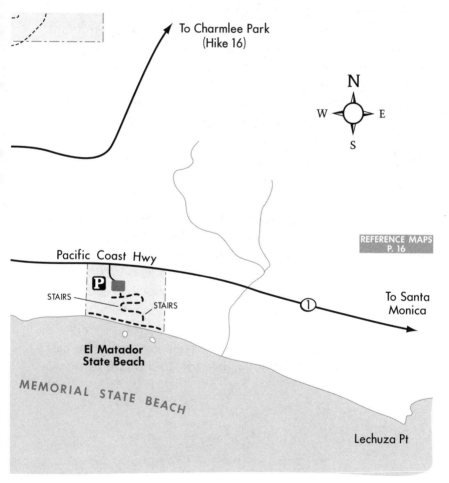

From the Pacific Coast Highway (Highway 1) and Las Posas Road in southeast Oxnard, drive 13.4 miles southbound to the posted El Pescador State Beach on the right (oceanside). The turnoff is 2.3 miles south of Leo Carrillo State Beach and just south of Decker Road.

LA PIEDRA STATE PARK: 32628 Pacific Coast Highway in Malibu. The turn-off is 0.2 miles east (southbound) from El Pescador State Park.

EL MATADOR STATE PARK: 32215 Pacific Coast Highway in Malibu. The turn-off is 0.9 miles east (southbound) from El Pescador State Park.

**Hiking directions:** EL PESCADOR STATE BEACH (10 acres): Walk across the grassy field to the bluffs. The path begins from the west side of the park. Descend the bluffs to the east, dropping onto the sandy beach. The small beach pocket is bordered on each end by blufftop homes.

LA PIEDRA STATE BEACH (9 acres): A side path by the picnic tables leads to an overlook on the edge of the 100-foot bluffs. The main trail begins at the upper west end of the parking lot. Drop down the sandstone cliffs through a draw to a long, narrow, sandy beach with a rocky west end. To the east, the beach ends at a home on the point at the base of the cliffs.

EL MATADOR STATE BEACH (18 acres): Walk towards the 100-foot bluffs to a picnic area overlooking the ocean and adjacent beachfront homes. Take the path to the left, looping clockwise down the eroding cliffs. Two sets of stairs lead down to the gorgeous beach with offshore rock outcroppings and caves. When the tide is right, water swirls through the caves and sea stack tunnels in the rock formations. To the east, beyond the state park boundary, are private homes. If strolling to the east, stay below the high-tide water line to avoid property owner hassles. ■

# 18. Point Dume Natural Preserve

**Hiking distance:** 1.5 miles round trip
**Hiking time:** 45 minutes
**Elevation gain:** 200 feet
**Maps:** U.S.G.S. Point Dume

map
page 60

**Summary of hike:** Point Dume Natural Preserve is a 35-acre preserve on the northwest tip of Santa Monica Bay. The triangular-shaped sandstone headland juts out to sea, surrounded by water on three sides (back cover photo). From the 203-foot perch at the tip, views extend across Santa Monica Bay from Point Mugu to Palos Verdes. From mid-December through March, the summit is among the finest sites to observe the migrating gray whales en route from the Bering Sea to Baja California. On the west side of the point is Point Dume State Beach, a popular swimming, sunbathing, and tidepooling beach with a rocky shoreline. To the east, tucked beneath the 200-foot sandstone cliffs, is Dume Cove (locally known as Pirates Cove), a secluded, unofficial clothing-optional beach between two rocky points.

**Driving directions:** From Santa Monica, drive 20 miles northbound on the Pacific Coast Highway (Highway 1) to Westward Beach Road by Point Dume and turn left/oceanside. (Westward Beach Road is 0.9 miles past Kanan Dume Road.) Turn left and drive 0.6 miles to the Point Dume State Beach entrance station. Continue 0.7 miles to the far south end of the parking lot. A parking fee is required.

For a second access point, just before reaching the beach entrance station, turn left on Birdview Avenue, and drive 1 mile to limited curbside parking spaces on the right. (Birdview Avenue becomes Cliffside Drive en route.)

**Hiking directions:** Walk towards the cliffs, past the trailhead gate, at the Point Dume Natural Preserve boundary. Wind up the hill on the footpath to a junction. The left fork leads to Birdview Avenue in a residential neighborhood. Stay to the right to a second junction. The right fork follows the ridge to a rocky point and ends at a fenced overlook. Return to the junction and take the other fork. A short distance ahead is a 4-way junction. The left fork loops around the terraced flat with coastal sage scrub to Birdview Avenue; it also connects with the beach access to Dume Cove. The right fork leads uphill to the summit, 203 feet above the ocean. The middle fork follows a boardwalk to a platform overlook. From the platform, a sandy path continues a short distance around to the point. Return to the beach access, and descend on the trail and stairs to Dume (Pirates) Cove at the base of the cliffs. At low tide, explore the tidepools and walk along the rocky shoreline northeast into Paradise Cove, a privately run, crescent-shaped beach with a small pier and concessions. ∎

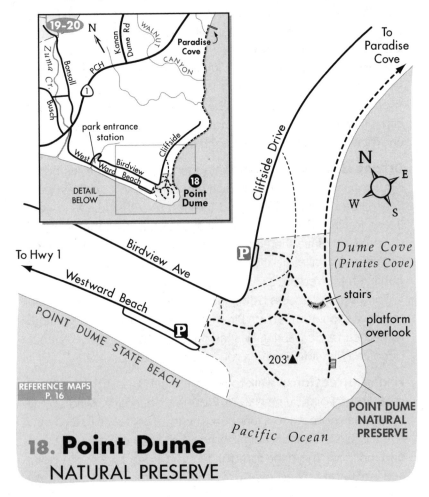

## 18. Point Dume
### NATURAL PRESERVE

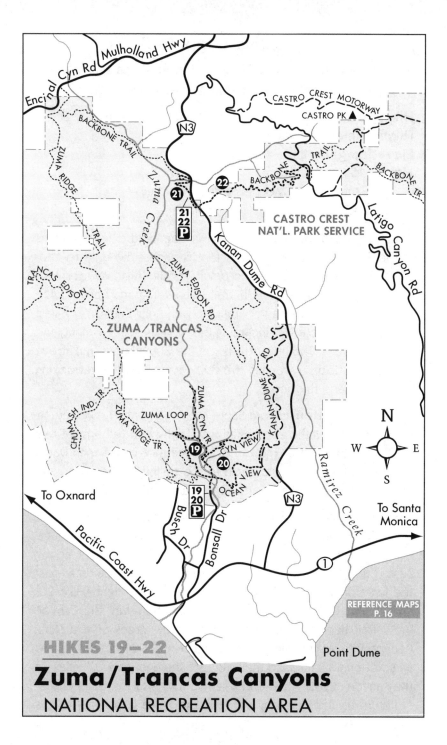

Mulholland Hwy

Encinal Cyn Rd

CASTRO CREST MOTORWAY

CASTRO PK ▲

BACKBONE TRAIL

N3

21

22

BACKBONE TRAIL

BACKBONE TR.

Zuma Creek

Latigo Canyon Rd

21 22 P

ZUMA RIDGE TRAIL

Kanan Dume Rd

CASTRO CREST NAT'L. PARK SERVICE

TRANCAS EDISON

ZUMA EDISON RD

ZUMA/TRANCAS CANYONS

CHUMASH IND. TR.

ZUMA RIDGE TR.

ZUMA LOOP

ZUMA CYN TR.

KANAN-DUME RD

CYN VIEW

19

20

OCEAN VIEW

Ramirez Creek

N3

19 20 P

To Oxnard

Busch Dr.

Bonsall Dr.

Pacific Coast Hwy

To Santa Monica

1

N
W ● E
S

REFERENCE MAPS
P. 16

**HIKES 19–22**

# Zuma/Trancas Canyons
## NATIONAL RECREATION AREA

Point Dume

# 19. Zuma Loop Trail

## ZUMA/TRANCAS CANYONS: Lower Zuma Canyon
## NATIONAL RECREATION AREA

**Hiking distance:** 1.7-mile loop plus optional 1.4-mile spur
**Hiking time:** 1—2 hours
**Elevation gain:** 250—450 feet
**Maps:** U.S.G.S. Point Dume
Santa Monica Mountains West Trail Map
N.P.S. Zuma/Trancas Canyons map

**Summary of hike:** Zuma Canyon is one of the few canyons in the Santa Monica Mountains that is accessible only to foot and horse traffic. There are no paved roads. This easy loop hike begins on the Zuma Canyon Trail in Lower Zuma Canyon. The trail heads up the drainage parallel to perennial Zuma Creek past lush riparian vegetation, including oak, willow, black walnut, and sycamore trees. The hike returns on the Zuma Loop Trail above the canyon floor, traversing the east-facing hillside overlooking the canyon and the ocean.

**Driving directions:** From Santa Monica, drive 21 miles north-bound on the Pacific Coast Highway/Highway 1 to Bonsall Drive and turn right/north. (The turnoff is one mile past Kanan Dume Road.) Continue one mile north to the trailhead parking area at road's end. The last 200 yards are on an unpaved lane.

**Hiking directions:** From the end of the road, hike north past the trailhead gate on the Zuma Canyon Trail. At 0.2 miles is a junction with the Zuma Loop Trail the return trail. Go straight on the Zuma Canyon Trail past oak and sycamore trees. Continue past the junction with the Ocean View Trail on the right (Hike 20), cross Zuma Creek, and continue to a junction with the Canyon View Trail. Bear left and remain close to the creek on the Zuma Canyon Trail. At 0.7 miles, cross Zuma Creek to a junction. To add an additional 1.4 miles to the hike, take the right fork 0.7 miles up the canyon, crossing the creek several times to the trail's end.

Return to the junction, and take the Zuma Loop Trail to the

west, traversing the hillside. Follow the ridge south, bearing left at three separate trail forks before returning down to the canyon floor and completing the loop. ■

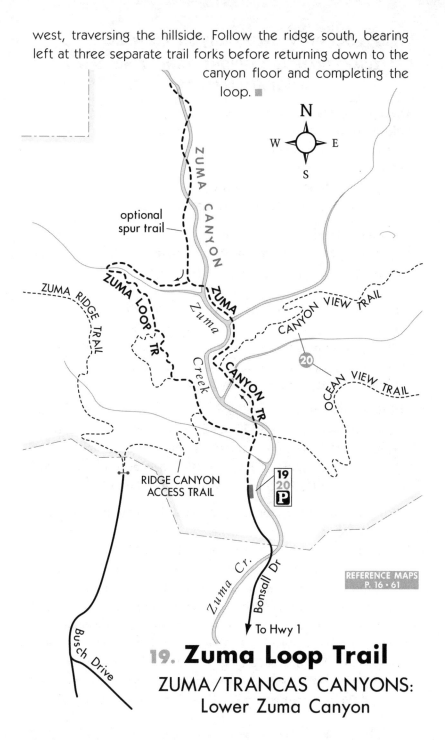

# 19. **Zuma Loop Trail**
## ZUMA/TRANCAS CANYONS:
### Lower Zuma Canyon

# 20. Ocean View—Canyon View Loop

## ZUMA/TRANCAS CANYONS: Lower Zuma Canyon
### NATIONAL RECREATION AREA

**Hiking distance:** 3.1 miles round trip
**Hiking time:** 1.5 hours
**Elevation gain:** 600 feet
**Maps:** U.S.G.S. Point Dume
Santa Monica Mountains West Trail Map
N.P.S. Zuma/Trancas Canyons map

**Summary of hike:** Zuma Canyon remains a beautiful, natural gorge with minimal development in Lower Zuma Canyon. The perennial stream makes its way down the canyon floor, reaching the ocean at the west end of Point Dume. From the parking area, a trail follows the canyon bottom and links to a network of hiking trails. This hike ascends the eastern hillside on the Ocean View Trail and returns back to the canyon on the Canyon View Trail. Throughout the hike are great views of Point Dume, the coastline, and upper Zuma Canyon.

**Driving directions:** From Santa Monica, drive 21 miles northbound on the Pacific Coast Highway/Highway 1 to Bonsall Drive and turn right/north. (The turnoff is one mile past Kanan Dume Road.) Continue one mile north to the trailhead parking area at road's end. The last 200 yards are on an unpaved lane.

**Hiking directions:** From the mouth of the canyon, head north up the canyon floor for 0.2 miles to a signed junction. The Zuma Canyon Loop (Hike 19) curves left. Stay on the canyon bottom 30 yards to the posted Ocean View Trail. Bear right to begin the loop. Cross a rocky streambed and ascend the east canyon wall. Wind up the hillside to views of Point Dume and the ocean, reaching the ridge at 1.3 miles. At the summit are sweeping coastal views that extend (on clear days) to Palos Verdes, Point Mugu, and Catalina. The Ocean View Trail ends at a T-junction, but the ocean views continue throughout the hike. Bear left 0.1 mile on the unpaved Kanan Edison Road to a junction with the Canyon View Trail. Curve left and follow the ridge across the head of the small side canyon. Weave down the hillside to the canyon floor and a junction at 2.6 miles. Bear left on the Zuma Canyon Trail and walk down canyon. Parallel the small stream past laurel sumac bushes and sycamore trees. Complete the loop and return to the trailhead. ■

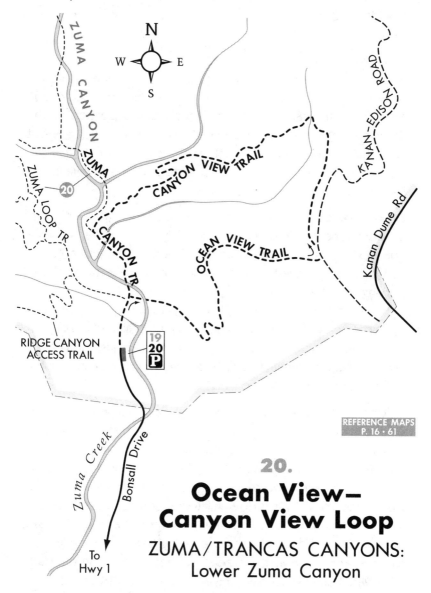

**20.**
# Ocean View–
# Canyon View Loop
## ZUMA/TRANCAS CANYONS:
### Lower Zuma Canyon

# 21. Newton Canyon Falls
## ZUMA/TRANCAS CANYONS: Upper Zuma Canyon
## NATIONAL RECREATION AREA

**Hiking distance:** 1.5 miles round trip
**Hiking time:** 1 hour
**Elevation gain:** 200 feet
**Maps:** U.S.G.S. Point Dume
      Santa Monica Mountains West Trail Map

**Summary of hike:** The Upper Zuma Canyon Trail is located in Newton Canyon in Zuma/Trancas Canyons National Recreation Area. The trail leads a short distance along a portion of the Backbone Trail to Newton Canyon Falls, a year-round, 30-foot waterfall in a lush, forested grotto with mossy rocks and a tangle of vines. There are large, shaded boulders to sit on while enjoying the falls by cascading Newton Creek.

**Driving directions:** From Santa Monica, drive 18 miles northbound on the Pacific Coast Highway/Highway 1 to Kanan Dume Road (5.8 miles past Malibu Canyon Road). Turn right and drive 4.4 miles north to the trailhead parking lot on the left (west). The parking lot is located just after the first tunnel (T-1).

From the Ventura Freeway/Highway 101 in Agoura Hills, exit on Kanan Road. Drive 7.9 miles south to the trailhead parking lot on the right (west). The parking lot is located just before entering the third tunnel (T-1). (Kanan Road becomes Kanan Dume Road after it crosses Mulholland Highway.)

**Hiking directions:** Hike west, away from Kanan Dume Road, on the signed Backbone Trail. The trail immediately begins its descent from the open chaparral into the shady canyon. After crossing the trickling Newton Creek, a side trail on the left leads 20 yards to sandstone rocks at the top of the falls. The main trail continues 100 yards downhill to a second cutoff trail on the left. Take this steep side path downhill through a forest of oaks, sycamores, and bay laurels to the creek, bearing to the left on the descent. Once at the creek, hike upstream along the path. Fifty yards up the narrow canyon is a lush grotto at the base of Newton Canyon Falls. The main Backbone Trail continues 1.9 miles northwest to the Zuma Ridge Trail, entering the rugged Zuma Canyon with its steep volcanic cliffs. Return by retracing your steps. ■

## 21.
# Newton Canyon Falls
## ZUMA/TRANCAS CANYONS:
### Upper Zuma Canyon

# 22. Newton Canyon
## ZUMA/TRANCAS CANYONS · CASTRO CREST N.P.S.

**Hiking distance:** 4.6 miles round trip
**Hiking time:** 2.5 hours
**Elevation gain:** 300 feet
**Maps:** U.S.G.S. Point Dume
Santa Monica Mountains West Trail Map

**Summary of hike:** This hike parallels Newton Canyon along a 2.3-mile section of the Backbone Trail between Kanan Dume Road and Latigo Canyon Road. The trail runs through the Castro Crest National Park Service corridor, which connects Zuma/Trancas Canyons to Malibu Creek State Park. The forested trail winds along the south ridge of the dense oak-filled canyon, with ocean views and seasonal stream crossings.

**Driving directions:** From Santa Monica, drive 18 miles northbound on the Pacific Coast Highway/Highway 1 to Kanan Dume Road (5.8 miles past Malibu Canyon Road). Turn right and drive 4.4 miles north to the trailhead parking lot on the left (west). The parking lot is located just after the first tunnel (T-1).

From the Ventura Freeway/Highway 101 in Agoura Hills, exit on Kanan Road. Drive 7.9 miles south to the trailhead parking lot on the right (west). The parking lot is located just before entering the third tunnel (T-1). (Kanan Road becomes Kanan Dume Road after it crosses Mulholland Highway.)

**Hiking directions:** The signed trail begins by Kanan Dume Road and heads south towards the ocean. The trail, an old fire road, climbs up to the tunnel and crosses over Kanan Dume Road. After crossing, the road narrows to a footpath and enters a forested canopy, slowly descending into Newton Canyon. The trail crosses a paved driveway, then enters the park and climbs to various overlooks. Continue along the winding mountainside above Newton Canyon. Near the end of the trail, maze-like switchbacks lead to Latigo Canyon Road, the turn-around spot.

To hike farther, cross the road to the trailhead parking area, and continue on the Backbone Trail. The trail leads another 1.4 miles

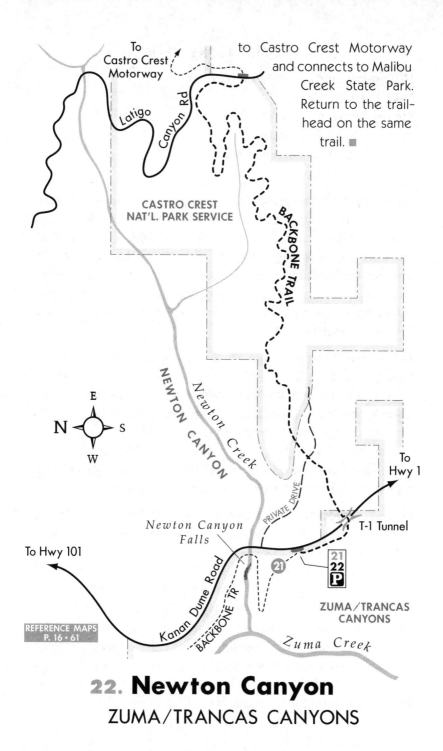

To
Castro Crest
Motorway

to Castro Crest Motorway and connects to Malibu Creek State Park. Return to the trailhead on the same trail. ▪

Latigo

Canyon Rd

CASTRO CREST
NAT'L. PARK SERVICE

BACKBONE TRAIL

E

N ← → S

W

NEWTON CANYON

Newton Creek

To
Hwy 1

PRIVATE DRIVE

T-1 Tunnel

Newton Canyon
Falls

To Hwy 101

Kanan Dume Road

BACKBONE TR

21

21
22
P

ZUMA/TRANCAS
CANYONS

REFERENCE MAPS
P. 16 • 61

Zuma Creek

## 22. **Newton Canyon**
### ZUMA/TRANCAS CANYONS

# 23. Rocky Oaks Park

**Hiking distance:** 2-mile loop
**Hiking time:** 1 hour
**Elevation gain:** 200 feet
**Maps:** U.S.G.S. Point Dume
Santa Monica Mountains West Trail Map
N.P.S. Rocky Oaks Site

**Summary of hike:** Rocky Oaks Park was once a working cattle ranch resting at the head of Zuma Canyon. The pastoral 200-acre ranch was purchased by the National Park Service in 1981. The park includes oak savannahs, rolling grasslands, chaparral covered hills, volcanic rock formations, scenic overlooks, picnic areas, and a pond in the grassy meadow. This easy loop hike meanders through the park, visiting each of these diverse ecological communities.

**Driving directions:** From Santa Monica, drive 18 miles northbound on the Pacific Coast Highway/Highway 1 to Kanan Dume Road (5.8 miles past Malibu Canyon Road). Turn right and drive 6.2 miles north to Mulholland Highway and turn left. Quickly turn right into the Rocky Oaks Park entrance and parking lot.

From the Ventura Freeway/Highway 101 in Agoura Hills, exit on Kanan Road. Drive 6.1 miles south to Mulholland Highway. Turn right and a quick right again into the park entrance.

**Hiking directions:** Hike north past the rail fence to the Rocky Oaks Loop Trail, which heads in both directions. Take the left fork a short distance to a 4-way junction. Continue straight ahead on the middle path towards the Overlook Trail. Ascend the hillside overlooking the pond, and take the horseshoe bend to the left. Beyond the bend is the Overlook Trail. This is a short detour on the left to a scenic overlook with panoramic views. Back on the main trail, continue northeast around the ridge, slowly descending to the valley floor near Kanan Road. Bear sharply to the right, heading south to the Pond Trail junction. Both the left and right forks loop around the pond and rejoin at the south end. At the junction, go south and back to the Rocky Oaks Loop, then retrace your steps back to the trailhead. ▪

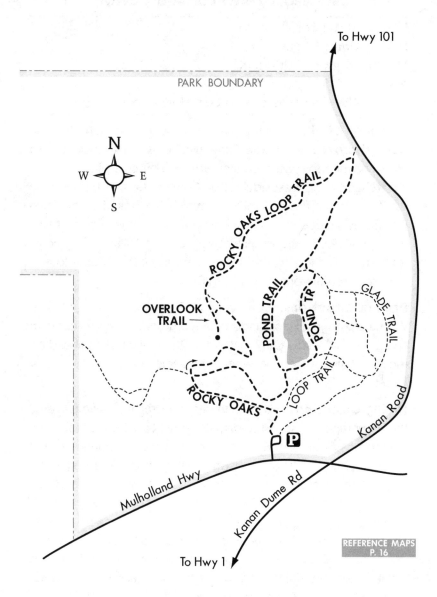

# 23.
# Rocky Oaks Park

# 24. China Flat Trail
## CHEESEBORO/PALO COMADO CANYONS

**Hiking distance:** 4-mile loop
**Hiking time:** 2 hours
**Elevation gain:** 1,000 feet
**Maps:** U.S.G.S. Thousand Oaks
      N.P.S. Cheeseboro/Palo Comado Canyons

**Summary of hike:** China Flat, a newer addition to the Cheeseboro/Palo Comado Canyons site, is a high, oak-dotted grassland meadow with sedimentary rock outcroppings. The flat is perched on the west side of Palo Comado Canyon beneath the shadows of Simi Peak, the highest peak in the Simi Hills. The China Flat Trail is a steep hike with awesome, panoramic views of Simi Valley, Oak Park, Agoura Hills, and Westlake Village. Connector trails link China Flat to the upper reaches of Palo Comado and Cheeseboro Canyons (Hikes 25—28).

**Driving directions:** From Ventura Freeway/Highway 101 in Westlake Village, exit on Lindero Canyon Road. Drive 4 miles north and park on Lindero Canyon Road by the China Flat Trailhead on the left. It is located between King James Court and Wembly Avenue.

**Hiking directions:** Hike north past the trailhead sign towards the mountains. Climb the short, steep hill to where a trail from King James Court merges with the main trail. Continue around the east side of a large sandstone outcropping. The trail levels out and heads east, following the contour of the mountain base, to an unsigned junction. Take the left fork north, heading uphill towards the ridge. Once over the ridge, the trail meets another unsigned junction. Take the left fork and head west, with views overlooking the canyon. Proceed uphill along the ridgeline to a flat area and trail junction. The right fork leads back towards Palo Comado and Cheeseboro Canyons. Take the left fork and descend to another junction. Again, take the left fork, winding downhill to a gate at King James Court. Leave the trail and walk one block on the sidewalk to Lindero Canyon Road. The trail-head is on the left. ■

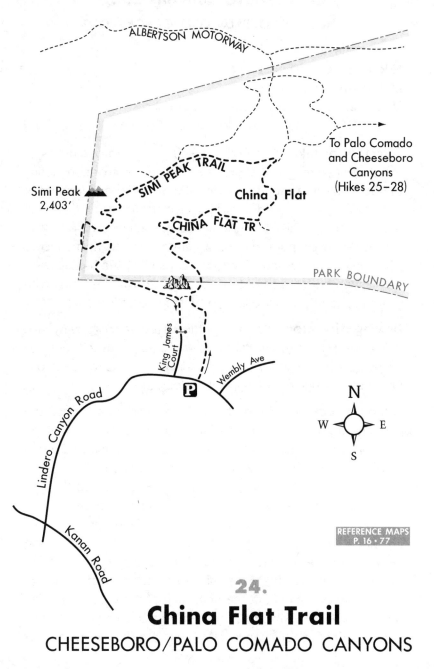

ALBERTSON MOTORWAY

SIMI PEAK TRAIL

Simi Peak
2,403'

China Flat

To Palo Comado
and Cheeseboro
Canyons
(Hikes 25–28)

CHINA FLAT TR

PARK BOUNDARY

King James Court

Wembly Ave

Lindero Canyon Road

P

N
W · E
S

Kanan Road

REFERENCE MAPS
P. 16 · 77

24.
**China Flat Trail**
CHEESEBORO/PALO COMADO CANYONS

# 25. Palo Comado — Cheeseboro Canyons Loop

## CHEESEBORO/PALO COMADO CANYONS

**Hiking distance:** 5-mile loop
**Hiking time:** 2.5 hours
**Elevation gain:** 800 feet
**Maps:** U.S.G.S. Thousand Oaks and Calabasas
N.P.S. Cheeseboro/Palo Comado Canyons

**Summary of hike:** Palo Comado and Cheeseboro Canyons, in the Simi Hills near Agoura Hills, is a wildlife corridor connecting the Santa Monica Mountains with the Santa Susana Mountains. This north-south corridor allows animals to move between the two ranges. This loop hike heads up the undeveloped Palo Comado Canyon parallel to a stream and adjacent meadows. After crossing over into Cheeseboro Canyon, the hike follows the canyon floor on an old ranch road through grasslands with groves of stately valley oaks and twisted coast live oaks.

**Driving directions:** From Ventura Freeway/Highway 101 in Agoura Hills, exit on Kanan Road. Head north 2.2 miles to Sunnycrest Drive and turn right. Continue 0.8 miles to the "Public Open Space" sign on the right. Park along the curb.

**Hiking directions:** From the trailhead, hike east past the gate and up a short hill on the Sunnycrest Connector Trail. As you top the hill, the trail descends into Palo Comado Canyon. Cross the stream at the canyon floor to a junction with the Palo Comado Canyon Trail, an old ranch road. Head left up the canyon through rolling grasslands with sycamore and oak groves. At one mile the trail begins to climb out of the canyon, winding along the contours of the mountain. Near the head of the canyon, the Palo Comado Canyon Trail curves left, heading to China Flat (Hike 24). There is an unmarked but distinct path leading sharply to the right at the beginning of this curve—the Old Sheep Corral Trail. Take this path uphill to a couple of ridges that overlook Cheeseboro Canyon. Descend into the canyon a short distance to the corral and a junction at Shepherds' Flat. Straight ahead the trail climbs up to Cheeseboro Ridge. Take the right fork and follow Cheeseboro Canyon gently downhill. At Sulphur Springs, identified by its smell, walk beneath the white sedimentary cliffs of the Baleen Wall on the east canyon wall. Continue down canyon through oak groves to the posted Ranch Center Connector Trail, 1.3 miles down the canyon on the right. Bear right and wind 1.1 mile up and over the chaparral hillside from Cheeseboro Canyon back to Palo Comado Canyon. Bear right a short distance, completing the loop. Return to the left on the Sunnycrest Connector Trail. ■

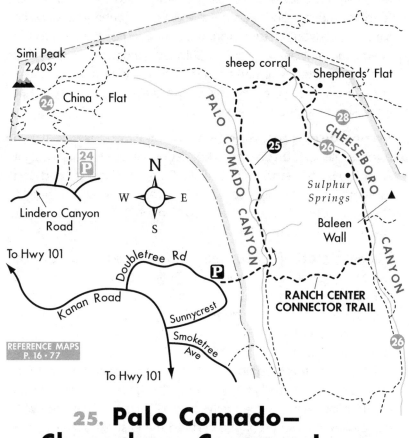

# 25. **Palo Comado–Cheeseboro Canyons Loop**
## CHEESEBORO/PALO COMADO CANYONS

# 26. Cheeseboro Canyon to Shepherds' Flat
## CHEESEBORO/PALO COMADO CANYONS

**Hiking distance:** 8.6 miles round trip
**Hiking time:** 4 hours
**Elevation gain:** 600 feet
**Maps:** U.S.G.S. Calabasas
        N.P.S. Cheeseboro/Palo Comado Canyons

**Summary of hike:** Cheeseboro Canyon is a lush stream-fed canyon with large valley oaks, gnarled coast live oaks, and syca-mores in the Cheeseboro/Palo Comado Canyons site. The hike follows an old abandoned ranch road on a gentle grade up the forested canyon bottom, from the south end of the park to the north. The trail passes fragrant Sulphur Springs as you pass be-neath the Baleen Wall, a vertical rock formation on the east can-yon wall. At the upper reaches of the canyon is Shepherds' Flat, a grassland flat and a sheep corral.

**Driving directions:** From Ventura Freeway/Highway 101 in Agoura Hills, exit on Chesebro Road. Continue one block straight ahead, past the stop sign, to Palo Comado Canyon Road and turn left. Drive 0.3 miles to Chesebro Road again and turn right. Continue 0.7 miles to Cheeseboro Canyon Road and turn right. The trailhead parking lot is 0.2 miles ahead.

**Hiking directions:** Take the service road east toward Cheeseboro Canyon to a road split. Bear left on the Cheeseboro Canyon Trail, heading into the canyon past the Modelo Trail and the Canyon View Trail. At 1.3 miles is a junction with the Cheeseboro Ridge Connector Trail (also known as the Baleen Wall Trail). Take the left fork towards Sulphur Springs to another junction with the Modelo Trail on the left. Proceed a short dis-tance on the main trail to a junction. Take the left branch. As you near Sulphur Springs, the white, jagged cliffs of the Baleen Wall can be seen towering on the cliffs to the east. At 3.5 miles, the canyon and trail both narrow as the smell of sulphur becomes stronger. At the head of the canyon is a three-way junction at Shepherds' Flat, the turn-around point.

To return, retrace your steps back on the Cheeseboro Canyon Trail to the Modelo Trail junction. Take the Modelo Trail along the western ridge of the canyon back to the trailhead. ■

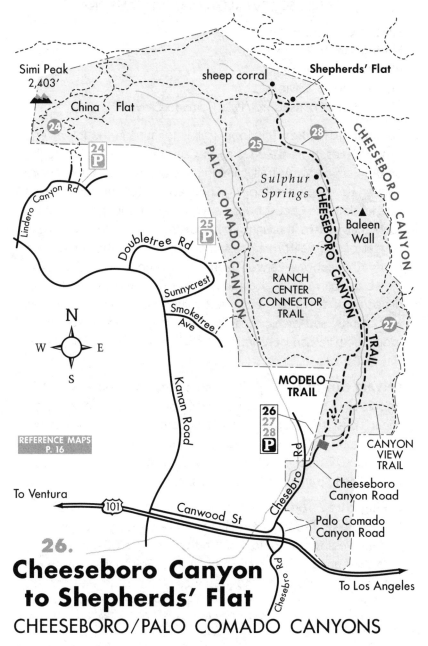

Simi Peak
2,403'

China Flat

sheep corral

**Shepherds' Flat**

24

24
P

Lindero Canyon Rd

Doubletree Rd

Sunnycrest

Smoketree Ave

25
P

PALO COMADO CANYON

25

*Sulphur Springs*

CHEESEBORO CANYON

28

Baleen Wall

CHEESEBORO CANYON

27

RANCH CENTER CONNECTOR TRAIL

N
W — E
S

Kanan Road

REFERENCE MAPS
P. 16

**MODELO TRAIL**

26
27
28
P

Cheesebro Rd

TRAIL

CANYON VIEW TRAIL

Cheeseboro Canyon Road

Palo Comado Canyon Road

To Ventura

101

Canwood St

To Los Angeles

Cheesebro Rd

# 26.
# **Cheeseboro Canyon to Shepherds' Flat**
## CHEESEBORO/PALO COMADO CANYONS

## 27. Canyon View—
## Cheeseboro Canyon Loop
### CHEESEBORO/PALO COMADO CANYONS

---

**Hiking distance:** 4-mile loop
**Hiking time:** 2 hours
**Elevation gain:** 500 feet
**Maps:** U.S.G.S. Calabasas
       N.P.S. Cheeseboro/Palo Comado Canyons

---

**Summary of hike:** This loop trail is located in the lower end of the Cheeseboro/Palo Comado Canyons site. The hike begins on the Canyon View Trail, climbing the east wall of Cheeseboro Canyon to a knoll overlooking Cheeseboro Canyon and the Lost Hills landfill. The Cheeseboro Canyon Trail is an abandoned ranch road that passes through groves of 200-year old valley oaks, largest of the California oaks. The hike follows the ridge separating Cheeseboro Canyon from Las Virgenes Canyon through native chaparral and coastal sage scrub communities. It then drops back down to the shaded valley oak savannahs, live oak woodlands, and picnic areas on the canyon floor. For a longer loop, the hike can be continued along the ridge to Shepherds' Flat—Hike 28.

**Driving directions:** From Ventura Freeway/Highway 101 in Agoura Hills, exit on Chesebro Road. Continue one block straight ahead, past the stop sign, to Palo Comado Canyon Road and turn left. Drive 0.3 miles to Chesebro Road again and turn right. Continue 0.7 miles to Cheeseboro Canyon Road and turn right. The trailhead parking lot is 0.2 miles ahead.

**Hiking directions:** Take the well-marked Cheeseboro Canyon Trail, and hike through the rolling hills filled with groves of stately oaks. Pass the Modelo Trail on the left to a posted junction with the Canyon View Trail at a half mile. Bear right, leaving the canyon floor, and climb the grassy canyon hillside. At 0.9 miles, the Canyon View Trail ends at a T-junction and a trail gate on

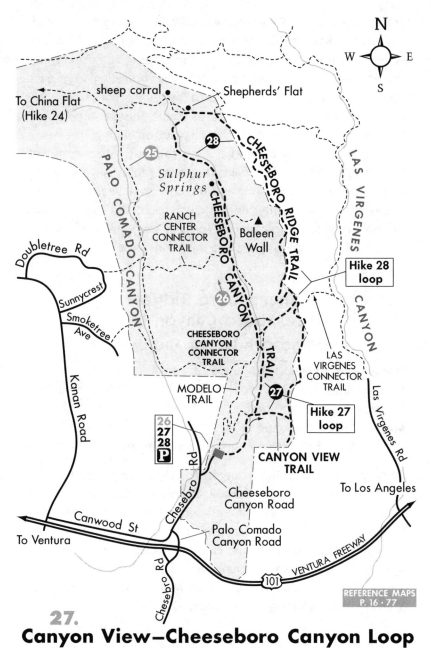

N
W · E
S

sheep corral •

Shepherds' Flat

To China Flat
(Hike 24)

25

28

*Sulphur Springs* •

PALO COMADO CANYON

CHEESEBORO RIDGE TRAIL

LAS VIRGENES CANYON

RANCH CENTER CONNECTOR TRAIL

CHEESEBORO CANYON

▲ Baleen Wall

Hike 28 loop

Doubletree Rd

Sunnycrest

Smoketree Ave

26

CHEESEBORO CANYON CONNECTOR TRAIL

LAS VIRGENES CONNECTOR TRAIL

MODELO TRAIL

TRAIL

27

Hike 27 loop

Kanan Road

26
27
28
P

Cheesboro Rd

CANYON VIEW TRAIL

Cheeseboro Canyon Road

To Los Angeles

Canwood St

To Ventura

Palo Comado Canyon Road

Las Virgenes Rd

VENTURA FREEWAY

Cheesboro Rd

101

REFERENCE MAPS
P. 16 · 77

# 27. Canyon View–Cheeseboro Canyon Loop
## 28. Cheeseboro Ridge and Canyon Loop
### CHEESEBORO/PALO COMADO CANYONS

Cheeseboro Ridge. Pass through the gate. The right fork leads 0.3 miles to an overlook of the canyon. Bear left (north) on the Cheeseboro Ridge Trail. Follow the ridge uphill to a Y-fork, enjoying the great canyon views. Stay left on the undulating ridge, passing power poles. Slowly descend to the Las Virgenes Connector Trail on the right. Stay left 120 yards to the Cheeseboro Canyon Connector Trail on the left. The Cheeseboro Ridge Trail—Hike 28—continues straight ahead along the ridge to Shepherds' Flat. Bear left and descend 0.7 miles down the grassy, sage-covered hillside to the canyon floor and a picnic area. Bear left on the Cheeseboro Canyon Trail, an old ranch road, and stroll through the oak groves, completing the loop at the Canyon View Trail junction. Return down canyon to the trailhead. ■

# 28. Cheeseboro Ridge— Cheeseboro Canyon Loop
## CHEESEBORO/PALO COMADO CANYONS

**Hiking distance:** 10-mile loop
**Hiking time:** 5 hours
**Elevation gain:** 900 feet
**Maps:** U.S.G.S. Calabasas
N.P.S. Cheeseboro/Palo Comado Canyons

**map page 79**

**Summary of hike:** This canyon-to-ridge loop explores a large tract of the Cheeseboro/Palo Comado Canyons site. The Cheeseboro Ridge Trail follows the ridge separating Cheeseboro Canyon and Las Virgenes Canyon in the Simi Hills above Agoura. From the ridge are bird's-eye views into both canyons that extend to the Santa Monica Mountains and across the San Fernando Valley. The hike returns through the shaded oak savannah, following a stream through Cheeseboro Canyon.

**Driving directions:** From Ventura Freeway/Highway 101 in Agoura Hills, exit on Chesebro Road. Continue one block straight ahead, past the stop sign, to Palo Comado Canyon Road and turn left. Drive 0.3 miles to Chesebro Road again and turn right. Continue 0.7 miles to Cheeseboro Canyon Road and turn right. The trailhead parking lot is 0.2 miles ahead.

**Hiking directions:** Take the well-marked Cheeseboro Canyon Trail, and hike through the rolling hills filled with groves of stately oaks. Pass the Modelo Trail on the left to a posted junction with the Canyon View Trail at a half mile. Bear right, leaving the canyon floor, and climb the grassy canyon hillside. At 0.9 miles, the Canyon View Trail ends at a T-junction and a trail gate on Cheeseboro Ridge. Pass through the gate. The right fork leads 0.3 miles to an overlook of the canyon. Bear left (north) on the Cheeseboro Ridge Trail. Follow the ridge uphill to a Y-fork, enjoying the great canyon views. Stay left on the undulating ridge, passing power poles. Slowly descend to the Las Virgenes Connector Trail on the right. Stay left 120 yards to the Cheeseboro Canyon Connector Trail on the left.

Stay to the right (north) on the old ranch road to begin the upper end of the loop. Wind up the ridge and skirt around the right side of a water tank. Gradually descend to the canyon floor and a trail split. Curve left and head west along the base of the mountain to a signed junction at Shepherds' Flat. The Sheep Corral Trail continues straight ahead to China Flat (Hike 24) and Palo Comado Canyon (Hike 25). Bear left on the Cheeseboro Canyon Trail (also called Sulphur Springs Trail), and follow the canyon floor steadily downhill. At Sulphur Springs, easily identified by its smell, walk beneath the white sedimentary cliffs of the Baleen Wall on the east canyon wall. Continue down canyon through oak groves and past shaded picnic areas. Pass the Ranch Center Connector Trail and the Palo Comado Connector Trail on the right, completing the loop at the Canyon View Trail junction. Return down canyon to the trailhead. ■

# 29. Chumash Trail
## ROCKY PEAK PARK

**Hiking distance:** 5 miles round trip
**Hiking time:** 2.5 hours
**Elevation gain:** 1,100 feet
**Maps:** U.S.G.S. Simi Valley East

**Summary of hike:** The Chumash Trail is located in Rocky Peak Park in the Santa Susana Mountains east of Simi Valley. This trail ascends the west flank of Rocky Peak, winding up the chaparral-cloaked mountainside to the ridge north of the peak. En route, the trail passes sculpted sandstone outcroppings, caves, and a series of scenic overlooks and highland meadows. From Hamilton Saddle and the Rocky Peak Trail junction are panoramic views of the Simi Hills, Simi Valley, San Fernando Valley, the Santa Susana Mountains, the Santa Monica Mountains, Blind Canyon, and Las Llajas Canyon.

**Driving directions:** From Highway 118/Ronald Reagan Freeway in Simi Valley, exit on Yosemite Avenue. Drive 0.4 miles north to Flanagan Drive and turn right. Continue 0.8 miles to the trailhead at the end of the road.

**Hiking directions:** Head north past the kiosk along the rolling hills and grassy meadows. The trail climbs steadily as you round the hillside to the first overlook of the Simi Hills to the south. The trail continues uphill through coastal sage scrub, curving left around the next rolling hill. The trail passes sculpted sand-stone formations. Arrow signposts are placed along the route. Continue to the east along the edge of the canyon to Hamilton Saddle. From the saddle, the trail sharply curves left (north), gaining elevation before leveling out again at Flat Rock. From Flat Rock, the trail begins its final ascent through chaparral, curving around the last ridge to the top. The trail ends at a junction with the Rocky Peak Trail at an elevation of 2,450 feet. Sixty yards to the left of the junction are views of Blind Canyon and Las Llajas Canyon. Reverse your route to return.

For a longer hike, the Rocky Peak Trail continues 1.3 miles southeast to the summit of Rocky Peak (Hike 31). ■

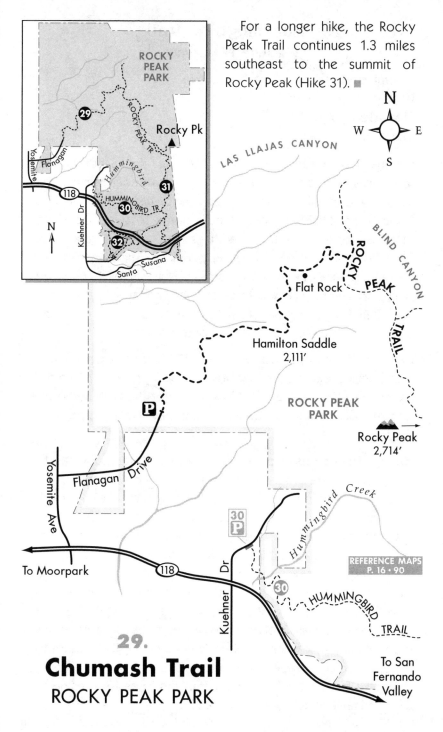

ROCKY PEAK PARK

ROCKY PEAK TR.

Rocky Pk

Hummingbird

HUMMINGBIRD TR.

Kuehner Dr.

Yosemite

Flanagan

118

Santa Susana

N

**29**

N
W          E
S

LAS LLAJAS CANYON

BLIND CANYON

ROCKY

Flat Rock

PEAK

Hamilton Saddle
2,111'

TRAIL

ROCKY PEAK PARK

Rocky Peak
2,714'

P

Yosemite Ave

Flanagan          Drive

Hummingbird Creek

30
P

To Moorpark

118

Kuehner Dr.

30

REFERENCE MAPS
P. 16 · 90

HUMMINGBIRD

TRAIL

To San Fernando Valley

# 29.
# **Chumash Trail**
## ROCKY PEAK PARK

# 30. Hummingbird Trail
## ROCKY PEAK PARK

**Hiking distance:** 4.6 miles round trip
**Hiking time:** 2 hours
**Elevation gain:** 1,000 feet
**Maps:** U.S.G.S. Simi Valley East

**Summary of hike:** Rocky Peak Park, in the Santa Susana Mountains, straddles the Los Angeles–Ventura county line at the eastern end of Simi Valley. A network of hiking trails weaves through the 4,815-acre park that is home to deep oak-lined canyons, trickling streams, and massive, sculpted sandstone formations with a moonscape appearance. The Hummingbird Trail, at the base of Rocky Peak, crosses Hummingbird Creek and climbs up a narrow canyon through open chaparral to the Rocky Peak Trail/fire road, passing stacks of giant sandstone boulders, sculpted caves, and dramatic rock outcroppings.

**Driving directions:** From Highway 118/Ronald Reagan Freeway in Simi Valley, exit on Kuehner Drive. Drive 0.3 miles north to the signed trailhead on the right. Park in one of the pullouts along-side the road. If full, additional parking is available just north of the freeway.

**Hiking directions:** From the trailhead kiosk, head downhill to the north. The trail soon U-turns southeast into the canyon to a defunct rock dam from 1917 and Hummingbird Creek. Proceed past the dam into an oak woodland and meadow. Once past the meadow, the trail crosses Hummingbird Creek and begins the ascent up the mountain through chaparral. Switchbacks lead up to sandstone caves and rock formations. After the rocks and caves, the trail levels out before the second ascent. Switchbacks make the climb easier as it heads up the canyon. At the head of the canyon, the trail levels out and passes more rock formations. The trail ends at a junction with the Rocky Peak Trail. Return to the trailhead by retracing your steps.

To hike farther, the Rocky Peak Trail continues 1.7 miles north to the summit of Rocky Peak—Hike 31. ■

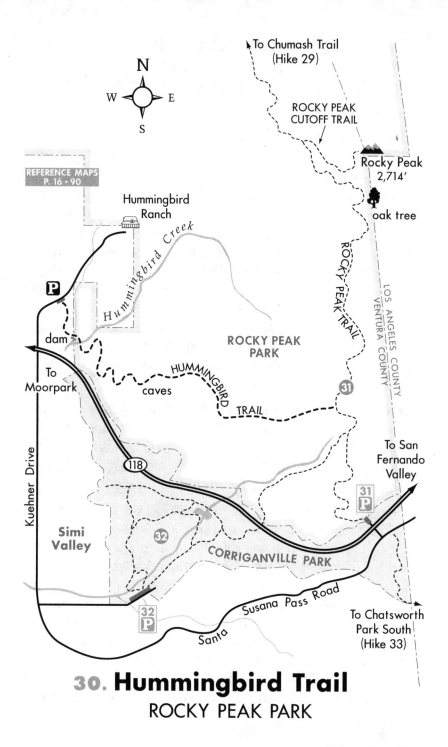

**N**
W   E
S

To Chumash Trail
(Hike 29)

ROCKY PEAK
CUTOFF TRAIL

Rocky Peak
2,714'

oak tree

REFERENCE MAPS
P. 16 • 90

Hummingbird
Ranch

Hummingbird Creek

**P**

dam

To
Moorpark

caves

HUMMINGBIRD TRAIL

ROCKY PEAK
PARK

ROCKY PEAK TRAIL

LOS ANGELES COUNTY
VENTURA COUNTY

31

To San
Fernando
Valley

118

Kuehner Drive

Simi
Valley

32

CORRIGANVILLE PARK

31
**P**

32
**P**

Susana Pass Road

Santa

To Chatsworth
Park South
(Hike 33)

# 30. **Hummingbird Trail**
## ROCKY PEAK PARK

# 31. Rocky Peak Trail
## ROCKY PEAK PARK

**Hiking distance:** 5–6 miles round trip
**Hiking time:** 2.5 hours
**Elevation gain:** 1,100 feet
**Maps:** U.S.G.S. Simi Valley East

**Summary of hike:** Rocky Peak Park is aptly named for the dramatic sandstone formations, fractured boulders, overhangs, and outcroppings. The 4,815-acre wilderness park is located in Simi Valley by Santa Susana Pass. The park is a critical wildlife habitat linkage between the Simi Hills and the Santa Susana Mountains. Rocky Peak Trail follows a winding fire road on the north side of the 118 Freeway to Rocky Peak, which lies on the Los Angeles-Ventura county line. There are a series of vista points along the route and at the jagged 2,714-foot peak, including top-of-the-world views of the San Fernando Valley, Simi Valley, the Santa Monica Mountains, and the many peaks of the Los Padres National Forest.

**Driving directions:** From Highway 118/Ronald Reagan Freeway in Simi Valley, exit on Kuehner Drive. Drive 3 miles south to the Highway 118 East on-ramp. (Along the way, Kuehner Drive becomes Santa Susana Pass Road.) Turn left, crossing over the freeway, and park 0.1 mile ahead at the end of the road.

**Hiking directions:** Hike past the trailhead kiosk up the winding fire road to an unsigned trail split at 0.9 miles. Stay to the left on the main trail, hiking steadily uphill to a signed junction with the Hummingbird Trail on the left (Hike 30). Proceed straight ahead on the Rocky Peak Trail, which levels out. The winding trail offers alternating views of the San Fernando Valley to the east and Simi Valley to the west. At the base of the final ascent is a singular, large oak tree. Begin the steep ascent, gaining 450 feet in a half mile, to the Rocky Peak Cutoff Trail. This is a good turn-around spot. However, if you wish to hike to the summit, the trail takes off to the right across the plateau for a half mile to Rocky Peak. The last section of the trail is a rock scramble to the peak. To return, reverse your route. ■

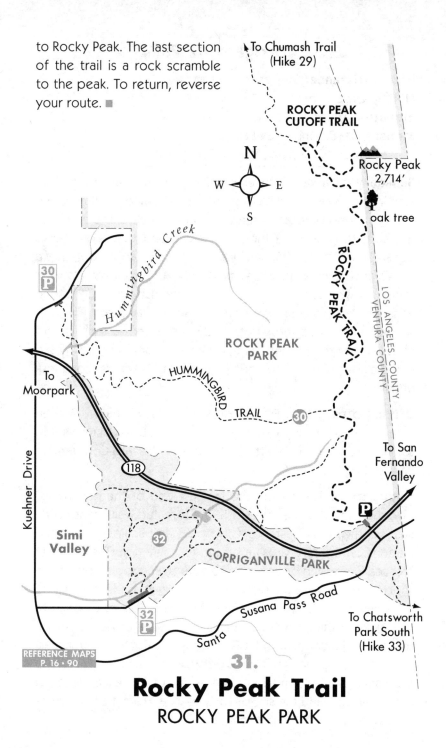

To Chumash Trail
(Hike 29)

**ROCKY PEAK
CUTOFF TRAIL**

Rocky Peak
2,714'

oak tree

ROCKY PEAK TRAIL

LOS ANGELES COUNTY
VENTURA COUNTY

N
W E
S

Hummingbird Creek

30
P

To
Moorpark

ROCKY PEAK
PARK

HUMMINGBIRD

TRAIL    30

To San
Fernando
Valley

Kuehner Drive

118

Simi
Valley

32

P

CORRIGANVILLE PARK

Susana Pass Road

Santa

To Chatsworth
Park South
(Hike 33)

32
P

REFERENCE MAPS
P. 16 • 90

**31.**

# Rocky Peak Trail
## ROCKY PEAK PARK

# 32. Corriganville Park

**Hiking distance:** 2 miles round trip
**Hiking time:** 1 hour
**Elevation gain:** 100 feet
**Maps:** U.S.G.S. Simi Valley East
     Rancho Simi Open Space: Corriganville Park

**Summary of hike:** Corriganville Park, at the eastern end of Simi Valley, was an old movie ranch. It is named for Ray "Crash" Corrigan, who purchased the ranch in the 1930s. The area was the setting to about a thousand movie and television shows between 1937 and 1965, including *The Lone Ranger, Gunsmoke, The Fugitive, Lassie, Mutiny on the Bounty, African Queen, How the West Was Won,* and *Fort Apache,* to name just a few. Old stone and concrete foundations from the sets still remain. The oak-shaded paths lead through the 225-acre park past prominent sandstone outcroppings, cliffs, caves, a stream, Jungle Jim Lake, and the Hangin' Tree, a towering oak used to "execute" countless outlaws.

**Driving directions:** From Highway 118/Ronald Reagan Freeway in Simi Valley, exit on Kuehner Drive. Drive 1.1 mile south to Smith Road and turn left. Continue 0.4 miles into Corriganville Park and park on the left.

**Hiking directions:** From the far east end of the parking lot, take the wide trail past the kiosk. The forested trail heads northeast up the draw past coast live oaks and sculpted rock formations on the left. Cross a bridge to a junction. The left fork crosses a wooden bridge, passes a pool, and loops back for a shorter hike. Stay to the right to the next junction. The right fork is a connector trail to Rocky Peak Park (Hike 31) via a concrete tunnel under the freeway. Curve to the left and cross the stream to another junction. Both trails lead west back to the trailhead. The footpath to the right travels between the sandstone cliffs to a dynamic overlook and a junction. The left fork descends to the old movie sets and the site of Fort Apache. From the sets, cross the bridge back to the parking lot. ■

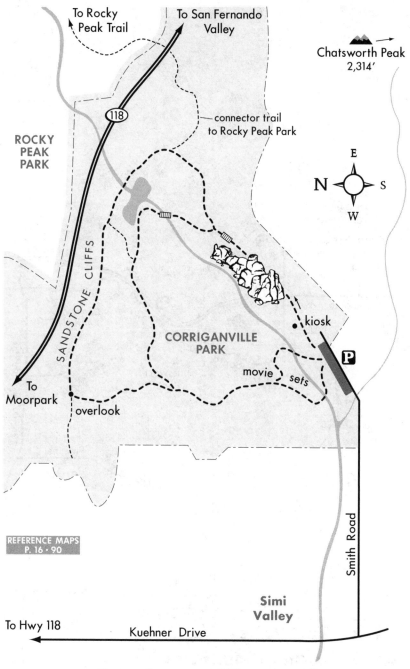

To Rocky
Peak Trail

To San Fernando
Valley

Chatsworth Peak
2,314'

118

ROCKY
PEAK
PARK

connector trail
to Rocky Peak Park

N E S W

SANDSTONE CLIFFS

CORRIGANVILLE
PARK

kiosk

P

movie sets

To
Moorpark

overlook

REFERENCE MAPS
P. 16 · 90

Smith Road

Simi
Valley

To Hwy 118

Kuehner Drive

## 32. Corriganville Park

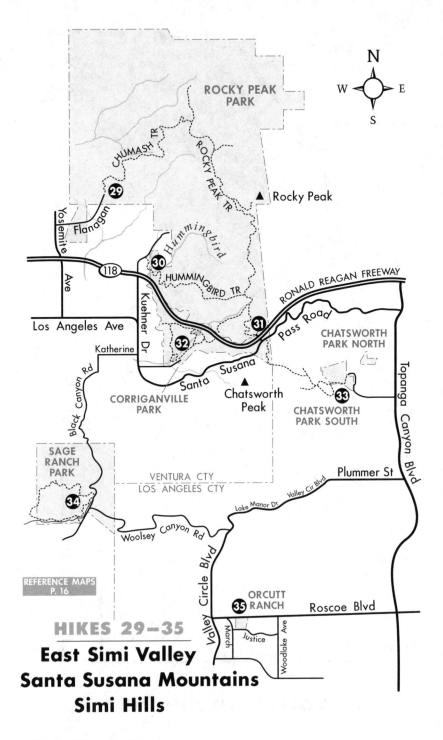

N
W · E
S

ROCKY PEAK PARK

CHUMASH TR

ROCKY PEAK TR

▲ Rocky Peak

Hummingbird

29

Yosemite

Flanagan

118

30

HUMMINGBIRD TR

Kuehner Dr

Los Angeles Ave

31

RONALD REAGAN FREEWAY

Pass Road

CHATSWORTH PARK NORTH

Katherine

32

Santa    Susana

Black Canyon Rd

CORRIGANVILLE PARK

▲ Chatsworth Peak

33

CHATSWORTH PARK SOUTH

Topanga Canyon Blvd

SAGE RANCH PARK

VENTURA CTY
LOS ANGELES CTY

Plummer St

34

Lake Manor Dr

Valley Cir Blvd

Woolsey Canyon Rd

Valley Circle Blvd

REFERENCE MAPS
P. 16

ORCUTT
35 RANCH

Roscoe Blvd

March

Justice

Woodlake Ave

**HIKES 29–35**
**East Simi Valley**
**Santa Susana Mountains**
**Simi Hills**

# 33. Old Stagecoach Trail

**Hiking distance:** 2.6 miles round trip
**Hiking time:** 1.5 hours
**Elevation gain:** 600 feet
**Maps:** U.S.G.S. Simi Valley East and Oat Mountain

map
page 92

**Summary of hike:** The Old Stagecoach Trail begins in Chatsworth Park South and climbs through the undeveloped wilderness of the Santa Susana Mountains. The trail follows a segment of the historic Santa Susana Stage Road that once linked Los Angeles with San Francisco from 1859—1890. The hike utilizes the old route, lined with interesting formations and bedrock worn down by stagecoach wheels. A web of unmarked and confusing trails weaves through rounded, fractured sedimentary rock to vistas of the city of Chatsworth, the San Fernando Valley, and the Santa Susana Mountains. Near the ridge is a plaque embedded into the sandstone rock. The marker was installed by the Native Daughters of the Golden West in 1937, designating the Old Santa Susana Stage Road.

**Driving directions:** From Highway 118/Ronald Reagan Freeway in Chatsworth, take the Topanga Canyon Boulevard exit. Drive 1.5 miles south to Devonshire Street and turn right. Continue a half mile to the end of Devonshire Street and enter Chatsworth Park South. Curve right and drive 0.2 miles to the main parking lot.

From Highway 101 (Ventura Freeway) in Woodland Hills, drive 5 miles north on Topanga Canyon Boulevard to Devonshire Street and turn left. Continue a half mile to the end of Devonshire Street and enter Chatsworth Park South. Curve right and drive 0.2 miles to the main parking lot.

**Hiking directions:** Follow the fire road/trail on the south (left) edge of Chatsworth Park South, skirting the wide park lawn. At the west end of the open grassland, take a gravel path towards the towering sandstone formations, just below the water tank on the right. Wind up the hillside past large boulders to an old paved road. Take the road 50 yards to the right, and bear left on the dirt path by two telephone poles. Climb to the ridge and a junction surrounded by the sculpted rocks. The left fork loops back to the park. Continue straight 50 yards and curve left towards Devil's Slide, a natural sandstone staircase. Follow the east edge of the chaparral-covered slope to an unsigned junction on the left. Bear left and climb the Devil's Slide, stair-stepping up the mountain on the stagecoach-worn bedrock. The sandstone slab leads to a huge rock with a historic plaque cemented into its face. From this overlook is a view into the Santa Susana railroad

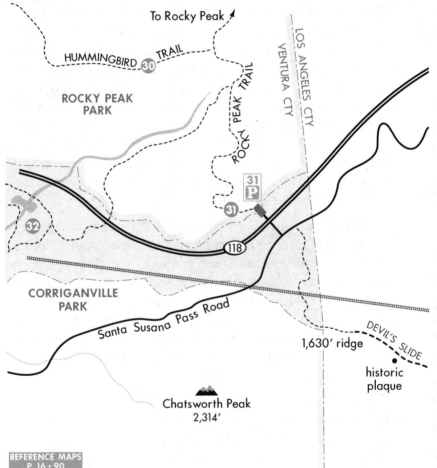

## 33.
# Old Stagecoach Trail

tunnel and across the San Fernando Valley. A quarter mile beyond the overlook is the 1,630-foot ridge atop the Devil's Slide, located near the Los Angeles—Ventura county line. Several trails wind through the hills and connect to Corriganville Park (Hike 32) and Rocky Peak Park (Hikes 29—31). Return on the same path or explore some of the side trails. ■

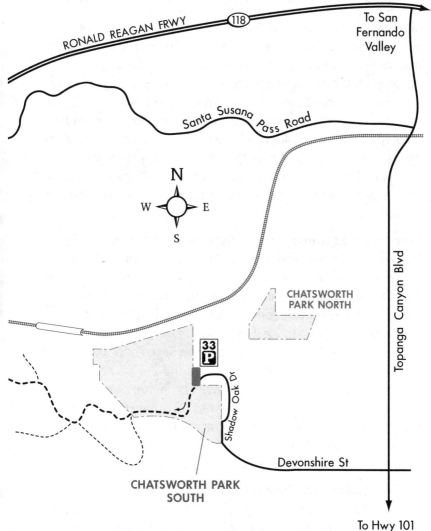

# 34. Sage Ranch Park

1 Black Canyon Road · Simi Valley

**Hiking distance:** 2.6-mile loop
**Hiking time:** 1.3 hours
**Elevation gain:** 300 feet
**Maps:** U.S.G.S. Calabasas
Santa Monica Mountains Conservancy: Sage Ranch Park

**Summary of hike:** Sage Ranch Park sits at 2,000 feet and has a garden-of-the-gods appearance. The ranch is located in the rocky Simi Hills overlooking a valley. The area is an inter-mountain habitat linkage connecting the Simi Hills with the Santa Monica and Santa Susana Mountains. This 635-acre park is rich with world-class sandstone formations, including an endless display of unique boulders and tilted sandstone outcroppings. Sandstone Ridge, a long, steep, weathered formation with caves and natural sculptures, rises 300 feet from the Sage Ranch Loop Trail. Beautiful carved boulders and eucalyptus trees fill the canyon.

**Driving directions:** From Highway 118/Ronald Reagan Freeway in the San Fernando Valley, exit on Topanga Canyon Boulevard. Drive south and turn right on Plummer Street. Continue 2.4 miles to Woolsey Canyon Road and turn right. (Along the way, Plummer Street becomes Valley Circle Boulevard and Lake Manor Drive.) Continue west on Woolsey Canyon Road 2.4 miles to Black Canyon Road and turn right. The Sage Ranch parking lot is 0.2 miles ahead on the left.

From Ventura Freeway/Highway 101 in the San Fernando Valley, exit on Valley Circle Boulevard. Drive north to Woolsey Canyon Road and turn left. Continue on Woolsey Canyon Road 2.4 miles to Black Canyon Road and turn right. The Sage Ranch parking lot is 0.2 miles ahead on the left.

**Hiking directions:** From the parking lot, hike west up the park service road. Proceed through the gate, passing orange groves on both sides. At the top of the hill next to the sandstone for-mations, the trail leaves the paved road and takes the gravel road to the right (north). Continue past a meadow dotted with oak trees and through an enormous garden of sandstone rocks. Watch for a short path on the right to a vista point overlooking Simi Valley. Back on the main trail, the trail parallels Sandstone Ridge before descending into the canyon. Once in the canyon, the trail curves back to the east past another series of large rock formations. Near the east end of the canyon is a trail split. Take the left fork, heading uphill and out of the canyon, back to the parking lot. ▪

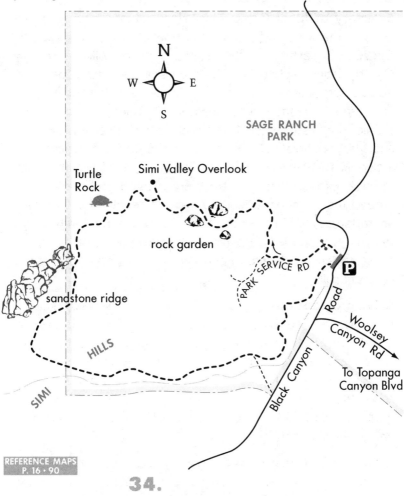

N
W ← → E
S

SAGE RANCH PARK

Simi Valley Overlook

Turtle Rock

rock garden

PARK SERVICE RD

P

sandstone ridge

Road

Woolsey Canyon Rd

HILLS

To Topanga Canyon Blvd

Black Canyon

SIMI

REFERENCE MAPS P. 16 · 90

## 34.
# Sage Ranch Park

# 35. Orcutt Ranch Horticulture Center

23600 Roscoe Boulevard · West Hills
Open daily 8 a.m. to 5 p.m.

**Hiking distance:** 1 mile round trip
**Hiking time:** 45 minutes
**Elevation gain:** Level
**Maps:** U.S.G.S. Calabasas and Canoga Park
Orcutt Ranch Horticulture Center map

**Summary of hike:** Orcutt Ranch Horticulture Center is tucked away at the west end of the San Fernando Valley in West Hills. The 200-acre estate was the vacation home of William and Mary Orcutt, dating back to 1917. The tree-studded estate, designated as a historical monument, was purchased by the Los Angeles Parks and Recreation Department in 1966 and opened to the public. The mission-style home with 16-inch thick adobe walls and a large patio area is nestled under the shade of ancient oaks, including a 700-year-old coastal live oak with a 33-foot circumference. Exotic plants and trees are planted on several acres around the former residence. Amid the fountains and statues are rattan palms, cork oaks, dogwoods, sycamores, birch, bunya bunya trees, purple lily magnolias, Chinese wisterias, bamboo, and a rose garden. An orchard of citrus and walnut groves covers the adjacent rolling hills.

**Driving directions:** From Highway 118 (Ronald Reagan Freeway) in Chatsworth, take the Topanga Canyon Boulevard exit. Drive 3.2 miles south to Roscoe Boulevard and turn right. Continue 2 miles to the posted park entrance on the left.

From Highway 101 (Ventura Freeway) in Woodland Hills, drive 3.4 miles north on Topanga Canyon Boulevard to Roscoe Boulevard and turn left. Continue 2 miles to the posted park entrance on the left.

**Hiking directions:** From the parking area, walk to the Parks and Recreation adobe buildings and the Orcutt estate house. After strolling through the patio areas, take the nature trail into the gardens. Dayton Creek flows through the south end of the gardens in a lush woodland. Along the creek are footbridges, statues and benches. Design your own route, meandering through the historic estate and gardens. ■

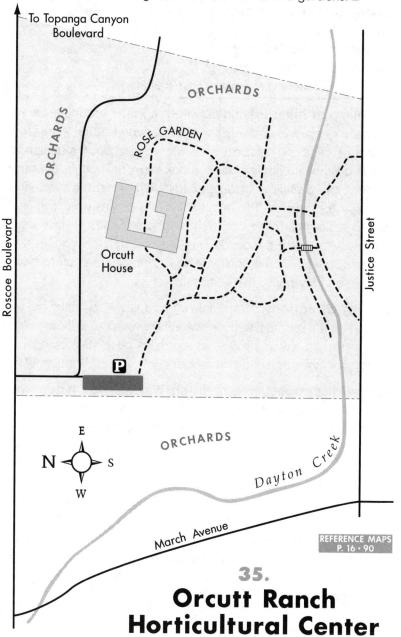

# 36. Escondido Falls

27200 Winding Way · Malibu

**Hiking distance:** 4.2 miles round trip
**Hiking time:** 2 hours
**Elevation gain:** 300 feet
**Maps:** U.S.G.S. Point Dume
    Santa Monica Mountains East Trail Map

**Summary of hike:** Escondido Falls is a 200-foot, multi-tiered cataract deep within the Escondido Canyon Natural Area. The upper cascade can be spotted during the hike, but the trail ends at the base of the lower falls in a box canyon. The falls tumbles 50 feet into a shallow pool, cascading off limestone cliffs into a mossy fern grotto. The hike to the falls begins on a winding, paved residential road due to trail access issues. In less than a mile, a footpath descends into the forested canyon. In the shade of oaks, willows and sycamores, the canyon trail follows a year-round creek to the waterfall.

**Driving directions:** From Santa Monica, drive 16.5 miles north-bound on the Pacific Coast Highway/Highway 1 to Winding Way and turn right. (Winding Way is 4.5 miles past Malibu Canyon Road.) The signed parking lot is on the left side of Winding Way.

**Hiking directions:** Hike north up Winding Way past some beautiful homes and ocean vistas on the south-facing slope. At 0.8 miles, leave the road on the well-defined trail, crossing the meadow to the left. Hike downhill into Escondido Canyon and cross the creek. After crossing, take the left fork upstream. (The right fork leads to Latigo Canyon.) Continue up the nearly level canyon trail beside the creek. The forested trail crosses the creek a few more times. After the fifth crossing, Escondido Falls comes into view. The trail ends by a shallow pool surrounded by travertine rock at the base of the waterfall. Return by reversing your route. (The upper falls is on private property and access is not permitted.) ∎

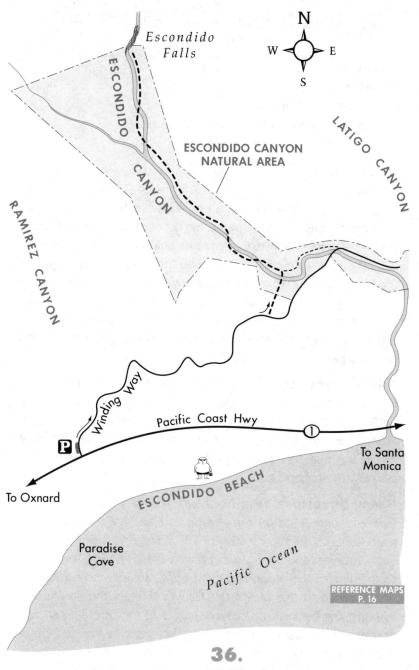

N
W E
S

*Escondido Falls*

ESCONDIDO CANYON

LATIGO CANYON

ESCONDIDO CANYON
NATURAL AREA

RAMIREZ CANYON

Winding Way

Pacific Coast Hwy

① To Santa
Monica

P

To Oxnard

ESCONDIDO BEACH

Paradise
Cove

*Pacific Ocean*

REFERENCE MAPS
P. 16

## 36.
# Escondido Falls

# 37. Rising Sun—Solstice Canyon Loop
## SOLSTICE CANYON

**Hiking distance:** 2.8-mile loop
**Hiking time:** 1.5 hours
**Elevation gain:** 400 feet
**Maps:** U.S.G.S. Point Dume and Malibu Beach
      N.P.S. Solstice Canyon map
      Santa Monica Mountains East Trail Map

**Summary of hike:** The hike up Solstice Canyon leads to Tropical Terrace, the ruins of a home built in the 1950s and destroyed by fire in 1982. The stone courtyard, garden terraces, stairways, and exotic tropical plants still remain. Near the ruins is Solstice Canyon Falls, cascading 30 feet over sandstone rocks. The Rising Sun Trail traverses the east wall of Solstice Canyon. The undulating path overlooks the lush canyon to the Pacific Ocean. The hike returns along the canyon floor parallel to Solstice Creek, passing through oak and walnut groves, grassy meadows, and picnic areas.

**Driving directions:** From Santa Monica, drive 14.3 miles northbound on the Pacific Coast Highway/Highway 1 to Corral Canyon Road and turn right. (Corral Canyon Road is 2.3 miles past Malibu Canyon Road.) Continue 0.2 miles to the gated entrance on the left. Turn left, entering the park, and drive 0.3 miles to the parking lot at road's end.

**Hiking directions:** Hike north up the steps past the TRW Trailhead sign. Wind up the hillside to a service road. Take the road uphill to the right to the TRW buildings, now home for the Santa Monica Mountains Conservancy. The Rising Sun Trail begins to the right of the second building. Long, wide switchbacks lead up to the east ridge of Solstice Canyon. Follow the ridge north towards the back of the canyon, and descend through lush vegetation. At the canyon floor, cross the creek to the ruins. Take the path upstream to the waterfalls and pools. After exploring, return on the service road parallel to Solstice Creek. A half mile

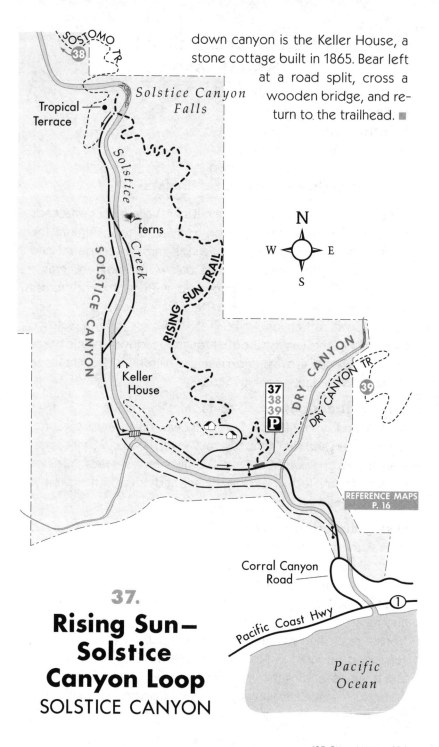

down canyon is the Keller House, a stone cottage built in 1865. Bear left at a road split, cross a wooden bridge, and return to the trailhead. ■

Solstice Canyon Falls

Tropical Terrace

SOSTOMO TR
38

Solstice Creek

ferns

SOLSTICE CANYON

RISING SUN TRAIL

N
W ⬥ E
S

Keller House

37
38
39
P

DRY CANYON

DRY CANYON TR
39

REFERENCE MAPS
P. 16

Corral Canyon Road

Pacific Coast Hwy

1

Pacific Ocean

## 37.
# Rising Sun– Solstice Canyon Loop
## SOLSTICE CANYON

# 38. Sostomo—Deer Valley Loop
## SOLSTICE CANYON

**Hiking distance:** 6.2 miles round trip
**Hiking time:** 3 hours
**Elevation gain:** 1,100 feet
**Maps:** U.S.G.S. Point Dume
      N.P.S. Solstice Canyon map
      Santa Monica Mountains East Trail Map

**Summary of hike:** The Sostomo–Deer Valley Loop ascends the west wall of Solstice Canyon to a 1,200-foot ridge at the preserve's north end. The trail winds through chaparral and coastal sage with stream crossings, oak woodlands, and grassy meadows. Sweeping vistas above Point Dume extend across Santa Monica Bay. The Sostomo–Deer Valley Loop is accessed by the Solstice Canyon Trail (Hike 37), which follows Solstice Creek along the canyon floor through meadows, picnic areas, oak and walnut groves, and past the historic Keller House, a stone building dating back to 1865.

**Driving directions:** From Santa Monica, drive 14.3 miles northbound on the Pacific Coast Highway/Highway 1 to Corral Canyon Road and turn right. (Corral Canyon Road is 2.3 miles past Malibu Canyon Road.) Continue 0.2 miles to the gated entrance on the left. Turn left, entering the park, and drive 0.3 miles to the parking lot at road's end.

**Hiking directions:** Take the posted Solstice Canyon Trail, and follow the paved road under sycamore trees alongside the creek. Cross a wood bridge to the west side of the creek at 0.2 miles. Continue up canyon past the historic Keller House. Just beyond the house is a trail split. The right fork leaves the main road and meanders through an oak grove, crossing the creek twice before rejoining the road. At 1.2 miles, just shy of the Tropical Terrace, is the posted Sostomo Trail. Bear left on the footpath, and begin ascending the west canyon wall. Climb at a moderate grade to magnificent views of Solstice Canyon. Rock hop over the creek in a narrow gorge. Wind up the canyon wall, passing

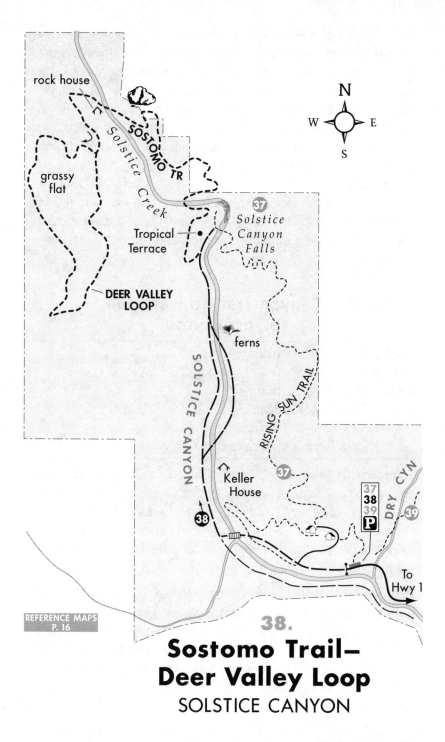

rock house

SOSTOMO TR

grassy
flat

Solstice Creek

Tropical
Terrace

37

*Solstice
Canyon
Falls*

DEER VALLEY
LOOP

ferns

SOLSTICE CANYON

RISING SUN TRAIL

Keller
House

37

38

37
**38**
39
P

DRY CYN

39

To
Hwy 1

38.

# Sostomo Trail—
# Deer Valley Loop
## SOLSTICE CANYON

the remnants of a home and chimney. At the head of the canyon is a towering sedimentary rock monolith. The trail skirts the park boundary and curves left before reaching the spectacular outcropping. Cross the creek again, passing the shell of a sturdy rock house. Climb to a junction with the Deer Valley Loop. Begin the loop to the right, leading to an open, grassy flat where the trail levels off. At an unpaved road, bear left for 50 yards and return to the footpath on the left. The sweeping coastal views extend across Santa Monica Bay, including a bird's-eye view of Point Dume. Switchback sharply left at the trail sign, and return on the lower loop. The Rising Sun Trail (Hike 37) can be seen across the canyon. Complete the loop and return by retracing your steps. ■

## 39. Dry Canyon Trail to waterfall
### SOLSTICE CANYON

**Hiking distance:** 1.2 miles round trip
**Hiking time:** 30 minutes
**Elevation gain:** 200 feet
**Maps:** U.S.G.S. Malibu Beach
      N.P.S. Solstice Canyon map
      Santa Monica Mountains East Trail Map

**Summary of hike:** Dry Canyon joins Solstice Creek at the lower end of Solstice Canyon near the Pacific Ocean. The Dry Canyon Trail leads up a canyon filled with oak and sycamore woodlands to an overlook of a seasonal, free-falling waterfall. After a rain, when the fall is active, the long, slender waterfall drops 150 feet off the hillside cliff.

**Driving directions:** From Santa Monica, drive 14.3 miles northbound on the Pacific Coast Highway/Highway 1 to Corral Canyon Road and turn right. (Corral Canyon Road is 2.3 miles past Malibu Canyon Road.) Continue 0.2 miles to the gated entrance on the left. Turn left, entering the park, and drive 0.3 miles to the parking lot at road's end.

**Hiking directions:** From the parking area, hike 20 yards back down the road to the signed Dry Canyon Trail on the left. Head north up the side canyon into a grassy oak grove. The well-defined trail parallels and crosses the creek. As you near the falls, the trail gains more elevation. The falls is across the narrow canyon on the left. This overlook is our turn-around spot. Return along the same path.

To hike farther, the trail continues a short distance to the end of the canyon before switchbacks lead up the canyon wall to Corral Canyon Road. Beyond the waterfall, the trail is not maintained and becomes overgrown with brush. ■

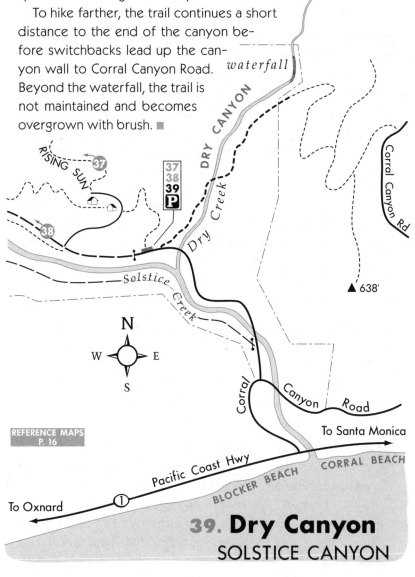

RISING SUN

37

38

37
38
**39**
P

*waterfall*

DRY CANYON

Dry Creek

Corral Canyon Rd

Solstice Creek

▲ 638'

N
W — E
S

Corral

Canyon Road

To Santa Monica

REFERENCE MAPS
P. 16

Pacific Coast Hwy

BLOCKER BEACH

CORRAL BEACH

To Oxnard

1

**39. Dry Canyon**
SOLSTICE CANYON

# 40. Corral Canyon Loop

### 25623 Pacific Coast Highway · Malibu

**Hiking distance:** 2.5-mile loop
**Hiking time:** 1.5 hours
**Elevation gain:** 400 feet
**Maps:** U.S.G.S. Malibu Beach
Malibu Creek State Park Trail Map

**Summary of hike:** Corral Canyon is an undeveloped, 2.5-mile-long watershed between Malibu Canyon and Latigo Canyon. The Canyon stretches from the crest of the Santa Monica Mountains to the Pacific Ocean. Seasonal Corral Canyon Creek, which runs through the steep draw, forms in Malibu Creek State Park, then drops 2,500 feet through the rugged canyon before emptying into the sea at Dan Blocker State Beach. The area was once owned by entertainer Bob Hope. It has since become Corral Canyon Park, encompassing 340 acres and this 2.5-mile loop trail. The well-maintained footpath climbs the east canyon slope on an ancient marine terrace with native bunch grasslands, providing wonderful ocean and mountain views. The trail climbs up through coastal sage scrub to the Peurco Canyon watershed divide. The return descends into the lush riparian canyon bottom among alder, coast live oak, California sycamore, and willow.

**Driving directions:** From Santa Monica, drive 13.8 miles northbound on the Pacific Coast Highway/Highway 1 to Malibu Seafood Fresh Fish Market on the right. Park along the side of the road for free or in the fee parking lot on the east side of the restaurant. The turnoff is located 1.8 miles past Malibu Canyon Road and 0.5 miles before Corral Canyon Road.

**Hiking directions:** From the parking lot on the east side of the restaurant, walk to the signed trailhead. Immediately drop into a shaded riparian corridor under oaks, sycamores and bays. Cross the creek and leave the lush vegetation to the exposed chaparral and veer left. Traverse the east slope of Corral Canyon to an unsigned fork. Begin the loop on the right fork, hiking counter-clockwise. Gently gain elevation to sweeping coastal and canyon views. Weave up the oceanfront hillside, with vistas stretching across Santa Monica Bay from Palos Verdes to Point Dume. Cut back to the left and continue climbing at a moderate grade on the east canyon wall. The path levels out, then begins to descend into the canyon with the aid of five switchbacks. Weave down-canyon, passing the remains of an old home on the left with an intact chimney. Return to the creekside vegetation, completing the loop. ■

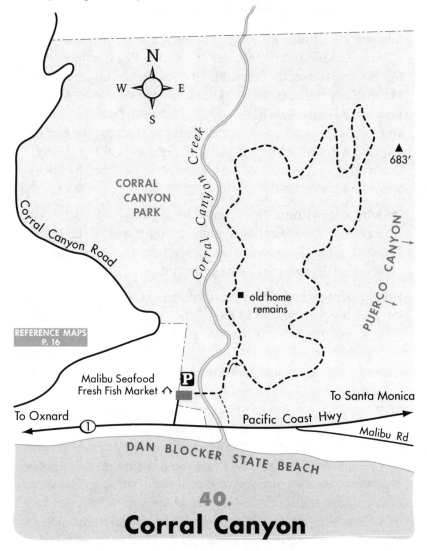

40.
**Corral Canyon**

# 41. Malibu Bluffs

## RECREATION AREA and COMMUNITY PARK

24250 Pacific Coast Highway · Malibu

---

**Hiking distance:** 2-mile loop
**Hiking time:** 1 hour
**Elevation gain:** 100 feet
**Maps:** U.S.G.S. Malibu Beach
Santa Monica Mountains East Trail Map

---

**Summary of hike:** Malibu Bluffs Recreation Area comprises 90 acres on the bluffs between the Pacific Coast Highway and Malibu Road, directly opposite of Pepperdine University and Malibu Canyon Road. The 100-foot bluffs rise above Amarillo Beach and Puerco Beach. Five public stairways (which adjoin private property) lead down to the shoreline from the base of the bluffs. The trails begin from the spacious lawns in Malibu Bluffs Community Park, a six-acre park with picnic facilities, ball fields, and a free parking lot.

**Driving directions:** From Santa Monica, drive 12 miles northbound on the Pacific Coast Highway (Highway 1) to Malibu Canyon Road by Pepperdine University. Turn left into the posted Malibu Bluffs Community Park parking lot.

**Hiking directions:** From the northwest corner of the parking lot, take the path closest to the Pacific Coast Highway and head west. Cross the meadow, passing a pocket of eucalyptus trees on the right, to a T-junction at the edge of deep Marie Canyon. The right fork exits the parkland to the Pacific Coast Highway, just east of John Tyler Drive. Bear left and follow the east ridge of the canyon to the bluffs closest to the ocean. Curve left along the edge of the bluffs to a junction. The right fork descends to the oceanfront homes and coastal access stairways at Malibu Road. Bear left and cross the footbridge over a minor drainage to another junction. The right fork gradually climbs to a picnic area at the southwest corner of Malibu Bluffs Community Park. Take the left fork 100 yards, following the east side of the gully. Two switchbacks zigzag up the hillside to great views of Pepperdine University and the Santa Monica Mountains. Continue to a trail fork. The left fork heads straight to the trailhead. Go to the right, climbing to a picnic area and paved path. Follow the blufftop path to the left and circle the park, passing the ball fields while overlooking Malibu Point (Hike 42). The path ends on the park road. Return along the road to the left. ■

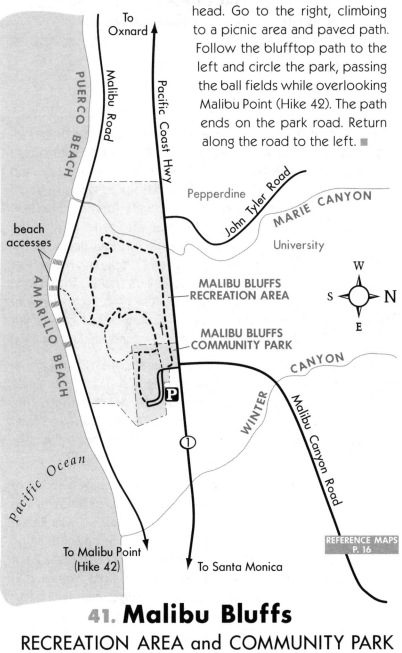

# 42. Malibu Lagoon State Beach
## MALIBU POINT
23200 Pacific Coast Highway · Malibu

**Hiking distance:** 1.5 miles round trip
**Hiking time:** 1 hour
**Elevation gain:** Level
**Maps:** U.S.G.S. Malibu Beach

**Summary of hike:** Malibu Lagoon State Beach encompasses 167 acres in the heart of Malibu, with 22 acres of wetlands, a brackish lagoon at the mouth of perennial Malibu Creek, and nearly a mile of ocean frontage. The sand-barred lagoon, just off Malibu Point, is a resting and feeding estuary for more than 200 species of migrating and native birds on the Pacific Flyway. The state beach includes a museum; 35-acre Surfrider Beach, popularized by surfing movies in the 1950s and 1960s; and Malibu Pier, a 700-foot long pier in a cove called Kellers Shelter. The historic pier dates back to 1903 and was rebuilt in 1946. To the west of Malibu Point is the exclusive Malibu Colony gated community. Nature trails meander to the beach and around the lagoon.

**Driving directions:** From Santa Monica, drive 11 miles northbound on the Pacific Coast Highway (Highway 1) to Cross Creek Road by the posted Malibu Lagoon State Beach turnoff. (The turnoff is 1.1 miles east/southbound of Malibu Canyon Road.) Turn left into the park, passing the entrance station to the parking lot. A parking fee is required.

**Hiking directions:** Take the paved path, crossing a series of bridges over the wetlands and lagoon. The path ends at the sandy beach on Malibu Point at the north end of Surfrider Beach. From here there are several walking options. Stroll south along Surfrider Beach to the Malibu Pier. Head north from Malibu Point along Malibu Beach in front of the Malibu Colony homes. (On this route, stay below the high-tide water line to avoid property owner hassles.) The third choice is to loop around the lagoon on the sandy beach.

Back at the trailhead on the far end of the parking lot, a bridge crosses an arm of the lagoon on estuary trails to a junction. The right fork leads through tall brush to a small opening on the lagoon. The left fork winds through the brush under the Pacific Coast Highway to the main lagoon channel. ■

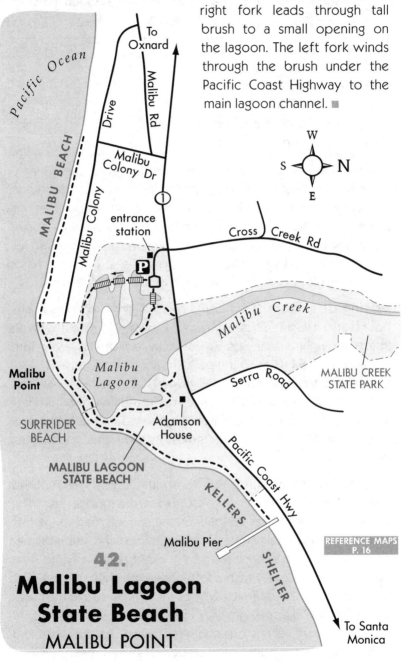

**42.**
# Malibu Lagoon
# State Beach
## MALIBU POINT

# 43. Peter Strauss Ranch

30000 Mulholland Hwy at Troutdale Drive · Agoura Hills

Open Daily: 8 a.m.—5 p.m.

**Hiking distance:** 1-mile loop
**Hiking time:** 30 minutes
**Elevation gain:** 200 feet
**Maps:** U.S.G.S. Point Dume
     N.P.S. Peter Strauss Ranch Site
     Santa Monica Mountains East Trail Map

**Summary of hike:** Triunfo Creek flows through the 65-acre Peter Strauss Ranch, with tree-shaded picnic areas along wide creekside lawns. This hike parallels the creek through an enchanting refuge. The trail traverses the hillside terraces above the creek through eucalyptus, oak, bay and sycamore groves with a lush understory of ferns and poison oak. The ranch has a giant outdoor aviary, amphitheater, and a 1926 stone house.

**Driving directions:** From Santa Monica, drive 12 miles northbound on the Pacific Coast Highway/Highway 1 to Malibu Canyon Road. Turn right and drive 6.5 miles to Mulholland Highway. Turn left and drive 5.1 miles to the park entrance on the left.

From the Ventura Freeway/Highway 101 in Agoura Hills, exit on Kanan Road. Head 3 miles south to Troutdale Drive. Turn left and drive 0.4 miles to Mulholland Highway. Turn left and immediately turn right into the Peter Strauss Park entrance and parking lot.

**Hiking directions:** Take the footpath towards Mulholland Highway and the entrance arch. Cross the bridge spanning Triunfo Creek, and enter the park on the service road to the left, across from Troutdale Drive. Head south past the amphitheater to the end of the service road by the old Lake Enchanto Dam, built in the 1940s. Stay to the left, parallel to Triunfo Creek. The forested Peter Strauss Trail traverses the hillside above the creek to a junction. Take the right fork up a series of switchbacks. At the top, the trail levels out and heads west. At the west end, switchbacks zigzag down the slope. Pass small meadows and cross a wooden bridge to a junction. The right fork leads to a picnic area. The left fork completes the loop at the amphitheater and aviary. ◼

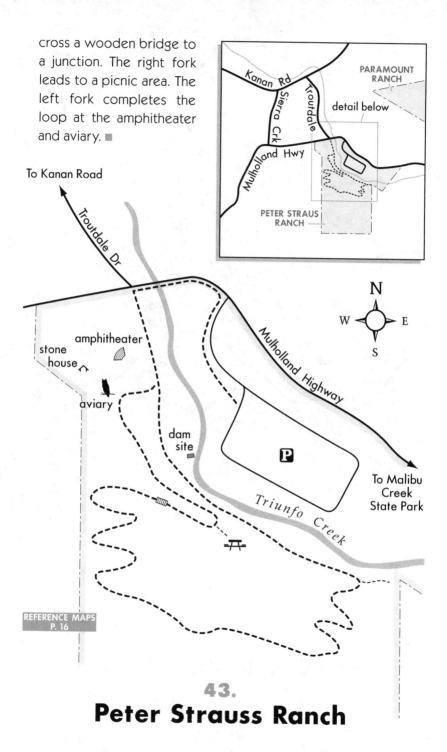

To Kanan Road

Troutdale Dr

PARAMOUNT RANCH

Kanan Rd

Sierra Crk

Troutdale

detail below

Mulholland Hwy

PETER STRAUS RANCH

amphitheater

stone house

aviary

dam site

Mulholland Highway

N
W · E
S

P

To Malibu Creek State Park

Triunfo Creek

REFERENCE MAPS
P. 16

## 43.
# Peter Strauss Ranch

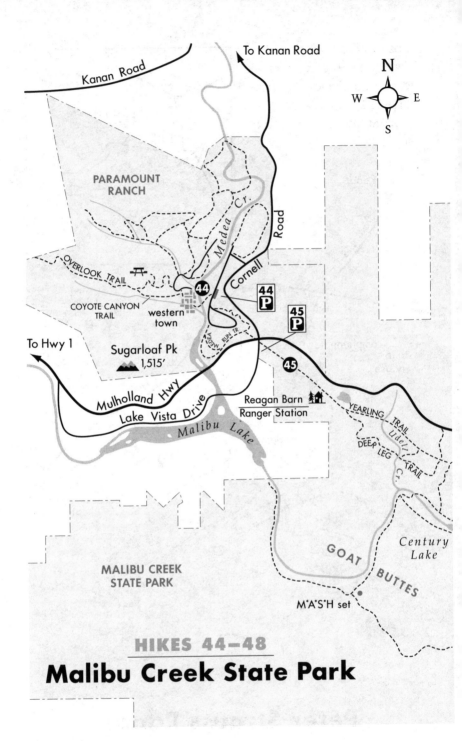

HIKES 44–48
# Malibu Creek State Park

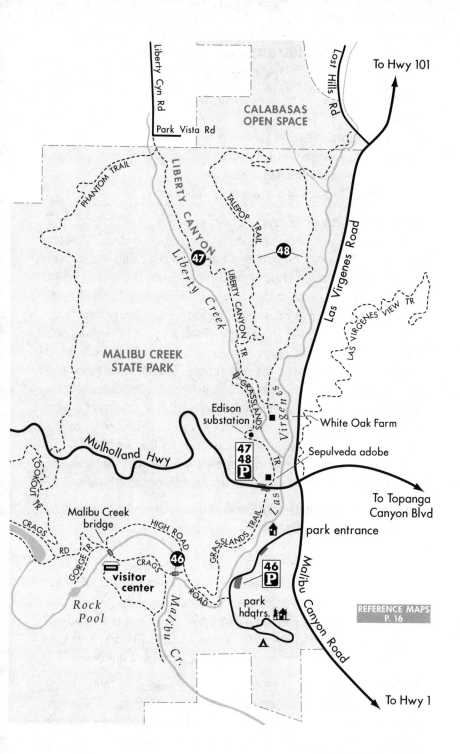

To Hwy 101

Liberty Cyn Rd

CALABASAS OPEN SPACE

Park Vista Rd

Lost Hills Rd

PHANTOM TRAIL

LIBERTY CANYON

Liberty Creek

TALEPOP TRAIL

LIBERTY CANYON TR.

**47**

**48**

Las Virgenes Road

LAS VIRGENES VIEW TR

MALIBU CREEK STATE PARK

GRASSLANDS TR.

Las Virgenes

Edison substation

White Oak Farm

Mulholland Hwy

LOOKOUT TR.

CRAGS RD.

Malibu Creek bridge

HIGH ROAD

CRAGS ROAD

GORGE TR.

visitor center

Rock Pool

Malibu Cr.

**47 48 P**

Sepulveda adobe

To Topanga Canyon Blvd

GRASSLANDS TRAIL

park entrance

**46**

**46 P**

park hdqtrs.

Malibu Canyon Road

REFERENCE MAPS P. 16

To Hwy 1

# 44. Paramount Ranch

2813 Cornell Road · Agoura Hills

**Hiking distance:** 2.75 miles round trip
**Hiking time:** 1.5 hours
**Elevation gain:** 200 feet
**Maps:** U.S.G.S. Point Dume
N.P.S. Paramount Ranch Site map
Santa Monica Mountains East Trail Map

**Summary of hike:** Paramount Ranch has a diverse and scenic landscape with oak savannahs, chaparral-covered hillsides, canyons, creekside thickets, rolling grasslands, and the prominent Sugarloaf Peak overlooking the parkland. The historic 326-acre ranch has been a motion picture filming site for hundreds of movies and television shows, including *Dr. Quinn, Medicine Woman*; *Have Gun Will Travel*; *The Cisco Kid*; *The Rifleman*; and *Tom Sawyer*. The hike takes in two short loop trails within the ranch that represent the diverse terrain. The Medea Creek Trail parallels the year-round creek through a riparian zone and circles an 860-foot hill near Sugarloaf Mountain. The Coyote Canyon Trail climbs the chaparral-covered canyon to a panorama of the ranch and an overlook of the mountains to the west. To reach the trail, wander through the streets of the realistic Western Town movie set with false store fronts, saloons and hotels.

**Driving directions:** From Santa Monica, drive 12 miles northbound on the Pacific Coast Highway/Highway 1 to Malibu Canyon Road. Turn right (north) and continue 6.5 miles to Mulholland Highway. Turn left and drive 3.2 miles to Cornell Road. Turn right and drive 0.4 miles to the Paramount Ranch entrance on the left. Turn left and continue 0.2 miles to the parking area.

From the Ventura Freeway/Highway 101 in Agoura Hills, exit on Kanan Road. Head 0.4 miles south to Cornell Road and turn left. Drive 1.8 miles to the ranch entrance on the right (west).

**Hiking directions:** COYOTE CANYON TRAIL—1.75 MILE LOOP: Cross the bridge over Medea Creek, and walk through Western Town to the signed Coyote Canyon Trail. Head west up the small ravine to a junction. The left fork is the half-mile Overlook Trail. The right (northeast) fork follows the ridgeline to another junction—the left fork leads to a picnic area, and the right fork heads down to a paved road. Return through Western Town.

MEDEA CREEK AND RUN TRAIL—1 MILE LOOP: From the parking area, head south on the service road parallel to Medea Creek. Take the signed trail bearing left. Switchbacks lead up to a junction. Continue straight ahead on the Run Trail to a trail split. Bear left towards Sugarloaf Peak. Curve to the right above the meadow at the base of the mountain. Descend into the wooded area parallel to Medea Creek, returning to the trailhead. ■

PARAMOUNT RANCH

Medea Creek

PAVED RD

SERVICE RD

Cornell

Road

OVERLOOK TRAIL

COYOTE CANYON TRAIL

Western Town

44 P

N

W E

S

RUN TRAIL

MEDEA

Sugarloaf Peak
1,515'

45 P

45

MALIBU CREEK STATE PARK

Mulholland Hwy

Lake Vista Drive

Malibu Lake

REFERENCE MAPS
P. 16 • 114

44. **Paramount Ranch**

# 45. Reagan Ranch
## MALIBU CREEK STATE PARK

**Hiking distance:** 3 miles round trip
**Hiking time:** 1.5 hours
**Elevation gain:** Level
**Maps:** U.S.G.S. Malibu Beach
　　　　Malibu Creek State Park map
　　　　Santa Monica Mountains East Trail Map

**Summary of hike:** The Reagan Ranch was President Ronald Reagan's home in the 1950s and 1960s before he was elected governor of California. The 305-acre ranch now occupies the northwest corner of Malibu Creek State Park. A network of trails, once used as horse riding paths for the Reagans, connects the ranch to the heart of the state park. This hike, the Yearling-Deer Leg Loop, includes a duck pond, a large rolling meadow, oak groves, stream crossings, magnificent vistas, and a visit to the Reagan barn.

**Driving directions:** From Santa Monica, drive 12 miles north-bound on the Pacific Coast Highway/Highway 1 to Malibu Canyon Road. Turn right (north) and continue 6.5 miles up this beautiful winding canyon road to Mulholland Highway. Turn left and drive 3.2 miles to Cornell Road. Turn left again and immediately park along the road wherever you find a spot.

From the Ventura Freeway/Highway 101 in Agoura Hills, exit on Kanan Road. Drive south 0.4 miles to Cornell Road. Turn left and continue 2.2 miles to the intersection of Mulholland Highway. Cross and park along the road.

**Hiking directions:** Enter the ranch at a gateway through the white rail fence on the southeast corner of Mulholland Highway and Cornell Road. Walk a quarter mile on the unpaved Yearling Road, lined with stately eucalyptus trees, to the old Reagan barn. Continue past the barn to a footpath—the Yearling Trail. The duck pond is on the left. Just beyond the pond is the beginning of the loop. Stay to the left on the Yearling Trail, heading towards the meadow. As you hike through the meadow, there are two side trails on the right that intersect with the Yearling Trail. You may bear right on either trail. They connect with the Deer Leg Trail for the return hike. Follow the Deer Leg Trail on the hillside slope as it winds past large oak trees. Cross Udell Creek and return through the meadow, past the pond, and back to the trailhead. ∎

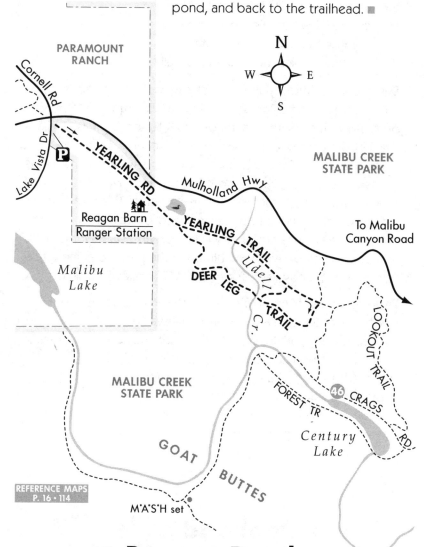

## 45. **Reagan Ranch**
### MALIBU CREEK STATE PARK

# 46. Rock Pool and Century Lake
## MALIBU CREEK STATE PARK

**Hiking distance:** 3 miles round trip
**Hiking time:** 2 hours
**Elevation gain:** 300 feet
**Maps:** U.S.G.S. Malibu Beach
  Malibu Creek State Park Map
  Santa Monica Mountains East Trail Map

**Summary of hike:** Malibu Creek State Park, purchased by the state from the 20th Century Fox movie studio in 1974, was originally home for thousands of years to the Chumash Indians. The 10,000-acre park contains a visitor center, campground, a manmade 7-acre lake, volcanic rock, sandstone outcroppings, majestic canyons, year-round streams, and over 30 miles of hiking trails that spread over its many acres. This hike follows Malibu Creek to Rock Pool, surrounded by towering volcanic cliffs, and continues to Century Lake. *Tarzan, Planet of the Apes,* and *South Pacific* have been filmed in the park, to name a few, but it is most recognized for the *M*A*S*H* television series.

**Driving directions:** From Santa Monica, drive 12 miles northbound on the Pacific Coast Highway/Highway 1 to Malibu Canyon Road. Turn right (north) and continue 6 miles up the winding canyon road. The Malibu Creek State Park entrance is located on the left, shortly before reaching Mulholland Highway. Turn left and park in the second parking lot on the left.

YEARLING

45

DEER LEG

Udell Cr.

FOREST

*Century Lake*

GOAT

TRIUNFO

BUTTES

• M·A·S·H set

LOST CABIN TR.

CANYON

# 46. Rock Pool and Century Lake
## MALIBU CREEK STATE PARK

From the Ventura Freeway/Highway 101, exit at Las Virgenes Road. Head south towards the mountains for 3.5 miles. The Malibu Creek State Park entrance is located on the right, just past Mulholland Highway. Turn right into the park.

**Hiking directions:** Cross the main road to the trailhead. Follow Crags Road as it slowly curves alongside Malibu Creek to a bridge. Crossing the bridge leads to the visitor center on Crags Road. The High Road stays on the north side of the creek. Both routes meet at Malibu Creek Bridge. At the bridge, take the posted Gorge Trail south. Bear left along the stream through a lava rock field to Rock Pool at the mouth of the gorge, 0.9 miles from the trailhead.

Return to the main trail back at the bridge. Continue on Crags Road (the main road) to the northwest. Continue uphill to a trail junction at the crest of the hill. From here is an overlook of Century Lake and a great view of Goat Buttes. The trail to the left leads down to the lake. Continuing right on Crags Road leads to the _M*A*S*H_ set one mile ahead. To return, retrace your steps. ■

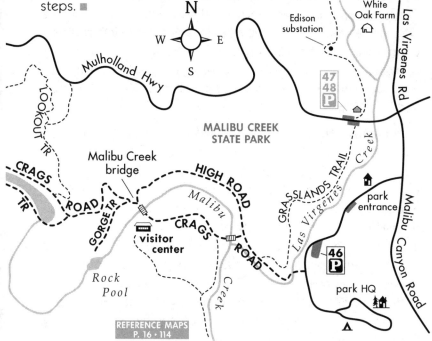

# 47. Liberty Canyon Natural Preserve
## MALIBU CREEK STATE PARK

**Hiking distance:** 3.8 miles round trip
**Hiking time:** 2 hours
**Elevation gain:** 100 feet
**Maps:** U.S.G.S. Malibu Beach and Calabasas
Malibu Creek State Park map
Santa Monica Mountains East Trail Map

**Summary of hike:** Liberty Canyon is one of three natural preserves in Malibu Creek State Park and is home to a rare stand of California valley oaks. The Grasslands Trail crosses rolling grasslands and merges with the Liberty Canyon Trail at a bridge spanning Liberty Creek. The Liberty Canyon Trail parallels the creek, gently climbing through oak woodlands to the head of the canyon.

**Driving directions:** From Santa Monica, drive 12 miles northbound on the Pacific Coast Highway/Highway 1 to Malibu Canyon Road. Turn right (north) and continue 6.5 miles up the winding canyon road to Mulholland Highway. Turn left and park 0.1 mile ahead in the parking pullouts on either side of the road.

From the Ventura Freeway/Highway 101, take the Las Virgenes Road exit. Drive 3.1 miles south to Mulholland Highway. Turn right and park 0.1 mile ahead in the parking pullouts.

**Hiking directions:** Begin on the signed Grasslands Trail, heading north past a white adobe house on the left. Cross the rolling grasslands, looping around the west side of an Edison substation. Continue north past oak trees, bearing right at a trail split. Cross a footbridge over Liberty Creek by a small waterfall and pools to a signed junction. Head left on the Liberty Canyon Trail past a junction at one mile with the Talepop Trail (Hike 48). Continue straight ahead, climbing the hillside through an oak grove overlooking the canyon, then return to the canyon bottom. The trail ends at the head of the canyon by Park Vista Road and Liberty Canyon Road. The Phantom Trail heads southwest to the left. Return along the same trail. ■

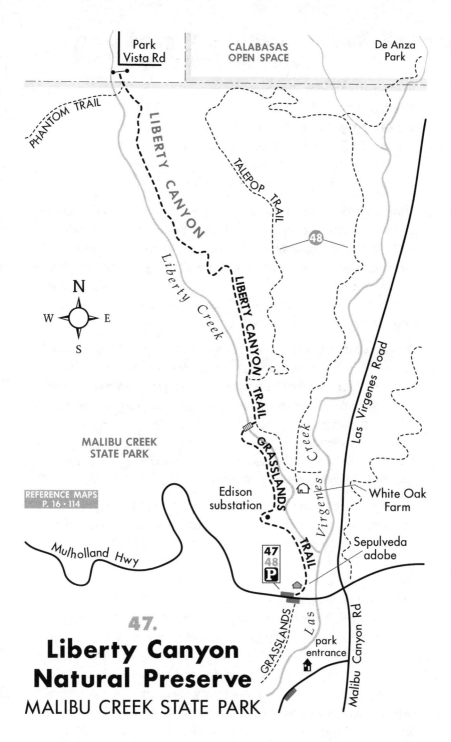

Park
Vista Rd

CALABASAS
OPEN SPACE

De Anza
Park

PHANTOM TRAIL

LIBERTY CANYON

Liberty Creek

TALEPOP TRAIL

48

N
W ·E
S

LIBERTY CANYON TRAIL

GRASSLANDS TRAIL

Las Virgenes Creek

Las Virgenes Road

MALIBU CREEK
STATE PARK

REFERENCE MAPS
P. 16 · 114

Edison
substation

White Oak
Farm

Mulholland Hwy

Sepulveda
adobe

47
48
P

GRASSLANDS

Las

park
entrance

Malibu Canyon Rd

**47.**
# Liberty Canyon
# Natural Preserve
## MALIBU CREEK STATE PARK

# 48. Talepop Trail—Las Virgenes Loop
## MALIBU CREEK STATE PARK

**Hiking distance:** 4.6 miles round trip
**Hiking time:** 2.5 hours
**Elevation gain:** 450 feet
**Maps:** U.S.G.S. Malibu Beach and Calabasas
Malibu Creek State Park map
Santa Monica Mountains East Trail Map

**Summary of hike:** This loop hike begins in Liberty Canyon, a natural preserve in Malibu Creek State Park. The Talepop Trail climbs to a grassy ridge overlooking Liberty Canyon, Las Virgenes Canyon, and the oak-dotted rolling hills. The path traverses the ridge, then returns in Las Virgenes Canyon parallel to Las Virgenes Creek. The Talepop Trail is named for a small Chumash Indian village once located in the area.

**Driving directions:** From Santa Monica, drive 12 miles northbound on the Pacific Coast Highway/Highway 1 to Malibu Canyon Road. Turn right and continue 6.5 miles up this beautiful, winding canyon road to Mulholland Highway. Turn left and park 0.1 mile ahead in the parking pullouts on either side of the road.

From the Ventura Freeway/Highway 101, take the Las Virgenes Road exit. Drive 3.1 miles south to Mulholland Highway. Turn right and park 0.1 mile ahead in the parking pullouts.

**Hiking directions:** Take the signed Grasslands Trail, and head north across the rolling meadow. Loop around an Edison substation. Continue north, bearing right at a trail split, to a footbridge over Liberty Creek by rock formations and pools. Cross the bridge to a signed junction. Take the left fork on the Liberty Canyon Trail, beginning the loop. At one mile is a signed junction with the Talepop Trail on the right. Head right (west) on the Talepop Trail, winding up the west canyon wall a half mile to the ridge. Follow the ridge north to the summit, overlooking Liberty Canyon on the west and Las Virgenes Canyon on the east. At the northern park boundary, bear right, down the hillside. Switchbacks lead to the Las Virgenes Canyon floor by Las

Virgenes Creek and a junction. The left fork crosses the creek and leads 0.3 miles to De Anza Park. Take the right fork—the Las Virgenes Trail—along the west side of the creek. As you approach White Oak Farm (a private residence) at the lower end of the loop, take the signed Liberty Canyon Trail to the right. A short distance ahead is the junction by the bridge, completing the loop. Bear left on the Grasslands Trail, cross the bridge, and retrace your steps. ■

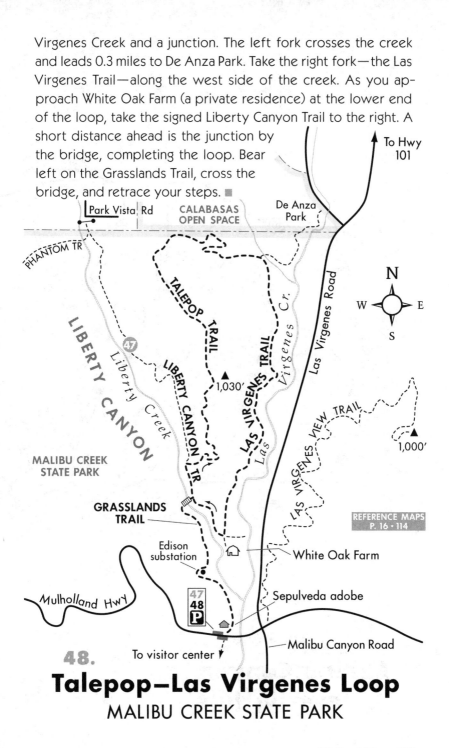

# 48.
# Talepop–Las Virgenes Loop
## MALIBU CREEK STATE PARK

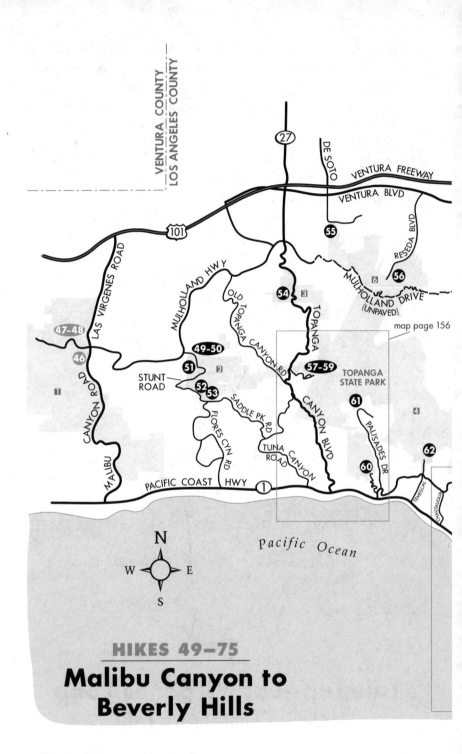

VENTURA COUNTY
LOS ANGELES COUNTY

27

DE SOTO

VENTURA FREEWAY

VENTURA BLVD

101

55

RESEDA BLVD

LAS VIRGENES ROAD

MULHOLLAND HWY

OLD TOPANGA CANYON RD

MULHOLLAND DRIVE
(UNPAVED)

6

56

54

3

map page 156

47-48

49-50

51

STUNT
ROAD

52 53

CANYON ROAD

MALIBU

2

SADDLE PK RD

FLORES CYN RD

TUNA
CANYON
ROAD

57-59

TOPANGA
STATE PARK

61

TOPANGA CANYON BLVD

PALISADES DR

60

4

62

TEMESCAL

CHAUTAUQUA

PACIFIC COAST HWY

1

N
W — E
S

Pacific Ocean

**HIKES 49–75**

# Malibu Canyon to
# Beverly Hills

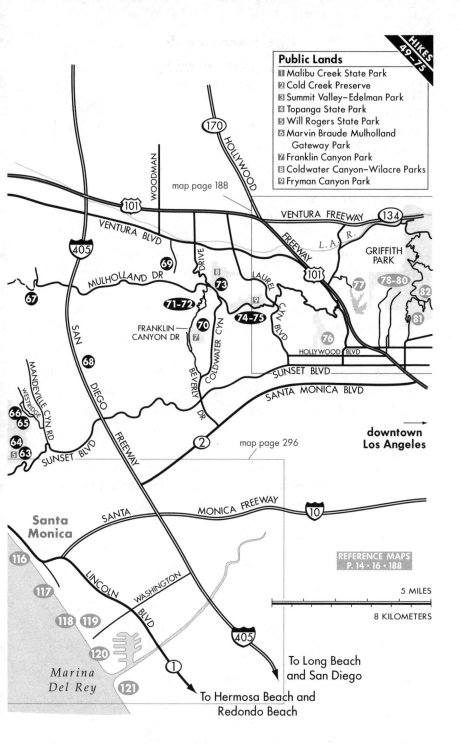

## Public Lands

1 Malibu Creek State Park
2 Cold Creek Preserve
3 Summit Valley–Edelman Park
4 Topanga State Park
5 Will Rogers State Park
6 Marvin Braude Mulholland Gateway Park
7 Franklin Canyon Park
8 Coldwater Canyon–Wilacre Parks
9 Fryman Canyon Park

HIKES 49–75

map page 188

VENTURA FREEWAY 134

L. A. R.

GRIFFITH PARK

VENTURA BLVD

101

WOODMAN

170 HOLLYWOOD

FREEWAY

101

405

MULHOLLAND DR

67

69

73 8

77

78-80

82

81

71-72

9

74-75

76

FRANKLIN CANYON DR

70

7

LAUREL CYN BLVD

COLDWATER CYN

BEVERLY DR

HOLLYWOOD BLVD

SAN

68

DIEGO

FREEWAY

SUNSET BLVD

SANTA MONICA BLVD

MANDEVILLE CYN RD

WESTRIDGE

66 65

64

5 63

SUNSET BLVD

2

downtown Los Angeles

map page 296

MONICA FREEWAY

10

Santa Monica

SANTA

116

117

118 119

120

LINCOLN

WASHINGTON BLVD

Marina Del Rey

121

1

405

REFERENCE MAPS
P. 14 · 16 · 188

5 MILES

8 KILOMETERS

To Long Beach and San Diego

To Hermosa Beach and Redondo Beach

# 49. Calabasas Peak

## COLD CREEK PRESERVE

**Hiking distance:** 4 miles round trip
**Hiking time:** 2 hours
**Elevation gain:** 900 feet
**Maps:** U.S.G.S. Malibu Beach
    Santa Monica Mountains East Trail Map

*map page 130*

**Summary of hike:** Calabasas Peak towers over Red Rock Canyon, Old Topanga Canyon, and bowl-shaped Cold Creek Canyon. The route to the 2,163-foot peak follows the Calabasas Motorway, a graded fire road. The vehicle-restricted road crosses the head of Red Rock Canyon past magnificent geological formations, including large, weathered sandstone outcroppings and tilted sandstone slabs with long ribs. Along the trail are spectacular 360-degree vistas into the surrounding canyons and the San Fernando Valley.

**Driving directions:** From Santa Monica, drive 12 miles northbound on the Pacific Coast Highway/Highway 1 to Malibu Canyon Road. Turn right and drive 6.5 miles to Mulholland Highway. Turn right and continue 4 miles to Stunt Road. Turn right again and drive one mile to the pullout on the right.

From the Ventura Freeway/Highway 101 in Calabasas, exit on Las Virgenes Road. Head 3 miles south to Mulholland Highway. Turn left and go 4 miles to Stunt Road. Turn right and drive one mile to the pullout on the right.

**Hiking directions:** Cross Stunt Road and walk 20 yards downhill to the trailhead. Walk up the unpaved fire road past the gate. The trail zigzags up the mountain to a junction at 0.7 miles on a saddle at the head of Red Rock Canyon. The right fork heads into Red Rock Canyon (Hike 50). Continue straight ahead to the north along the cliff's edge, passing large eroded sandstone slabs while overlooking Red Rock Canyon. As Calabasas Peak comes into view, the trail curves sharply to the right, circling the peak along an eastern ridge. From the ridge are views into Old Topanga Canyon to the northeast. The trail heads gently downhill before a steep descent. Just before the descent, watch for a narrow path on the left. Take this side path west up to the chaparral-covered summit. After lingering at the peak, retrace your steps.

From Calabasas Peak, the Calabasas Motorway continues to Old Topanga Canyon Road. ■

# 50. Red Rock Canyon
## COLD CREEK PRESERVE

**Hiking distance:** 4 miles round trip
**Hiking time:** 2 hours
**Elevation gain:** 700 feet
**Maps:** U.S.G.S. Malibu Beach
Santa Monica Mountains East Trail Map

map
page 130

**Summary of hike:** Red Rock Canyon is a beautiful, multi-colored canyon that looks similar to the canyons in the southwest. Huge weather-sculpted red sandstone formations and conglomerate rocks dominate a landscape that is dotted with oaks and sycamores. Shell fossils can be spotted in the eroded rocks, shallow caves, overhangs, and arches. The riparian canyon is a wildlife corridor connecting Topanga State Park and Malibu Creek State Park. The trail follows the first portion of the Calabasas Motorway—a graded fire road—to the head of Red Rock Canyon.

**Driving directions:** From Santa Monica, drive 12 miles north-bound on the Pacific Coast Highway/Highway 1 to Malibu Canyon Road. Turn right and drive 6.5 miles to Mulholland Highway. Turn right and continue 4 miles to Stunt Road. Turn right again and drive one mile to the pullout on the right.

From the Ventura Freeway/Highway 101 in Calabasas, exit on Las Virgenes Road. Head 3 miles south to Mulholland Highway. Turn left and go 4 miles to Stunt Road. Turn right and drive one mile to the pullout on the right.

**Hiking directions:** Cross Stunt Road and walk 20 yards west downhill to the trailhead. Take the unpaved road past the gate and wind up the mountain. At 0.7 miles is a junction on a saddle at the head of Red Rock Canyon. The trail straight ahead to the north leads to Calabasas Peak (Hike 49). Take the right fork east into Red Rock Canyon. Continue downhill, deeper into the canyon. Pass numerous red sandstone formations to the signed Red Rock Canyon Trail on the left at 1.4 miles. Bear left on the footpath, and walk up wooden steps to the base of some formations. The trail curves up the draw, crosses a seasonal stream, and passes additional sandstone formations along the north wall

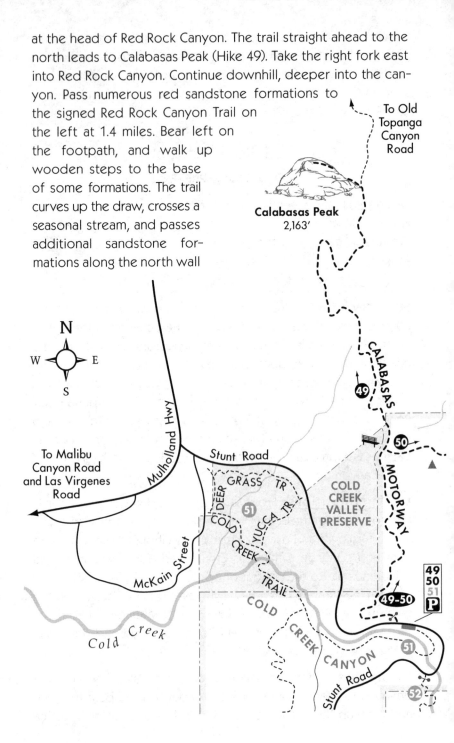

To Old Topanga Canyon Road

Calabasas Peak
2,163'

of the canyon. Continue uphill to the trail's end at an overlook. Return along the same path back to the canyon floor.

Before returning, take a short detour 200 yards to the left (east) on the main trail to an awesome red rock formation with shallow caves and arches. The trail continues a half mile to the Red Rock Canyon picnic area by Red Rock Road. Return by retracing your steps. ■

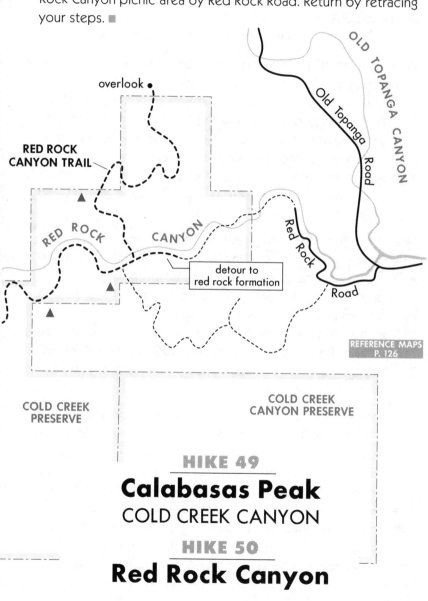

overlook •

OLD TOPANGA CANYON

Old Topanga Road

RED ROCK CANYON TRAIL

RED ROCK CANYON

Red Rock

detour to red rock formation

Road

REFERENCE MAPS P. 126

COLD CREEK PRESERVE

COLD CREEK CANYON PRESERVE

HIKE 49

# Calabasas Peak
## COLD CREEK CANYON

HIKE 50

# Red Rock Canyon

# 51. Cold Creek Trail
## COLD CREEK VALLEY PRESERVE

**Hiking distance:** 3 miles round trip
**Hiking time:** 1.5 hours
**Elevation gain:** 300 feet
**Maps:** U.S.G.S. Malibu Beach
Santa Monica Mountains East Trail Map

**Summary of hike:** The Cold Creek Valley Preserve sits in a flat bowl set among craggy sandstone peaks. It is home to a wide assortment of plant communities and flowers. Cold Creek flows through the valley preserve and Cold Creek Canyon. The Cold Creek Trail leads to the 57-acre preserve, parallel to the creek. The trail meanders through riparian woodlands and a gently rolling grass meadow. En route, the trail crosses the creek three times and traverses the hillside under the shade of oaks and sycamores.

**Driving directions:** From Santa Monica, drive 12 miles northbound on the Pacific Coast Highway/Highway 1 to Malibu Canyon Road. Turn right and drive 6.5 miles to Mulholland Highway. Turn right and continue 4 miles to Stunt Road. Turn right again and drive one mile to the pullout on the right.

From the Ventura Freeway/Highway 101 in Calabasas, exit on Las Virgenes Road. Head 3 miles south to Mulholland Highway. Turn left and go 4 miles to Stunt Road. Turn right and drive one mile to the pullout on the right.

**Hiking directions:** Take the trail southeast for a short distance, parallel to the road. Curve right and cross Cold Creek. Follow the creek downstream on the Lower Stunt High/Cold Creek Trail, and head into the forested canyon. Cross a tributary stream to a junction at a half mile. The left fork—the Lower Stunt High Trail—leaves the riparian canopy and heads up the hillside to Stunt Road. Go to the right on the Cold Creek Trail, staying close to Cold Creek. Continue northwest as the path rises above and returns to the creek. Cross Cold Creek to a junction in the preserve at one mile. This is the beginning of the Deer

Grass-Yucca Trail loop within the preserve, which may be hiked in either direction. The loop is one mile, connecting to McKain Street and Stunt Road. After hiking the loop, return on the same path. ∎

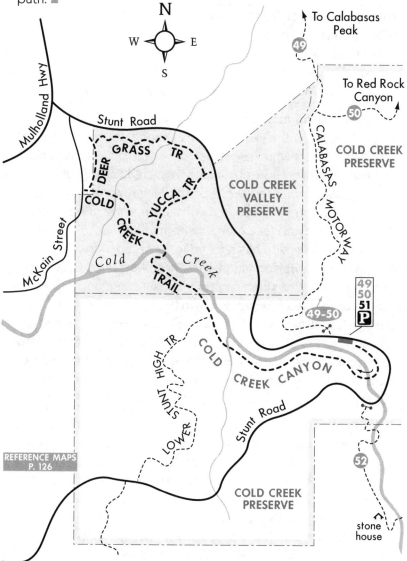

## 51. Cold Creek Trail
### COLD CREEK VALLEY PRESERVE

# 52. Cold Creek Canyon Preserve

A free access permit is required from
The Mountains Restoration Trust: (818) 346-9675

**Hiking distance:** 3.3 miles round trip
**Hiking time:** 1.5 hours
**Elevation gain:** 800 feet
**Maps:** U.S.G.S. Malibu Beach
Santa Monica Mountains East Trail Map

**Summary of hike:** Cold Creek Canyon is a pristine, bowl-shaped canyon with a year-round creek and a diverse ecosystem. The 1,100-acre nature preserve is owned by the Mountains Restoration Trust, a non-profit land trust created to protect and enhance the natural resources of the Santa Monica Mountains. To protect the fragile resources of the preserve, a free access permit is requested (see contact information above).

Cold Creek Canyon has high ridges, a steep slope, and magnificent sandstone formations. The headwaters of Cold Creek originate within the preserve, rising from springs and cascading down canyon. This hike winds down the north-facing watershed through lush streamside vegetation and jungle-like ferns, passing cascades and small waterfalls. The trail weaves through the natural basin in an idyllic setting under oak, maple, sycamore, and bay woodlands. Watch for the remains of a 1900s-era homesteader house, hand-carved into the giant split sandstone boulders.

**Driving directions:** From Santa Monica, drive 12 northbound on the Pacific Coast Highway/Highway 1 to Malibu Canyon Road and turn right. Drive 6.5 miles to Mulholland Highway. Turn right and continue 4 miles to Stunt Road. Turn right and drive 3.3 miles to the Cold Creek parking pullout on the left by a chain-link fence. Park off road on the shoulder.

From the Ventura Freeway/Highway 101 in Calabasas, exit on Las Virgenes Road. Head 3 miles south to Mulholland Highway. Turn left and continue 4 miles to Stunt Road. Turn right and drive 3.3 miles to the Cold Creek parking pullout on the left.

**Hiking directions:** Walk through the gate in the chain-link fence, and head east through the tall chaparral. The trail leads gradually downhill along the contours of the hillside and across a wooden bridge over Cold Creek at 0.6 miles. Pass moss-covered rocks and a rusty classic Dodge truck as you make your way into the lush vegetation and open oak woodland to the canyon floor. Cross Cold Creek again and continue past large sandstone boulders to the remains of Herman Hethke's stone house. Several switchbacks lead downhill across side streams and past small waterfalls. At 1.6 miles, the path reaches the locked lower gate at Stunt Road. Return by retracing your steps up canyon. ■

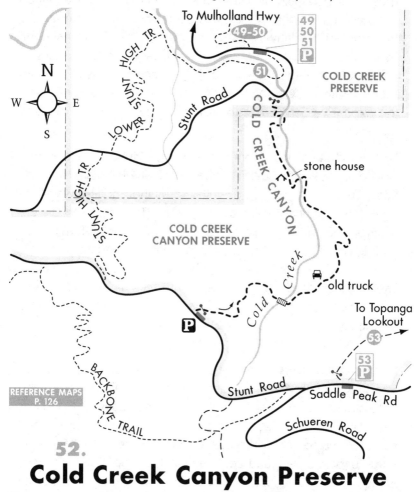

**52.**
# Cold Creek Canyon Preserve

# 53. Topanga Fire Lookout
## COLD CREEK CANYON PRESERVE

**Hiking distance:** 2 miles round trip
**Hiking time:** 1 hour
**Elevation gain:** 200 feet
**Maps:** U.S.G.S. Malibu Beach
Santa Monica Mountains East Trail Map

**Summary of hike:** The Topanga Fire Lookout, destroyed in a 1970 fire, was, ironically, used by the fire department to spot fires. All that remains is a large multi-level concrete foundation perched at the edge of the 2,469-foot mountain. This one-mile trail follows a relatively easy grade along the Topanga Ridge Trail, a fire road along the east ridge of the Cold Creek Canyon Preserve. From the lookout are spectacular views into Old Topanga Canyon, Cold Creek Canyon Preserve, Red Rock Canyon, the expansive San Fernando Valley to Los Angeles, and Santa Monica Bay.

**Driving directions:** From Santa Monica, drive 12 miles northbound on the Pacific Coast Highway/Highway 1 to Malibu Canyon Road. Turn right and drive 6.5 miles to Mulholland Highway. Turn right and continue 4 miles to Stunt Road. Turn right and drive 5 miles up the winding road to the end of Stunt Road. Turn left on Saddle Peak Road, and park in the pullout on the right.

From the Ventura Freeway/Highway 101 in Calabasas, exit on Las Virgenes Road. Head 3 miles south to Mulholland Highway. Turn left and go 4 miles to Stunt Road. Turn right and drive 4 miles up the road to the end of Stunt Road. Turn left on Saddle Peak Road, and park in the pullout on the right.

**Hiking directions:** From the parking pullout, cross Saddle Peak Road to the gated service road. Head northeast on the paved road along the ridge, high above Cold Creek Canyon. Calabasas Peak (Hike 49) can be seen to the north. At a quarter mile is a road split. The paved right fork leads to a radar tower. Bear left on the wide, unpaved path and continue gradually uphill. At one mile is the concrete foundation at the mountain's edge, overlooking

Hondo Canyon, Old Topanga Canyon, the Cold Creek drainage, the San Fernando Valley, and sections of Los Angeles. Return by retracing your steps. ■

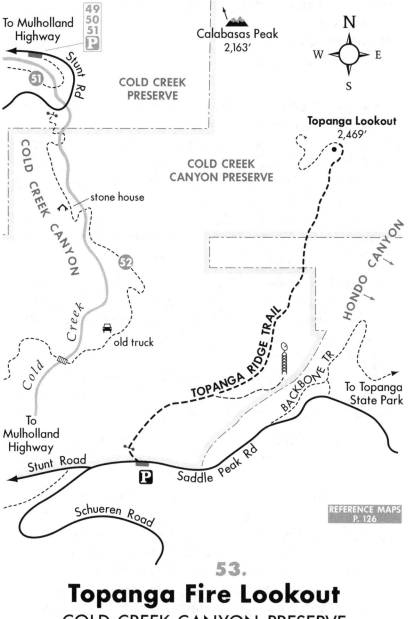

## 53.
# Topanga Fire Lookout
## COLD CREEK CANYON PRESERVE

# 54. Summit Valley Trail
## EDMUND D. EDELMAN PARK

**Hiking distance:** 2 miles round trip
**Hiking time:** 1 hour
**Elevation gain:** 300 feet
**Maps:** U.S.G.S. Canoga Park
Santa Monica Mountains East Trail Map

**Summary of hike:** Edmund D. Edelman Park is located in bowl-shaped Summit Valley at the head of Topanga Canyon. The 1,500-foot ridge at the north end of this 662-acre park separates rural Topanga Canyon from the urban San Fernando Valley. The park's wildlife corridor includes oak woodlands, mixed chaparral communities, native grasslands, and the headwaters of Topanga Creek. The network of trails are open to hikers, bikers, and equestrians. This hike loops through two valleys, crosses the gently rolling hills, and parallels Topanga Creek.

**Driving directions:** From Santa Monica, drive 4 miles northbound on the Pacific Coast Highway/Highway 1 to Topanga Canyon Boulevard and turn right. Continue 8.2 miles to the signed Summit Valley/Edmund D. Edelman parking area on the left (west).

From the Ventura Freeway/Highway 101 in Woodland Hills, exit on Topanga Canyon Boulevard, and drive 4 miles south to the parking area on the right (west).

**Hiking directions:** Head west past the trailhead gate, and descend into the forested stream-fed draw, crossing the headwaters of Topanga Creek. At 0.2 miles is a five-way junction. Take the far right trail—the Summit Valley Canyon Trail—to begin the loop. Head north along the canyon floor, parallel to the seasonal Topanga Creek on the right. At one mile, just before descending into a eucalyptus grove, the unsigned Summit Valley Loop Trail bears left. Take this trail as it zigzags up the hillside. Heading south, traverse the edge of the hill to a ridge and a junction. (For a shorter hike, the left fork returns to the five-way junction along the ridge.) Take the middle fork straight ahead, and descend into the next drainage. The trail curves south, returning down the draw to the five-way junction. ■

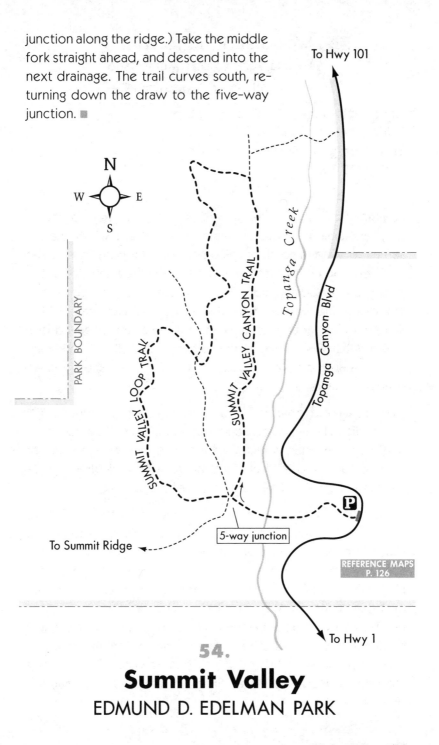

## 54.
# Summit Valley
## EDMUND D. EDELMAN PARK

# 55. Woodland Ridge Trail
## Serrania Park to Dirt Mulholland
20864 Wells Drive, Woodland Hills

**Hiking distance:** 2.3 miles round trip
**Hiking time:** 1 hour
**Elevation gain:** 500 feet
**Maps:** U.S.G.S. Conoga Park
Topanga State Park Trail Map

**Summary of hike:** Serrania Park is a popular neighborhood dog park tucked into a small canyon in Woodland Hills on the San Fernando Valley's south rim. A paved, circular path follows the perimeter of the tree-dotted grassland. On the east edge of the park is the Woodland Ridge Trail, a natural footpath connecting Woodland Hills with Dirt Mulholland, just below the crest of the Santa Monica Mountains. (Dirt Mulholland is the unpaved portion of Mulholland Drive.) The trail climbs the hillside, following the ridge across several knolls while offering sweeping views across the valley.

**Driving directions:** From the Ventura Freeway/Highway 101 in Woodland Hills, exit on De Soto Avenue. Drive 0.8 miles south on De Soto Avenue (which becomes Serrania Avenue south of Ventura Boulevard) and veer left on Wells Drive. Park alongside the road or turn right into the Serrania Park parking lot.

**Hiking directions:** From the east edge of Serrania Park, take the footpath, which is set off by a wood railing. Head up the slope through chaparral on the dirt and rock path, with vistas across Woodland Hills and Conoga Park to the Santa Susana Mountains. Follow a narrow ridge above Serrania Park to views of the Santa Monica Mountains backcountry and the San Gabriel Mountains. Continue along the exposed ridge and veer left, just before reaching a steep slope. Follow the serpentine ridge to a knoll with a survey marker and 360-degree vistas. While staying atop the ridge, descend and climb, reaching Dirt Mulholland at the trail's end. ∎

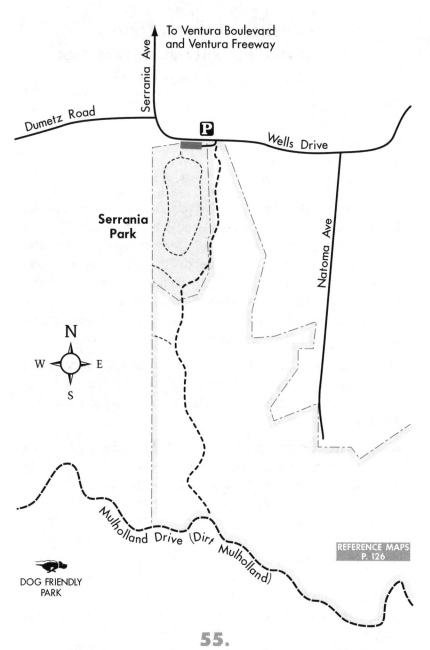

To Ventura Boulevard
and Ventura Freeway

Serrania Ave

Dumetz Road

**P**

Wells Drive

Natoma Ave

Serrania
Park

N

W    E

S

Mulholland Drive (Dirt Mulholland)

REFERENCE MAPS
P. 126

DOG FRIENDLY
PARK

**55.**

# Woodland Ridge Trail
## SERRANIA PARK to DIRT MULHOLLAND

# 56. Caballero Canyon Loop

## MARVIN BRAUDE MULHOLLAND GATEWAY PARK

3600 Reseda Boulevard · Tarzana

**Hiking distance:** 3.7-mile loop
**Hiking time:** 2 hours
**Elevation gain:** 600 feet
**Maps:** U.S.G.S. Conoga Park
Santa Monica Mountains East Trail Map

**Summary of hike:** Caballero Canyon, on the north border of Topanga State Park, offers easy access to a network of hiking and biking trails. The trailhead is in Marvin Braude Mulholland Gateway Park, a grassy hillside park with picnic sites in the San Fernando Valley near Tarzana. From the north slope of the Santa Monica Mountains, the trail connects with an unpaved section of Mulholland Drive. This hike follows the ridge and returns down Caballero Canyon through sycamore and willow groves.

**Driving directions:** From the Ventura Freeway/Highway 101 in Tarzana, exit on Reseda Boulevard. Drive 3.4 miles south into Marvin Braude Mulholland Gateway Park, and park at the end of the road.

**Hiking directions:** From the south end of Reseda Boulevard, take the gated, unpaved fire road up the hill into Topanga State Park. Pass a second vehicle gate to Dirt Mulholland at 0.2 miles. Bear left on the wide road, and follow the ridge across the head of Caballero Canyon, curving south then east. From the ridge are southern views into Temescal and Rustic Canyons and northern views into Caballero Canyon. At 0.7 miles, pass the Bent Arrow Trail, a connector trail to Temescal Ridge Fire Road, and continue along the ridge. Just before the road curves left around a prominent hill known as Farmer Ridge, watch for the Caballero Canyon Trail on the left. Bear left and descend down the east flank of the canyon. Wind downhill to the canyon floor dotted with sycamore trees. Head north, parallel to an intermittent stream, and meander through the canyon to Reseda Boulevard at the old Caballero Canyon trailhead. Bear left and follow land-scaped Reseda Boulevard above Caballero Canyon for 1.2 miles, back to the trailhead. ■

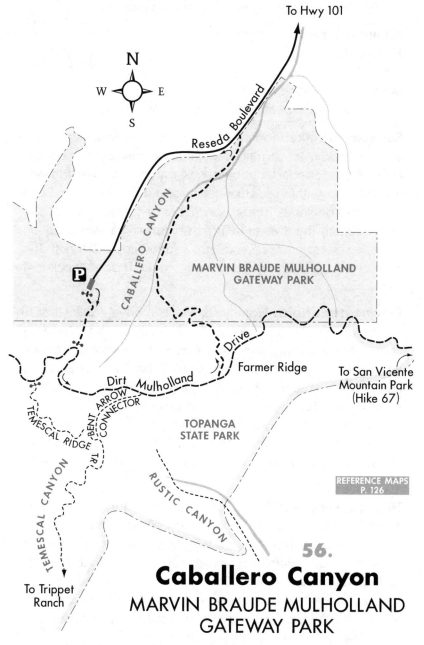

**56.**
# Caballero Canyon
## MARVIN BRAUDE MULHOLLAND GATEWAY PARK

# 57. Dead Horse Trail

## TOPANGA STATE PARK

20825 Entrada Road · Topanga

**Hiking distance:** 2.5 miles round trip
**Hiking time:** 1.5 hours
**Elevation gain:** 400 feet
**Maps:** U.S.G.S. Topanga
      Santa Monica Mountains East Trail Map

**map
page 146**

**Summary of hike:** Topanga State Park covers more than 11,000 acres with 36 miles of trails through open grasslands, chaparral, and oak woodlands. It has been designated as the world's largest wildland within the boundaries of a major city. The Dead Horse Trail begins at Trippet Ranch, the park headquarters and visitor center. The diverse trail crosses rolling grasslands, enters a riparian forest, and descends into a streamside oak forest. The path crosses a rustic wooden bridge over Trippet Creek in a rocky grotto.

**Driving directions:** From Santa Monica, drive 4 miles northbound on the Pacific Coast Highway/Highway 1 to Topanga Canyon Boulevard and turn right. Continue 4.6 miles to Entrada Road on the right and turn right again. Drive 0.7 miles and turn left, following the posted state park signs. Turn left again in 0.3 miles into the Topanga State Park parking lot.

From the Ventura Freeway/Highway 101 in Woodland Hills, exit on Topanga Canyon Boulevard, and drive 7.6 miles south to Entrada Drive. Turn left and follow the posted state park signs to the parking lot.

**Hiking directions:** Take the signed Musch Trail for 50 yards, heading north to a pond on the right. The Dead Horse Trail heads left (west) across from the pond. The footpath parallels a wood rail fence, rolling grasslands, and an oak woodland. At 0.5 miles is a trail split. Take the right fork along the contours of the ridge. The trail descends into a shady riparian forest of bay and sycamore trees. A wooden bridge crosses the rocky streamed of

Trippet Creek in a narrow draw. After crossing, steps lead up to a junction. Take the middle fork downhill to a trail split. Bear right and loop around to the lower parking lot near Topanga Canyon Boulevard. Return by retracing your steps. ■

## 58. Eagle Rock Loop
### TOPANGA STATE PARK
20825 Entrada Road · Topanga

**Hiking distance:** 4 miles round trip
**Hiking time:** 2.5 hours
**Elevation gain:** 800 feet
**Maps:** U.S.G.S. Topanga
      Santa Monica Mountains East Trail Map

*map
page 146*

**Summary of hike:** This hike begins at a beautiful picnic area with a pond and a one-mile nature trail at the Trippet Ranch visitor center in Topanga State Park. The hike follows a fire road through grasslands and oak groves up to Eagle Rock, an impressive sandstone rock pitted with crevices and caves (cover photo). The views of the mountains, valleys, and the Santa Ynez Canyon are superb. The return on the Musch Trail descends past oak, sycamore, and bay trees. The footpath includes lush vegetation, ferns, moss-covered rocks, and stream crossings.

**Driving directions:** From Santa Monica, drive 4 miles northbound on the Pacific Coast Highway/Highway 1 to Topanga Canyon Boulevard and turn right. Continue 4.6 miles to Entrada Road on the right and turn right again. Drive 0.7 miles and turn left, following the posted state park signs. Turn left again in 0.3 miles into the Topanga State Park parking lot.

From the Ventura Freeway/Highway 101 in Woodland Hills, exit on Topanga Canyon Boulevard, and drive 7.6 miles south to Entrada Drive. Turn left and follow the posted state park signs to the parking lot.

**Hiking directions:** The trailhead is located at the end of the parking lot by the picnic area. Follow the trail uphill a short distance to a posted junction. Take the left trail—the Santa Ynez

Fire Road (also known as Eagle Springs Fire Road). Continue along this gradual uphill trail, passing the Santa Ynez Canyon Trail on the right at 0.5 miles. One mile farther is the Musch Trail on the left. For now, follow the ridge a short distance to a trail fork. Bear left to Eagle Rock ,which is close and visually prominent at the head of Santa Ynez Canyon.

After exploring the caves and hollows of the rock and enjoying the 360-degree views, return to the Musch Trail junction. Take the footpath to the right as it winds down to the valley. Cross a couple of ravines through lush foliage and dense oak, sycamore, and laurel woodlands. One mile down this trail is a junction at Musch Camp. Follow the trail sign and walk across the meadow. Turn left a short distance ahead at an unmarked junction and left again at a second unmarked junction. The trail winds back down to the main Topanga parking lot, passing a pond along the way. ■

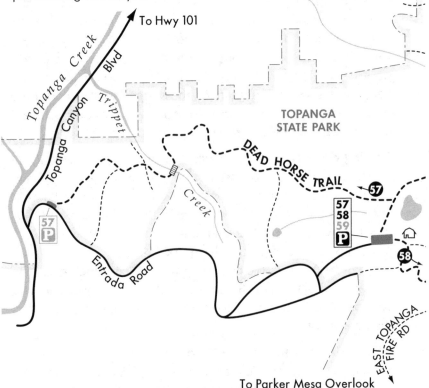

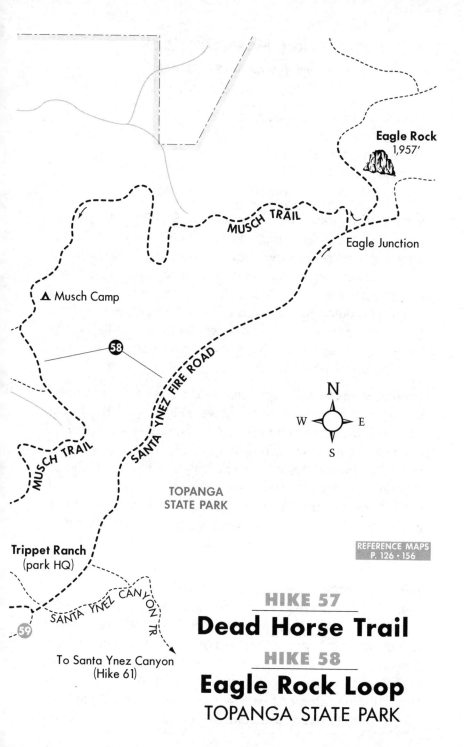

Eagle Rock
1,957'

MUSCH TRAIL

Eagle Junction

▲ Musch Camp

58

SANTA YNEZ FIRE ROAD

MUSCH TRAIL

N
W    E
S

TOPANGA
STATE PARK

REFERENCE MAPS
P. 126 • 156

Trippet Ranch
(park HQ)

SANTA YNEZ CANYON TR

59

To Santa Ynez Canyon
(Hike 61)

**HIKE 57**
# Dead Horse Trail
**HIKE 58**
# Eagle Rock Loop
## TOPANGA STATE PARK

# 59. Parker Mesa Overlook

## from TOPANGA STATE PARK

20825 Entrada Road · Topanga

**Hiking distance:** 6 miles round trip
**Hiking time:** 3 hours
**Elevation gain:** 800 feet
**Maps:** U.S.G.S. Topanga
Santa Monica Mountains East Trail Map

**Summary of hike:** This hike follows the East Topanga Fire Road along the ridge dividing Topanga Canyon and Santa Ynez Canyon. There are spectacular views into both canyons, including numerous ravines and enormous slabs of sandstone. This hike begins in Topanga State Park at Trippet Ranch (the park headquarters) and heads south. The trail leads to Parker Mesa Overlook, a barren knoll overlooking Topanga Beach, Santa Monica Bay, Pacific Palisades, and Santa Monica. The overlook can also be accessed from the south (Hike 60).

**Driving directions:** From Santa Monica, drive 4 miles northbound on the Pacific Coast Highway/Highway 1 to Topanga Canyon Boulevard and turn right. Continue 4.6 miles to Entrada Road on the right and turn right again. Drive 0.7 miles and turn left, following the posted state park signs. Turn left again in 0.3 miles into the Topanga State Park parking lot.

From the Ventura Freeway/Highway 101 in Woodland Hills, exit on Topanga Canyon Boulevard, and drive 7.6 miles south to Entrada Drive. Turn left and follow the posted state park signs to the parking lot.

**Hiking directions:** Head southeast on the signed trail towards Eagle Rock to a fire road. Bear left up the road to a junction at 0.2 miles. The left fork leads to Eagle Rock (Hike 58). Take the right fork on the East Topanga Fire Road past a grove of coastal oaks. Continue uphill to a ridge and a bench with panoramic views from Topanga Canyon to the Pacific Ocean. A short distance ahead, the trail crosses a narrow ridge overlooking Santa Ynez Canyon and its tilted sandstone slabs. Follow the ridge south, with alternating views of both canyons. At 2.5 miles is a junction with a trail on the right. The main trail on the left (east) leads to Paseo Miramar (Hike 60). Leave the fire road, and take the right trail a half mile to Parker Mesa Overlook at the trail's end. After enjoying the views, return to Trippet Ranch along the same route. ■

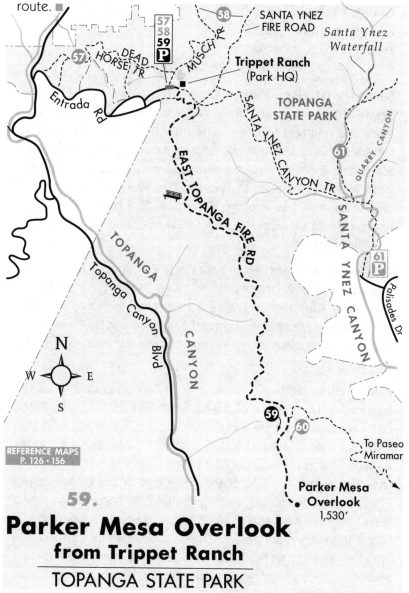

## 59.
# Parker Mesa Overlook
### from Trippet Ranch
#### TOPANGA STATE PARK

# 60. Parker Mesa Overlook
## from PASEO MIRAMAR
### TOPANGA STATE PARK

**Hiking distance:** 5 miles round trip
**Hiking time:** 2.5 hours
**Elevation gain:** 1,200 feet
**Maps:** U.S.G.S. Topanga
Santa Monica Mountains East Trail Map

**Summary of hike:** The strenuous hike to Parker Mesa Overlook from Paseo Miramar in Pacific Palisades has spectacular vistas along the trail and from the overlook. The trail follows a ridge separating Santa Ynez Canyon and Los Liones Canyon in Topanga State Park. There are expansive views from Venice to Malibu and from West Los Angeles to Topanga. The Parker Mesa Overlook (also known as the Topanga Overlook) is a barren knoll overlooking Santa Monica Bay to Palos Verdes and, on clear days, Catalina Island.

**Driving directions:** From Santa Monica, drive 3 miles northbound on the Pacific Coast Highway/Highway 1 to Sunset Boulevard. Turn right and drive 0.3 miles to Paseo Miramar. Turn left on Paseo Miramar, and drive 1.2 miles to the trailhead at the end of the road. Park alongside the curb on the west side of the street.

**Hiking directions:** From the end of Paseo Miramar, pass the trailhead gate, entering Topanga State Park. Hike north on the dirt fire road along the ridge, overlooking Santa Ynez Canyon and Santa Monica. Bend left to a junction with the Los Liones Canyon Trail on the left at 0.2 miles. (The trail leads 1.6 miles downhill to the trailhead at the north end of Los Liones Drive.) Continue straight ahead, staying on the East Topanga Fire Road. Traverse the hillside above Santa Ynez Canyon to a junction at 2 miles. The main road leads 2.7 miles to Trippet Ranch (Hike 59) and 4 miles to Eagle Rock (Hike 58). Instead, leave the fire road and take the trail to the left. Head a half mile south to Parker

Mesa Overlook at the end of the trail. From the bald knoll are great vistas overlooking the ocean and coastline. After savoring the views, return along the same route. ■

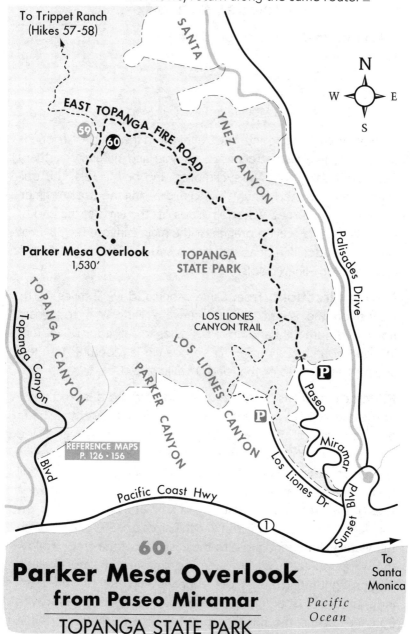

To Trippet Ranch
(Hikes 57-58)

EAST TOPANGA FIRE ROAD

59

60

SANTA

YNEZ CANYON

TOPANGA
STATE PARK

Parker Mesa Overlook
1,530'

Palisades Drive

LOS LIONES
CANYON TRAIL

TOPANGA CANYON

Topanga Canyon

PARKER CANYON

LOS LIONES CANYON

P

P

Paseo

Miramar

Los Liones Dr

Sunset Blvd

REFERENCE MAPS
P. 126 · 156

Blvd

N
W · E
S

Pacific Coast Hwy

1

To
Santa
Monica

60.
**Parker Mesa Overlook**
from Paseo Miramar

Pacific
Ocean

TOPANGA STATE PARK

# 61. Santa Ynez Canyon Trail to Santa Ynez Waterfall

## TOPANGA STATE PARK

**Hiking distance:** 3 miles round trip
**Hiking time:** 1.5 hours
**Elevation gain:** 300 feet
**Maps:** U.S.G.S. Topanga
Santa Monica Mountains East Trail Map

**Summary of hike:** Santa Ynez Canyon, in the heart of Topanga State Park, is a lush stream-fed canyon and natural sanctuary filled with oaks, willows, sycamores, and bay laurels. The trail follows the forested canyon bottom, crossing the stream numerous times. Santa Ynez Waterfall drops off the cliffs at the end of a narrow, steep-walled branch of the main canyon. The 18-foot cataract resides in a peaceful grotto surrounded by sandstone cliffs and fern-lined pools.

**Driving directions:** From Santa Monica, drive 3 miles northbound on the Pacific Coast Highway/Highway 1 to Sunset Boulevard. Turn right and drive 0.4 miles to Palisades Drive. Turn left and continue 2.4 miles to Vereda de la Montura. Turn left and park at the end of the road 0.1 mile ahead.

**Hiking directions:** Pass the trailhead gate and descend steps to the creek. Follow the east bank of the creek under the shade of sycamore and oak trees. Cross stepping stones over a side stream and continue up canyon. Cross the creek four consecutive times. After a huge, sculpted sandstone outcrop is a trail split at Quarry Canyon. Stay to the left and cross to the west side of the creek and a posted trail split at a half mile. The left fork leads 1.5 miles to Trippet Ranch (Hikes 57—59). Bear right on the Waterfall Trail, and cross to the east side of the creek. Follow the watercourse, crossing four more times as the steep-walled canyon tightly narrows. Work your way up the canyon, passing a jumble of boulders and sandstone formations with caves. Boulder-hop up the fern-lined rock grotto to the waterfall at the end of the box canyon. Just before reaching the falls, a path on the right climbs the east canyon wall to an overlook of the canyon. ■

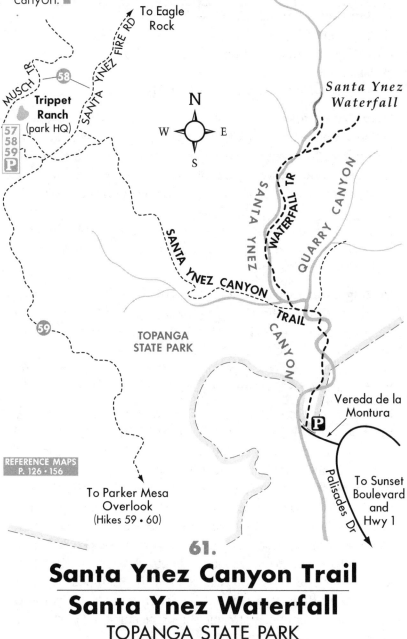

# 61.
# Santa Ynez Canyon Trail
# Santa Ynez Waterfall
## TOPANGA STATE PARK

# 62. Temescal Canyon Loop

## TOPANGA STATE PARK

**Hiking distance:** 4.2-mile loop
**Hiking time:** 2 hours
**Elevation gain:** 1,000 feet
**Maps:** U.S.G.S. Topanga
       Santa Monica Mountains East Trail Map

**Summary of hike:** Temescal Canyon is a creek-fed canyon within Topanga State Park that is shaded by oaks, maples, and sycamores. This canyon-to-ridgetop loop hike climbs the hillside cliffs on the west side of the canyon and follows the ridge, offering far-reaching views of Los Angeles and the Pacific coastline. The return route drops into the tree-shaded canyon to a footbridge at the seasonal Temescal Canyon Falls, framed by huge volcanic rocks. The trail begins at Temescal Gateway Park in Pacific Palisades.

**Driving directions:** From Santa Monica, drive 2 miles northbound on the Pacific Coast Highway/Highway 1 to Temescal Canyon Road. Turn right and drive 1.3 miles to the end of Temescal Canyon Road, crossing Sunset Boulevard en route. Park in the Temescal Gateway parking lot at the conference and retreat center. A parking fee is required.

**Hiking directions:** Walk to the top of the road, and follow the trail signs on the left to a posted junction. The Temescal Canyon Trail to the right is our return route. Begin the loop to the left on the Temescal Ridge Trail. Zigzag up the west canyon wall, entering Topanga State Park at 0.3 miles. Short switchbacks continue uphill to the open ridge, with sweeping views of Santa Ynez Canyon, Pacific Palisades, Santa Monica, and the entire Santa Monica Bay. Continue up the ridge overlooking Temescal Canyon to a posted 4-way junction at 1.8 miles. The left fork leads 1 mile to Bienveneda Avenue in Pacific Palisades. The right fork descends into the canyon, our return route. For a side trip to Skull Rock, continue straight ahead, climbing a half mile the wind-sculpted rock.

After viewing the carved sandstone formation, return to the 4-way junction. Take the Temescal Canyon Trail to the left and steeply descend into the densely wooded canyon, passing the Trailer Canyon Trail on the left. At the canyon floor is a wooden footbridge over the creek in the rock grotto just below Temescal Canyon Falls. The trail parallels the creek downstream on the east canyon wall. At the canyon floor, wind through the parklands under groves of eucalyptus, sycamore, and coastal oak, back to the trailhead. ■

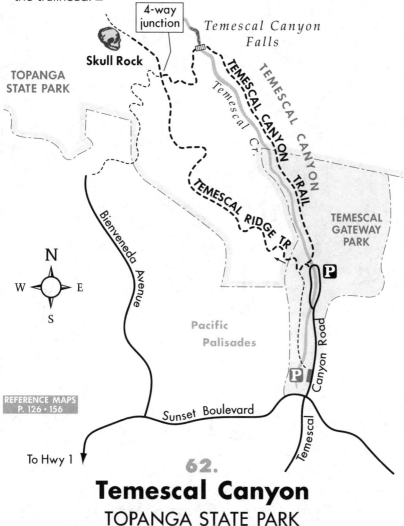

## 62.
# Temescal Canyon
## TOPANGA STATE PARK

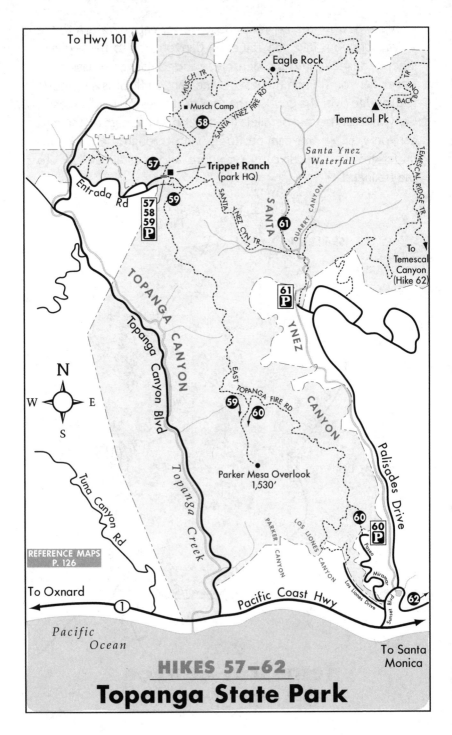

To Hwy 101

Eagle Rock

MUSCH TR

BACK BONE TR

Musch Camp

Temescal Pk

**58**

SANTA YNEZ FIRE RD

**57**

**Trippet Ranch**
(park HQ)

*Santa Ynez
Waterfall*

SANTA

Entrada Rd

**59**

57
58
59
**P**

SANTA YNEZ CYN TR

YNEZ

QUARRY CANYON

TEMESCAL RIDGE TR

To
Temescal
Canyon
(Hike 62)

**61**

**61**
**P**

TOPANGA

CANYON

Topanga Canyon Blvd

N
W        E
S

YNEZ

EAST
TOPANGA FIRE RD

CANYON

**59**

**60**

Palisades Drive

Parker Mesa Overlook
1,530'

Tuna Canyon Rd

Topanga Creek

**60**

**60**
**P**

Paseo

REFERENCE MAPS
P. 126

PARKER

CANYON

LOS LIONES CANYON

Los Liones Drive

Miramar

To Oxnard

1

Pacific Coast Hwy

Sunset Blvd

**62**

*Pacific
Ocean*

To Santa
Monica

**HIKES 57–62**

# Topanga State Park

# 63. Inspiration Point

## WILL ROGERS STATE HISTORIC PARK

1501 Will Rogers State Park Road · Open 8 a.m. to 5 p.m. daily

**Hiking distance:** 2-mile loop
**Hiking time:** 1 hour
**Elevation gain:** 300 feet
**Maps:** U.S.G.S. Topanga
Santa Monica Mountains East Trail Map
Will Rogers State Historic Park Trail map

map
page 158

**Summary of hike:** Will Rogers State Historic Park is a 186-acre retreat in the hills above Santa Monica. At the upper reaches of the park is Inspiration Point, a broad, flat knoll overlooking the beautiful park grounds and the rugged mountain canyons and ridges. The expansive views extend from downtown Los Angeles to Santa Monica and across Santa Monica Bay to Palos Verdes. Inspiration Point Loop Trail, designed by Rogers himself, is a two-mile trail that climbs the undeveloped hillside behind the ranch to Inspiration Point. The top of the loop connects with the eastern terminus of the Backbone Trail, which crosses the spine of the Santa Monica Mountains for 64 miles to Point Mugu State Park. Picnic grounds, horse riding stables, and daily tours of Will Rogers' 31-room ranch home make visiting this state park a great way to spend the day. For a longer hike, continue with Hike 64.

**Driving directions:** From Santa Monica, drive 1.6 miles northbound on the Pacific Coast Highway/Highway 1 to Chautauqua Boulevard. Turn right and continue 0.9 miles to Sunset Boulevard. Turn right again. Drive 0.5 miles and turn left at Will Rogers State Park Road. The parking area is 0.7 miles ahead at the end of the road. A parking fee is required.

**Hiking directions:** Begin the hike from the visitor center and Will Rogers' home, built in 1928. Head west (left) past the tennis courts to a fire road—the Inspiration Point Loop Trail. Take the fire road to the right and climb the ridge, heading north above Rivas Canyon. Climb steadily, reaching the Inspiration Point junction at 0.8 miles near the top of the knoll. Bear right to the overlook on the flat knoll. After resting and savoring the views of the entire ranch, return to the main loop. Continue north past the Backbone Trail by an information kiosk. The main loop continues northeast and descends to the south, overlooking the polo grounds. Walk through a eucalyptus-shaded lane, returning to the well-kept park grounds and visitor center. ∎

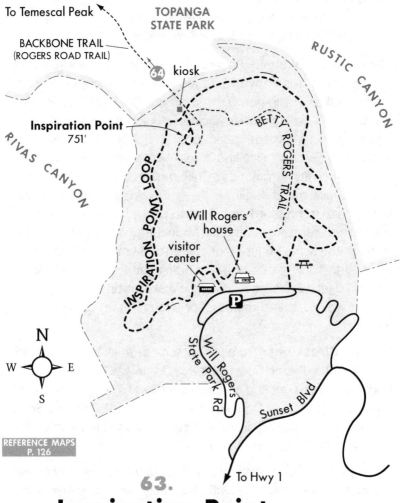

## 63.
# Inspiration Point
## WILL ROGERS STATE HISTORIC PARK

# 64. Rustic Canyon Loop

## WILL ROGERS STATE HIST. PARK • TOPANGA STATE PARK

### 1501 Will Rogers State Park Road

**Hiking distance:** 5 miles round trip
**Hiking time:** 3 hours
**Elevation gain:** 1,000 feet
**Maps:** U.S.G.S. Topanga
Santa Monica Mountains East Trail Map

map
page 161

**Summary of hike:** Rustic Canyon is a lush, stream-fed canyon on the east side of Will Rogers State Historic Park. The narrow, steep-walled canyon has a few old abandoned structures from Anatol Josepho's ranch, a friend of Will Rogers. The hike begins in the state park on the Inspiration Point Loop Trail (Hike 63). The loop trail connects with Rogers Road Trail, the easternmost segment of the Backbone Trail that was designed by both Rogers and Josepho. The trail straddles the razor-point ridge between Rustic and Rivas Canyons. The canyon and ocean views are spectacular. The hike returns to the state park along the floor of secluded Rustic Canyon, following the year-round watercourse of Rustic Creek.

**Driving directions:** From Santa Monica, drive 1.6 miles northbound on the Pacific Coast Highway/Highway 1 to Chautauqua Boulevard. Turn right and continue 0.9 miles to Sunset Boulevard. Turn right again. Drive 0.5 miles and turn left at Will Rogers State Park Road. The parking area is 0.7 miles ahead at the end of the road. A parking fee is required.

**Hiking directions:** Begin the hike from visitor center and Will Rogers' home, built in 1928. Head west (left) past the tennis courts to a fire road—the Inspiration Point Loop Trail. Take the fire road to the right and climb the ridge, heading north above Rivas Canyon. Climb steadily, reaching the Inspiration Point junction at 0.8 miles near the top of the knoll (Hike 63). A short distance ahead is the information kiosk.

Leave the Inspiration Point Loop Trail, and take the Rogers Road Trail (Backbone Trail). Climb north on the narrow ridge between Rustic Canyon and Rivas Canyon. At 1.5 miles, cross Chicken Ridge Bridge and follow the steep knife-edged slope. At just under 2 miles is a junction on a saddle. Leave the Backbone Trail and steeply descend into Rustic Canyon on the right, dropping nearly 700 feet in a half mile. At the canyon floor, cross Rustic Creek to the Rustic Canyon Trail and an old barn from the Josepho Ranch. The left fork heads up canyon and connects with Camp Josepho (a Boy Scout camp) and the Sullivan Ridge Fire Road (Hike 65).

For this hike, bear right and head south, crisscrossing Rustic Creek downstream through a forest of sycamore, walnut, cottonwood, and thick pockets of poison oak. Weave through the canyon bottom past abandoned structures and a small dam. The vertical rock-walled canyon narrows, then widens out. The path leaves the canyon and returns to the polo field across from Will Rogers' home. ■

# 65. Sullivan Canyon

**Hiking distance:** 8.6 miles round trip
**Hiking time:** 4 hours
**Elevation gain:** 1,200 feet
**Maps:** U.S.G.S. Topanga
        Santa Monica Mountains East Trail Map

map
page 163

**Summary of hike:** Sullivan Canyon is a secluded steam-fed canyon with huge stands of sycamore, oak, willow, and walnut trees. The trail follows the intermittent stream through the steep-walled canyon beneath a rich canopy of green foliage. After meandering up the long, pristine canyon, the trail climbs the chaparral-covered slopes to Sullivan Ridge and magnificent canyon views. This hike can be combined with Hike 66 for a 10-mile loop.

**Driving directions:** From Santa Monica, drive 1.6 miles northbound on the Pacific Coast Highway/Highway 1 to Chautauqua Boulevard and turn right. Continue 0.9 miles to Sunset Boulevard and turn right. Drive 2.8 miles and turn left on Mandeville Canyon

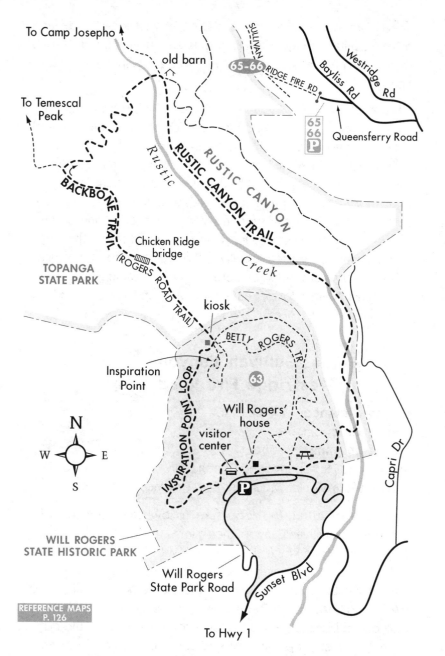

To Camp Josepho

old barn

SULLIVAN RIDGE FIRE RD.

65-66

Westridge Rd

Bayliss Rd

To Temescal Peak

RUSTIC CANYON

65 66 P

Queensferry Road

Rustic

BACKBONE TRAIL

RUSTIC CANYON TRAIL

(ROGERS ROAD TRAIL)

Creek

Chicken Ridge bridge

TOPANGA STATE PARK

kiosk

BETTY ROGERS TR.

63

Inspiration Point

Will Rogers' house

INSPIRATION POINT LOOP

visitor center

Capri Dr

N
W E
S

WILL ROGERS STATE HISTORIC PARK

P

WILL ROGERS STATE PARK ROAD

Will Rogers State Park Road

Sunset Blvd

REFERENCE MAPS P. 126

To Hwy 1

# 64. **Rustic Canyon Loop**
## WILL ROGERS STATE HISTORIC PARK

Road. Turn left again at the first street—Westridge Road—and drive 1.2 miles to Bayliss Road. Turn left on Bayliss Road, and go 0.3 miles to Queensferry Road. Turn left and park near the trail-head gate.

**Hiking directions:** Step around the vehicle-restricting gate. Walk 0.2 miles down the paved service road to the floor of Sullivan Canyon. Head right, up the serene canyon floor under a lush forest canopy. At 1 mile, cross a seasonal stream and pass sandstone outcroppings. At 3.5 miles, Sullivan Canyon curves right (northeast). The trail curves left (northwest) up a narrow side canyon. Climb the west canyon wall overlooking Sullivan Canyon. Follow the contours of the mountain up to the ridge and a T-junction with the Sullivan Ridge Fire Road at 4.3 miles. This is the turn-around spot. Return along the same route.

To hike a 10-mile loop, bear right (north) up to Dirt Mulholland, and continue with Hike 53. ■

## 66. Sullivan Canyon— Westridge Fire Road Loop

**Hiking distance:** 10-mile loop
**Hiking time:** 5 hours
**Elevation gain:** 1,300 feet
**Maps:** U.S.G.S. Topanga and Conoga Park
      Santa Monica Mountains East Trail Map

**map
page 165**

**Summary of hike:** This loop hike follows the forested canyon floor of Sullivan Canyon, then climbs the chaparral-covered slopes to Sullivan Ridge. The trail follows Dirt Mulholland Drive a short distance, an unimproved road along the ridge overlooking the west end of Los Angeles, the San Fernando Valley, and the Encino Reservoir. (Dirt Mulholland is the unpaved portion of Mulholland Drive.) The loop returns southward down the ridge from 1, formerly the NIKE Missile Control Site, an old military outpost active from 1956 through 1968. The 10-acre park (Hike 67) includes a self-guided interpretive center with descriptions of its former life. The trail descends on the Westridge Fire Road,

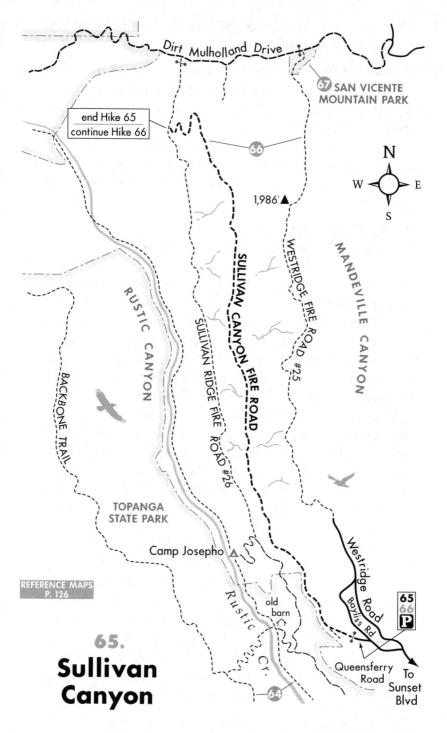

Dirt Mulholland Drive

**67** SAN VICENTE
MOUNTAIN PARK

end Hike 65
continue Hike 66

**66**

1,986'▲

N
W E
S

SULLIVAN CANYON FIRE ROAD

WESTRIDGE FIRE ROAD #25

MANDEVILLE CANYON

RUSTIC CANYON

SULLIVAN RIDGE FIRE ROAD #26

BACKBONE TRAIL

TOPANGA
STATE PARK

Camp Josepho ▲

Rustic Cr.

old
barn

Westridge Road

Bayliss Rd

**65**
**66**
**P**

REFERENCE MAPS
P. 126

**65.**
# Sullivan
# Canyon

Queensferry
Road

To
Sunset
Blvd

**64**

a hiking and biking route straddling the ridgeline between Sullivan and Mandeville Canyons.

**Driving directions:** From Santa Monica, drive 1.6 miles northbound on the Pacific Coast Highway/Highway 1 to Chautauqua Boulevard and turn right. Continue 0.9 miles to Sunset Boulevard and turn right. Drive 2.8 miles and turn left on Mandeville Canyon Road. Turn left again at the first street—Westridge Road—and drive 1.2 miles to Bayliss Road. Turn left on Bayliss Road, and go 0.3 miles to Queensferry Road. Turn left and park near the trailhead gate.

**Hiking directions:** Step around the vehicle-restricting gate. Walk 0.2 miles down the paved service road to the floor of Sullivan Canyon. Head right, up the serene canyon floor under a lush forest canopy. At 1 mile, cross a seasonal stream and pass sandstone outcroppings. At 3.5 miles, Sullivan Canyon curves right (northeast). The trail curves left (northwest) up a narrow side canyon. Climb the west canyon wall overlooking Sullivan Canyon. Follow the contours of the mountain up to the ridge and a T-junction with the Sullivan Ridge Fire Road, the turn-around point for Hike 65.

Bear right and head north on the ridge between Rustic Canyon and Sullivan Canyon, reaching Dirt Mulholland at a half mile. Walk around the gate and follow Dirt Mulholland to the right for 0.8 miles, overlooking the Encino Reservoir and the San Fernando Valley. Pass another gate and bear right into San Vicente Mountain Park, the defunct missile silo site (Hike 67). Walk up the paved road and through the park, passing picnic areas and vista overlooks. Take the Westridge Fire Road (also known as Sullivan Ridge East) along the narrow ridge that divides Sullivan and Mandeville Canyons. Follow the ridge south to the high point of the hike at 1,986 feet. Gradually descend along the contours of the ridge, overlooking Sullivan Canyon, Rustic Canyon, the west ridge of Temescal Canyon, and the Los Angeles basin. The fire road exits at Westridge Road. Walk a half mile down Westridge Road, and turn right on Bayliss Road. Walk another half mile to Queensferry Road and turn right, returning to the trailhead. ∎

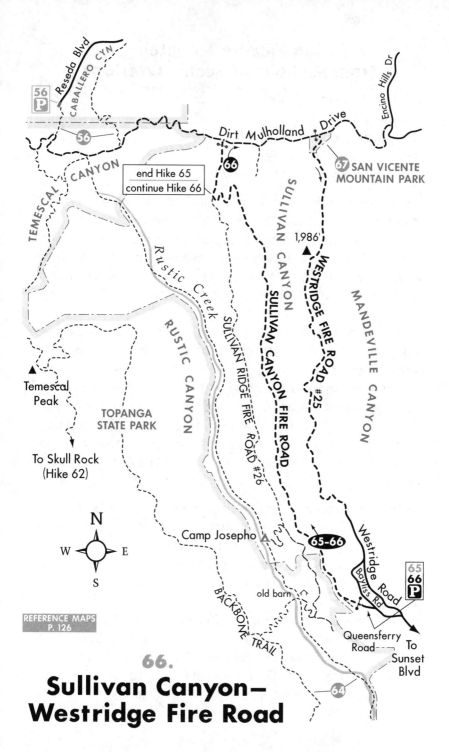

Reseda Blvd

CABALLERO CYN

56 P

56

Dirt Mulholland Drive

Encino Hills Dr

TEMESCAL CANYON

66

end Hike 65
continue Hike 66

57 SAN VICENTE
MOUNTAIN PARK

SULLIVAN CANYON

Rustic Creek

1,986 ▲

WESTRIDGE FIRE ROAD #25

SULLIVAN CANYON FIRE ROAD

MANDEVILLE CANYON

RUSTIC CANYON

SULLIVAN RIDGE FIRE ROAD #26

▲ Temescal
Peak

TOPANGA
STATE PARK

To Skull Rock
(Hike 62)

N
W   E
S

Camp Josepho ▲

65-66

Westridge Road

Bayliss Rd

65
66
P

REFERENCE MAPS
P. 126

old barn

BACKBONE TRAIL

Queensferry
Road

To
Sunset
Blvd

64

**66.**
# Sullivan Canyon—
# Westridge Fire Road

# 67. San Vicente Mountain from Mulholland Scenic Overlook

**Hiking distance:** 2 miles round trip
**Hiking time:** 1 hour
**Elevation gain:** 300 feet
**Maps:** U.S.G.S. Conoga Park
　　　 Topanga State Park Trail Map

**Summary of hike:** San Vicente Mountain Park was the former NIKE Missile Control Site. From 1956 through 1968, this Cold War sentry post was utilized to guard Los Angeles from Soviet attacks. The site contained radar towers atop the 1,950-foot peak to neutralize Soviet planes. The radar would guide missiles launched from the Sepulveda Basin below to destroy any invading aircraft.

The 10-acre mountaintop park sits at the head of Mandeville Canyon nearly 2,000 feet above the city. It is now home to a self-guided interpretive center with information panels, a radar tower, guard shack, picnic areas, and a variety of overlooks. This hike follows Dirt Mulholland, an unpaved portion of the famous ridge road, to San Vicente Mountain Park. The scenic parkway corridor, constructed in 1924, offers spectacular panoramic vistas across the San Fernando Valley and the Los Angeles Basin to the ocean.

**Driving directions:** Heading northbound from Los Angeles on the San Diego Freeway/Interstate 405, exit on Mulholland Drive. Turn right and drive 0.3 miles to Mulholland Drive. Turn left and follow the scenic winding road 2 miles to the end of the paved road by Encino Hills Drive on the right. Curve left on Dirt Mulholland and park.

Heading southbound from the San Fernando Valley on the San Diego Freeway/Interstate 405, exit on Mulholland Drive. Turn left and drive 0.4 miles to Mulholland Drive. Turn left and follow the winding road 2 miles to the end of the paved road by Encino Hills Drive on the right. Curve left on Dirt Mulholland and park.

**Hiking directions:** From the overlook of the San Fernando Valley, walk up unpaved Dirt Mulholland. Curve to the southern slope and a view towards Los Angeles, then return to the sweeping valley vistas that span to the San Gabriel Mountains and the Santa Susana Mountains. Continue on a gentle incline above the Encino Reservoir to a fork at the top of Mandeville Canyon at 1 mile. Dirt Mulholland continues straight ahead for one mile to Sullivan Canyon (Hike 66). Caballero Canyon (Hike 56) is 2.7 miles ahead. For this hike, bear left into San Vicente Mountain Park, the former Cold War sentry post. At the 1,950-foot rim above Mandeville Canyon, stairs lead up to an overlook platform with expansive views. The 360-degree vistas stretch from the San Gabriel Mountains and Burbank, across the Los Angeles Basin to the sea, and across the San Fernando Valley, from the Santa Susana Mountains to the Santa Monica Mountains. Explore the former helicopter platform and tower platform while savoring the views from the overlooks. Return by retracing your steps. ■

# San Vicente Mountain Park
## from MULHOLLAND SCENIC OVERLOOK

# 68. Getty View Trail

**Hiking distance:** 3.6 miles round trip
**Hiking time:** 2 hours
**Elevation gain:** 600 feet
**Maps:** U.S.G.S. Beverly Hills
　　　　Santa Monica Mountains Conservancy map

**Summary of hike:** The Getty View Trail in Bel Air ascends the steep hillside from Sepulveda Pass to Casiano Fire Road, an unpaved road on the ridgeline. A three-quarter mile climb through chaparral and pockets of live oak and toyon provides access to a section of the 376-acre Sepulveda Pass Open Space. The ridge-top trail overlooks Hoag Canyon, with sweeping vistas of the Getty Center Museum, West Los Angeles, Santa Monica, and the Pacific Ocean.

**Driving directions:** Heading northbound from Los Angeles on the San Diego Freeway/Interstate 405, take the Getty Center Drive exit. Turn left (north) 0.1 mile to the trailhead parking lot on the right, just before crossing under the freeway.

Heading southbound from the San Fernando Valley on the San Diego Freeway/Interstate 405, take the Getty Center Drive exit. Turn left (south) and cross under the freeway to the trailhead parking lot, immediately on the left.

**Hiking directions:** From the trailhead map, bear left (north) on the signed trail, and head up the side canyon past sycamore trees. Switchbacks lead up the chaparral-covered hillside east of Sepulveda Pass. The views improve with every step. Switchbacks make the elevation gain very easy. At 0.6 miles, the trail reaches the ridge and a T-junction with the Casiano Fire Road.

Bear left on the ridge-hugging dirt road above the deep and undeveloped Hoag Canyon. A footpath parallels the road on the west, gaining elevation to an incredible overlook by an isolated oak tree. The footpath parallels the cliffs and rejoins the fire road. A short distance ahead, a second side path on the left parallels the road to additional overlooks before rejoining the road again. At 0.4 miles, the pavement begins at a gated residential area.

Return south, back to the Getty View Trail junction. Continue south on the fire road while descending along the ridge. An undulating footpath parallels the east side of the road, overlooking Hoag Canyon. At 0.7 miles the fire road ends at Casiano Road in Bel Air Estates, where views open up across West Los Angeles. Return along the same route. ■

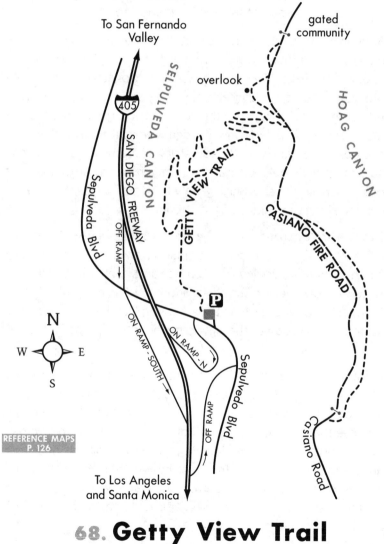

# 68. Getty View Trail

# 69. Dixie Canyon Park

## Barbara Asa—Dorian Trail

South end of Dixie Canyon Place · Sherman Oaks

---

**Hiking distance:** 0.7-mile loop
**Hiking time:** 30 minutes
**Elevation gain:** 300 feet
**Maps:** U.S.G.S. Van Nuys
      Santa Monica Mountains Recreation Topo Map

---

**Summary of hike:** Dixie Canyon Park is a small, twenty-acre, heavily wooded canyon overlooking the San Fernando Valley in Sherman Oaks. The open space was donated to the Santa Monica Mountains Conservancy by actor/director Warren Beatty in 1986. Tucked into the north slope of the Santa Monica Mountains, the shaded canyon is rich with California black walnut and coast live oak, with an understory of mushrooms, ferns, fungus, and poison oak. A perennial stream flows through the heart of the parkland. A short hiking-only loop trail winds through the canyon along both sides of the stream.

**Driving directions:** From the Ventura Freeway/Highway 101 in Sherman Oaks, exit on Woodman Avenue. Drive a half mile south to Ventura Boulevard. Turn left and continue 0.4 miles to Dixie Canyon Avenue. Turn right and go 0.7 miles south to Dixie Canyon Place. Veer left on Dixie Canyon Place and go 0.2 miles up the narrow road to the signed trailhead at the end of the cul-de-sac. Park along the side of the road.

**Hiking directions:** Walk to the end of the cul-de-sac, and pass the trailhead sign. Climb the concrete steps and cross to the east side of the stream. Follow the lush, narrow canyon upstream. Recross the drainage on the second bridge. At the third crossing is a bridge and a junction. Begin the loop on the right fork and head up the hillside. Traverse the west canyon wall on the serpentine path. At 0.3 miles, cross the waterway and loop back on the east side of the canyon. Weave down the hillside with the aid of four switchbacks, completing the loop at the third bridge. ∎

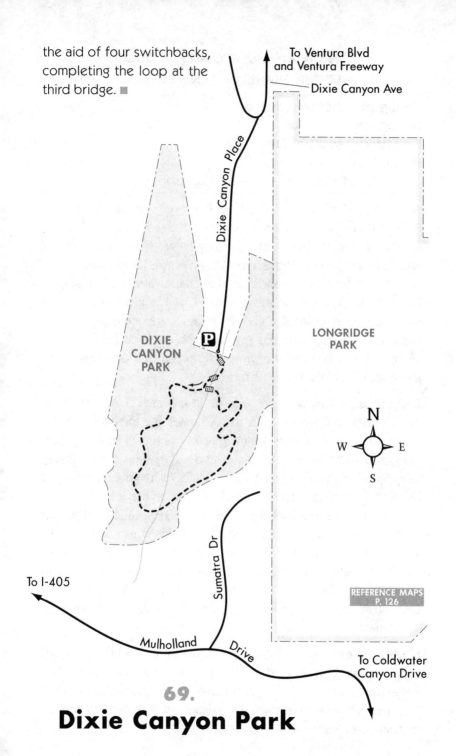

To Ventura Blvd
and Ventura Freeway

Dixie Canyon Ave

Dixie Canyon Place

LONGRIDGE
PARK

**P**

DIXIE
CANYON
PARK

N
W E
S

To I-405

Sumatra Dr

REFERENCE MAPS
P. 126

Mulholland Drive

To Coldwater
Canyon Drive

**69.**
# Dixie Canyon Park

# 70. Hastian—Discovery Loop
## LOWER FRANKLIN CANYON PARK

**Hiking distance:** 3-mile loop
**Hiking time:** 1.5 hours
**Elevation gain:** 400 feet
**Maps:** U.S.G.S. Beverly Hills
Franklin Canyon Park Nature Trails map

**Summary of hike:** The Hastian—Discovery Loop in Lower Franklin Canyon Park winds through the 105-acre Franklin Canyon Ranch site. The ranch is nestled in a deep valley in the mountains above Beverly Hills. These two trails form a loop through the canyon bottom woodlands to the chaparral-covered slopes. The Hastian Trail climbs the east wall of Franklin Canyon on a fire road to spectacular vistas of the lower canyon, Franklin Canyon Reservoir, West Los Angeles, and the Pacific Ocean. The Discovery Trail follows the canyon floor through groves of sycamore, oak, and black walnut trees.

**Driving directions:** From Sunset Boulevard in Beverly Hills, head north on Beverly Drive for 0.6 miles. At the fork, go left on Beverly Drive, where the main road continues as Coldwater Canyon Drive. Continue 0.8 miles and curve right onto Franklin Canyon Drive. Drive 1.1 mile to Lake Drive. Turn right and drive 0.3 miles to the posted trailhead parking area on the left.

From the Ventura Freeway/Highway 101 in Studio City, exit on Coldwater Canyon Drive. Head 2.5 miles south to the intersection with Mulholland Drive by the Coldwater Canyon Park/TreePeople Park. Make a 90-degree right turn onto Franklin Canyon Drive. Continue 1.4 miles to Lake Drive. Curve left onto Lake Drive, and go 0.3 miles to the posted trailhead parking area on the left.

**Hiking directions:** Take the posted Hastian Trail (a fire road) past the trail gate. Traverse the hillside high above Lake Drive. The easy uphill grade climbs the east canyon wall. The trail curves left and makes a wide sweeping loop around a side canyon, steadily gaining elevation to an overlook of Lower Franklin Canyon,

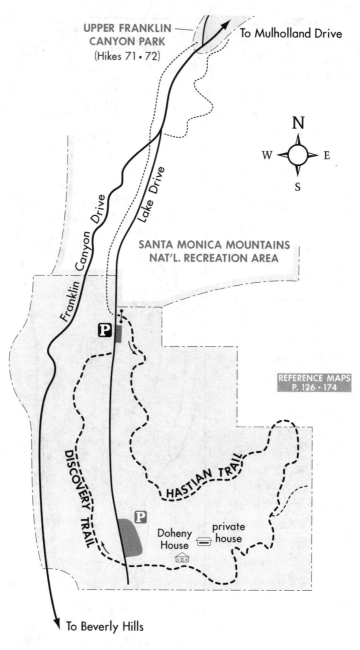

UPPER FRANKLIN
CANYON PARK
(Hikes 71 • 72)

To Mulholland Drive

N
W   E
S

Franklin Canyon Drive

Lake Drive

SANTA MONICA MOUNTAINS
NAT'L. RECREATION AREA

P

REFERENCE MAPS
P. 126 • 174

DISCOVERY TRAIL

HASTIAN TRAIL

P

Doheny
House

private
house

To Beverly Hills

# 70. **Hastian Discovery Loop**
## LOWER FRANKLIN CANYON PARK

Westwood, Santa Monica, and the ocean. The main trail curves left and continues up to the ridge, leaving Franklin Canyon and the park. Take the narrow footpath on the right by the wood pole and wind down the hill. The serpentine path exits the hillside at 2.3 miles on a broad grassy lawn by the old Doheny house, a Spanish-style stucco house built in 1935. Cross Lake Road to the Discovery Trail. Curve right and head north, parallel to the park road along the lower west canyon slope. The trail joins Lake Drive 50 yards south of the trailhead. Return to the left. ■

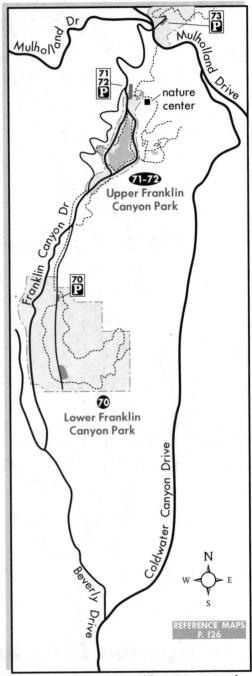

**Upper and Lower Franklin Canyon Parks**

# 71. Franklin Canyon Lake Loop

## UPPER FRANKLIN CANYON PARK

1500 Franklin Canyon Drive · Beverly Hills

---

**Hiking distance:** 1-mile loop
**Hiking time:** 30 minutes
**Elevation gain:** 30 feet
**Maps:** U.S.G.S. Beverly Hills
       N.P.S. Franklin Canyon Site
       Franklin Canyon Park Nature Trails map

*map page 177*

---

**Summary of hike:** Franklin Canyon Park is a 605-acre wildlife refuge and tranquil retreat just minutes from Beverly Hills. The pastoral open space of Upper Franklin Canyon centers around Franklin Canyon Lake, a beautiful, 9-acre man-made lake which is part of the California migratory bird route. The famous opening sequence of the *Andy Griffith Show* was filmed on the trail near the lake. This hike circles the serene lake under sycamores and oaks. To the east of the lake is Heavenly Pond. Circling the pond is the Wodoc Nature Trail, a wheelchair-accessible path through a natural riparian habitat.

**Driving directions:** From Sunset Boulevard in Beverly Hills, head north on Beverly Drive for 0.6 miles. At the fork, go left on Beverly Drive, where the main road continues as Coldwater Canyon Drive. Continue 0.8 miles and curve right onto Franklin Canyon Drive. Drive 1.8 miles, winding through Franklin Canyon Park, to the large William O. Douglas Outdoor Classroom and Sooky Goldman Nature Center parking lot on the right.

From the Ventura Freeway/Highway 101 in Studio City, exit on Coldwater Canyon Drive. Head 2.5 miles south to the intersection with Mulholland Drive by the Coldwater Canyon Park/TreePeople Park. Make a 90-degree right turn onto Franklin Canyon Drive. Continue 0.7 miles to the William O. Douglas Outdoor Classroom and Sooky Goldman Nature Center parking lot on the left.

**Hiking directions:** Follow the park road to the left (south) for 30 yards to a road on the right by the maintenance shop. To hike counter-clockwise around Franklin Canyon Lake, curve right and descend steps on the left to the trail. Pass the surge basin to a trail split. Both paths parallel the lake and merge at a picnic area by the park road. (The left fork skirts the edge of the lake.) Follow the road to the left 50 yards to the Wodoc Nature Trail at Heavenly Pond. Loop around the serene pond on the paved path. Back at the road, continue south above the lake, and cross the dam at the end of the lake. After crossing, descend steps on the Chernoff Trail, and follow the east banks of the lake through a shady woodland and a picnic area. At the Franklin Lake spillway, curve right to the road, and bear left 100 yards, returning to the parking area. (If the spillway is dry, you may cross over it to complete the loop and return to the right.) ■

## 72. Blinderman Trail
### UPPER FRANKLIN CANYON PARK
1500 Franklin Canyon Drive · Beverly Hills

**Hiking distance:** 1.5-mile loop
**Hiking time:** 40 minutes
**Elevation gain:** 200 feet

map
page 179

**Maps:** U.S.G.S. Beverly Hills and Van Nuys
N.P.S. Franklin Canyon Site
Franklin Canyon Park Nature Trails map

**Summary of hike:** Upper Franklin Canyon Park is home to the Sooky Goldman Nature Center and the William O. Douglas Outdoor Classroom, providing educational programs to the public and local schools. The Blinderman Trail is adjacent to the nature center. The path traverses the canyon slopes through chaparral, strolls along stream-fed side canyons with meadows, and climbs to overlooks of Franklin Canyon Lake and the entire canyon oasis.

**Driving directions:** From Sunset Boulevard in Beverly Hills, head north on Beverly Drive for 0.6 miles. At the fork, go left on Beverly Drive, where the main road continues as Coldwater

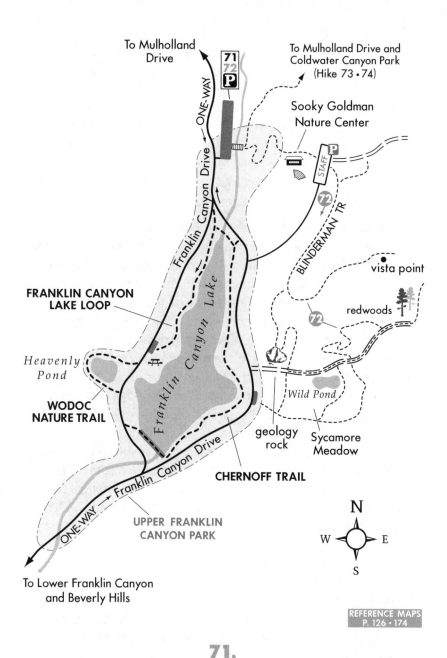

To Mulholland Drive

**71** **72** **P**

ONE-WAY

Franklin Canyon Drive

To Mulholland Drive and Coldwater Canyon Park (Hike 73 • 74)

Sooky Goldman Nature Center

**P** STAFF

**72** BLINDERMAN TR

vista point

redwoods

**72**

**FRANKLIN CANYON LAKE LOOP**

Franklin Canyon Lake

Heavenly Pond

*Wild Pond*

**WODOC NATURE TRAIL**

Franklin Canyon Drive

geology rock

Sycamore Meadow

**CHERNOFF TRAIL**

ONE-WAY ← Franklin Canyon Drive

**UPPER FRANKLIN CANYON PARK**

N
W — E
S

To Lower Franklin Canyon and Beverly Hills

REFERENCE MAPS
P. 126 • 174

## 71.
# Franklin Canyon Lake Loop
## UPPER FRANKLIN CANYON PARK

Canyon Drive. Continue 0.8 miles and curve right onto Franklin Canyon Drive. Drive 1.8 miles, winding through Franklin Canyon Park, to the large William O. Douglas Outdoor Classroom and Sooky Goldman Nature Center parking lot on the right.

From the Ventura Freeway/Highway 101 in Studio City, exit on Coldwater Canyon Drive. Head 2.5 miles south to the intersection with Mulholland Drive by the Coldwater Canyon Park/TreePeople Park. Make a 90-degree right turn onto Franklin Canyon Drive. Continue 0.7 miles to the William O. Douglas Outdoor Classroom and Sooky Goldman Nature Center parking lot on the left.

**Hiking directions:** Cross the wooden bridge to the information board. The left fork is a northbound connector trail to Coldwater Canyon Park (Hikes 73 and 74). Bear right and wind up the hill to the Sooky Goldman Nature Center. Walk through the courtyard to the back (east) side of the buildings and the posted Blinderman Trail. Twenty yards up the footpath is a trail fork. The left fork leads through walnut groves to a maintenance road. Head right and traverse the hillside, curving left to a trail split. Take the left fork and climb up the hillside to an overlook of Franklin Lake. Continue uphill to the ridge, with views down the entire length of Franklin Canyon. The ridge path leads to additional observation points.

Return to the main trail, and continue on the south fork to the canyon floor by Geology Rock. Bear left on the dirt road, passing Wild Pond on the right to a 4-way junction. (En route, a short side path loops around the pond to Sycamore Meadow.) Bear left and climb steps up the hillside. The undulating path crosses a wooden bridge and returns to the canyon floor at a T-junction. The left fork leads 100 yards to a large grassy flat with towering redwoods at the park boundary. The right fork returns to the 4-way junction. Take the left fork and climb the hill through a eucalyptus grove. Curve right to the park road by Franklin Canyon Lake. Follow the one-way road to the right, returning to the trailhead parking lot. ■

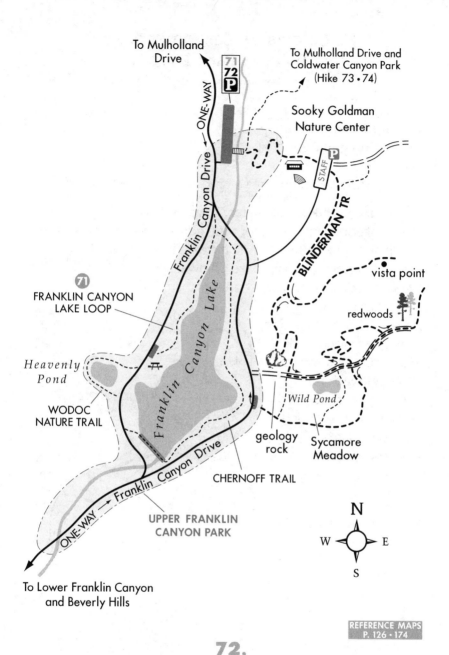

To Mulholland
Drive

71
72
P

ONE-WAY

Franklin Canyon Drive

To Mulholland Drive and
Coldwater Canyon Park
(Hike 73·74)

Sooky Goldman
Nature Center

P

STAFF

BLINDERMAN TR

vista point

redwoods

71
FRANKLIN CANYON
LAKE LOOP

Franklin Canyon Lake

*Heavenly
Pond*

WODOC
NATURE TRAIL

*Wild Pond*

geology
rock

Sycamore
Meadow

CHERNOFF TRAIL

Franklin Canyon Drive

ONE-WAY

UPPER FRANKLIN
CANYON PARK

N

W       E

S

To Lower Franklin Canyon
and Beverly Hills

REFERENCE MAPS
P. 126·174

## 72.
# Blinderman Trail
## UPPER FRANKLIN CANYON PARK

# 73. Coldwater Canyon Park—
## Wilacre Park Loop

12601 Mulholland Drive

**Hiking distance:** 2.7-mile loop
**Hiking time:** 1.5 hours
**Elevation gain:** 500 feet
**Maps:** U.S.G.S. Van Nuys
  Trails Illustrated Santa Monica Mountains Nat'l. Rec. Area

**Summary of hike:** Coldwater Canyon Park (44 acres) is home to TreePeople Park, a non-profit educational facility known for planting more than a million trees. TreePeople, which maintains and improves Coldwater Canyon Park, includes a tree nursery, fruit orchard, organic garden, and the Magic Forest Nature Trail. The adjacent Wilacre Park, in Studio City, is a 128-acre undeveloped greenbelt of chaparral-covered ridges and wooded canyons surrounded by residential homes.

To Hwy 101

Coldwater Cyn Dr

WILACRE PARK

DEARING MTN

TREEPEOPLE PARK

MAGIC FOREST NATURE TRAIL

Mulholland Drive

P

COLDWATER CANYON PARK

To San Diego Freeway (405)

Coldwater Canyon Dr

Franklin Canyon Drive

Sooky Goldman Nature Center

UPPER FRANKLIN CANYON PARK

71

72

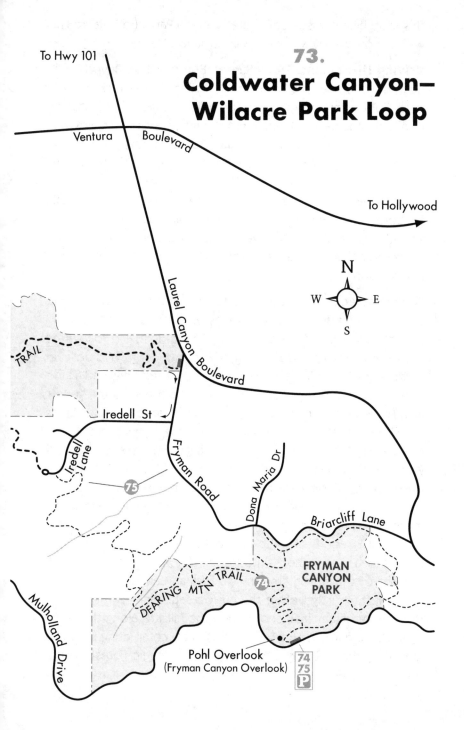

**73.**
# Coldwater Canyon–
# Wilacre Park Loop

To Hwy 101

Ventura Boulevard

To Hollywood

N
W E
S

Laurel Canyon Boulevard

TRAIL

Iredell St

Iredell Lane

75

Fryman Road

Dona Maria Dr

Briarcliff Lane

FRYMAN
CANYON
PARK

DEARING MTN TRAIL

74

Mulholland Drive

Pohl Overlook
(Fryman Canyon Overlook)

74
75
P

This loop hike crosses Coldwater Canyon Park and Wilacre Park with panoramic views of the San Fernando Valley.

**Driving directions:** From Sunset Boulevard in Beverly Hills, head north on Beverly Drive for 0.6 miles. At the fork, go right onto Coldwater Canyon Drive. Continue 3 miles to an intersection with Mulholland Drive. Go to the left, staying on Coldwater Canyon Drive, and drive 0.4 miles to the posted Coldwater Canyon/TreePeople Park on the right. Turn right into the parking area.

From the Ventura Freeway/Highway 101 in Studio City, exit on Coldwater Canyon Drive. Head 2.5 miles south to the intersection with Mulholland Drive. The posted Coldwater Canyon/TreePeople Park entrance is on the left (east) side of the intersection.

**Hiking directions:** From the information kiosk at the far end of the parking area, bear left on the nature trail, and head 30 yards to a junction. Cut back sharply to the right, and follow the wide path on an easy downhill grade to the second hillside level. Switchback to the left and descend to the third level and a junction with the Dearing Mountain Trail. Begin the loop to the left, gaining elevation while crossing the head of Iredell Canyon. Cross a small saddle and curve around the hillside to sweeping bird's-eye views of the valley. Continue on a slow but steady descent with wide curves. Along the way, the trail becomes a narrow, paved path, winding through cypress and pine tree groves. The trail ends at the Wilacre Park trailhead on Fryman Road at 1.5 miles. For a loop hike, follow Fryman Road 0.15 miles to the right to Iredell Street. Bear right and walk a half mile through a residential area, curving left onto Iredell Lane to the cul-de-sac at the end of the street. (The trail to Fryman Canyon—Hike 74—is to the left, shortly before the cul-de-sac.) Pick up the posted Dearing Mountain Trail, and ascend the hillside along the open space boundary. Make a wide right curve, completing the loop. Return to the left and stroll through the Magic Forest Nature Trail. ▪

# 74. Dearing Mountain Tra´
## Fryman Canyon Park to TreePec

**Hiking distance:** 5 miles round trip
**Hiking time:** 2.5 hours
**Elevation gain:** 500 feet
**Maps:** U.S.G.S. Beverly Hills and Van Nuys
      Trails Illustrated Santa Monica Mountains Nat'l. Rec. Area

**Summary of hike:** Fryman Canyon Park, which encompasses more than 120 acres, sits on a north-facing hillside bordering Mulholland Drive. At the trailhead, the Nancy Hoover Pohl Overlook (formerly known as the Fryman Canyon Overlook) provides views across the wooded canyon to the San Fernando Valley, Santa Susana Mountains, and the San Gabriel Mountains. This hike on the Dearing Mountain Trail descends into the canyon from the overlook, connecting Fryman Canyon Park with Coldwater Canyon Park and Wilacre Park.

**Driving directions:** From Sunset Boulevard in Beverly Hills, head north on Beverly Drive for 0.6 miles. At the fork, go right onto Coldwater Canyon Drive. Continue 3 miles to an intersection with Mulholland Drive. Turn right on Mulholland Drive, and go 2 miles to the posted Fryman Canyon Park entrance on the left. Turn left into the parking lot.

From the Ventura Freeway/Highway 101 in Studio City, exit on Laurel Canyon Boulevard. Head 2.8 miles south to the intersection with Mulholland Drive. Turn right on Mulholland Drive, and drive 0.8 miles to the posted Fryman Canyon Park entrance on the right.

**Hiking directions:** To the left of the trailhead, steps lead up to the Pohl (Fryman Canyon) Overlook. The posted Dearing Mountain Trail descends to a junction a short distance ahead (also known as the Betty B. Dearing Trail). Bear left and zigzag down seven switchbacks into Fryman Canyon. Follow the contours of the hillside, and make a horseshoe right bend across a spring-fed drainage. Pass remnants of a few old cars, and continue on

nyon wall to a T-junction. Take the left fork and stroll through
ture grove of oak and eucalyptus trees. Cross a stream in a ra-
e and bear left. Cross another drainage by a huge sandstone
utcrop, and pass an overlook of a few showcase homes. Curve
right on a footpath and traverse the sloping hillside. Descend
steps and emerge on Iredell Lane at 2 miles. Bear left for 0.1
mile to the cul-de-sac. Pick up the posted Dearing Mountain Trail,
and ascend the hillside for a half mile to a junction. Bear left and
stroll through the Magic Forest Nature Trail, or ascend the steps
to the park headquarters and an educational facility at TreePeople
Park.

To return to the trailhead, there are three hiking options. Return
along the same route for the shortest option. Continue with Hike 73
for a loop through Wilacre Park. Or loop back through residential
areas utilizing Iredell Street and Fryman Road—Hike 75. ■

## 75. Fryman Canyon Loop
### FRYMAN CANYON PARK

#### CROSS MOUNTAIN PARK SYSTEM

**Hiking distance:** 4-mile loop
**Hiking time:** 2 hours
**Elevation gain:** 500 feet

**map
page 187**

**Maps:** U.S.G.S. Beverly Hills and Van Nuys
Trails Illustrated Santa Monica Mountains Nat'l. Rec. Area

**Summary of hike:** This hike passes through Fryman Canyon
Park and a quiet residential area along the border, turning Hike
74 into a loop hike. Several parks in this area are collectively
referred to as Cross Mountain Park: Fryman Canyon Park (Hikes
74 and 75), Coldwater Canyon Park (Hike 73), Wilacre Park (Hike
73), and Franklin Canyon Park (Hikes 70—72). The mountain paths
through this 1,000-acre park system cross ridges, wind through
chaparral-covered hillsides, and meander up stream-fed canyons.
All of the parks are connected with hiking paths, offering many
opportunities for extending your hike.

**Driving directions:** From Sunset Boulevard head north on Beverly Drive for 0.6 miles. At onto Coldwater Canyon Drive. Continue 3 r tion with Mulholland Drive. Turn right on Mu. go 2 miles to the posted Fryman Canyon Park en. left. Turn left into the parking lot.

From the Ventura Freeway/Highway 101 in Studio City, ex. Laurel Canyon Boulevard. Head 2.8 miles south to the intersec-tion with Mulholland Drive. Turn right on Mulholland Drive, and drive 0.8 miles to the posted Fryman Canyon Park entrance on the right.

**Hiking directions:** To the left of the trailhead, steps lead up to the Nancy Hoover Pohl Overlook (formerly the Fryman Canyon Overlook). The posted Dearing Mountain Trail gradually descends on the chaparral-covered slope. A short distance ahead is a junc-tion on the left, our return route. Stay straight, following the con-tours of the hillside on a near-level grade that overlooks Fryman Canyon. Pass oak groves to a trail split at 0.4 miles. The right (upper trail) dead-ends in a quarter mile near Laurel Canyon Boulevard. Take the lower (left) fork, dropping down into the canyon to a T-junction with an unpaved road behind a row of homes fronted on Briarcliff Lane. Follow the road downhill to the left for 0.3 miles along the park boundary to the base of Fryman Canyon, where the road becomes paved. Detour left for 100 yards up the canyon on the footpath. Cross a ravine and meander up the canyon floor on the tree-shaded path. Curving right is a narrow, stream-fed canyon where the trail fades and becomes hard to follow.

Return to the road. Bear left 0.1 mile to the south end of Fryman Road. Follow Fryman Road to the left 0.4 miles to Iredell Street. Bear left and walk up the residential road, curving left on Iredell Lane. One hundred yards before the cul-de-sac, pick up the Dearing Mountain Trail on the left. Climb the steps and wind through Fryman Canyon under the shade of eucalyptus and oak groves. Cross a spring-fed drainage, and steadily climb seven switchbacks to the head of Fryman Canyon, completing the loop at the T-junction. Return to the trailhead on the right. ▪

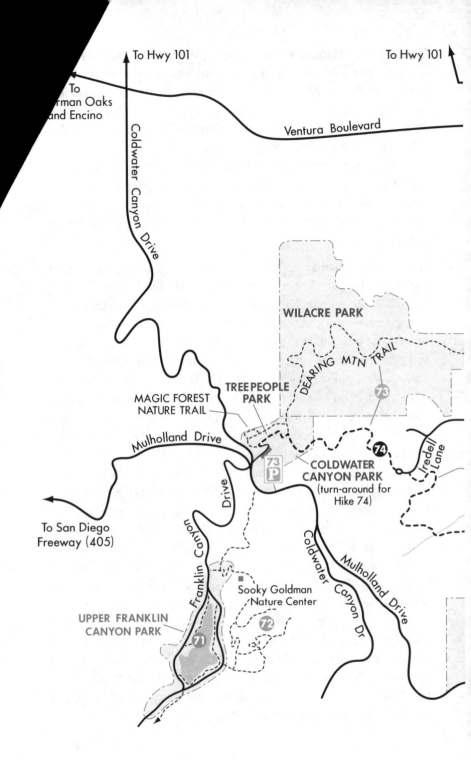

To Hwy 101

To Hwy 101

To
rman Oaks
and Encino

Ventura Boulevard

Coldwater Canyon Drive

WILACRE PARK

DEARING MTN TRAIL

73

MAGIC FOREST
NATURE TRAIL

TREE PEOPLE
PARK

74

Iredell Lane

Mulholland Drive

73
P

COLDWATER
CANYON PARK
(turn-around for
Hike 74)

Drive

To San Diego
Freeway (405)

Coldwater Canyon Dr

Mulholland Drive

Franklin Canyon

Sooky Goldman
Nature Center

72

UPPER FRANKLIN
CANYON PARK

71

# 74. Dearing Mountain Trail
## Fryman Canyon Park to TreePeople Park

# 75. Fryman Canyon Loop

## FRYMAN CANYON PARK
## CROSS MOUNTAIN PARK SYSTEM

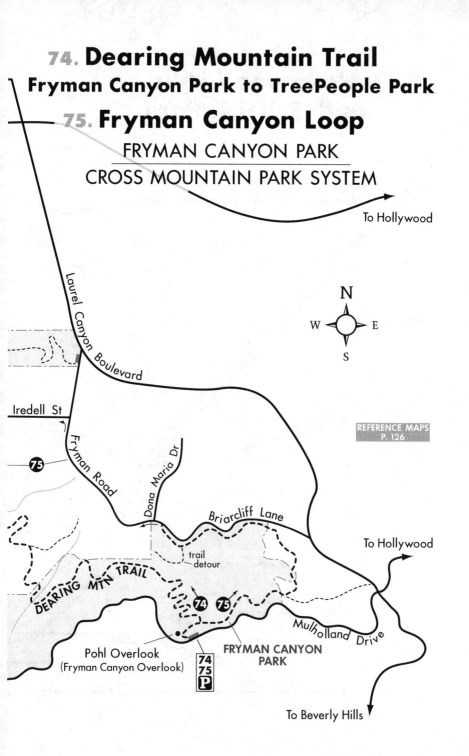

To Hollywood

Laurel Canyon Boulevard

N
W E
S

Iredell St

Fryman Road

75

Dona Maria Dr

Briarcliff Lane

REFERENCE MAPS
P. 126

To Hollywood

trail
detour

DEARING MTN TRAIL

74 75

Mulholland Drive

Pohl Overlook
(Fryman Canyon Overlook)

74
75
P

FRYMAN CANYON
PARK

To Beverly Hills

# Hollywood Hills
# and Griffith Park

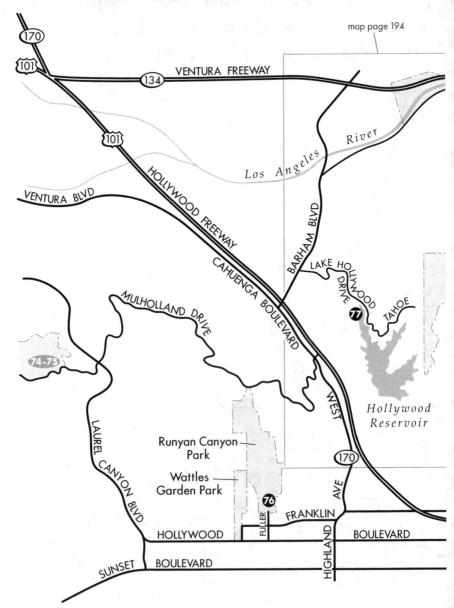

map page 194

170

101

134   VENTURA FREEWAY

101

*Los Angeles River*

VENTURA BLVD

HOLLYWOOD FREEWAY

CAHUENGA BOULEVARD

BARHAM BLVD

LAKE HOLLYWOOD DRIVE

TAHOE

77

MULHOLLAND DRIVE

74-75

WEST

*Hollywood Reservoir*

LAUREL CANYON BLVD

Runyan Canyon Park

Wattles Garden Park

170

76

FULLER

FRANKLIN

HIGHLAND AVE

HOLLYWOOD   BOULEVARD

SUNSET   BOULEVARD

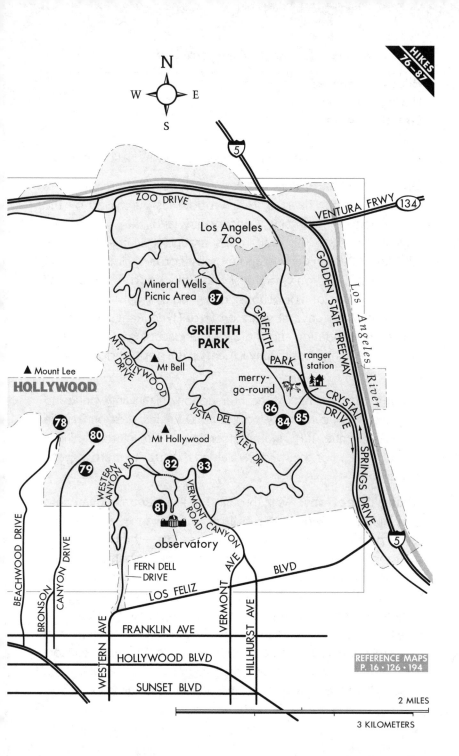

N
W · E
S

ZOO DRIVE

Los Angeles Zoo

VENTURA FRWY 134

GOLDEN STATE FREEWAY

Los Angeles River

Mineral Wells Picnic Area **87**

**GRIFFITH PARK**

GRIFFITH PARK

ranger station

▲ Mount Lee

**HOLLYWOOD**

MT. HOLLYWOOD DRIVE

▲ Mt Bell

merry-go-round

CRYSTAL DRIVE

VISTA DEL VALLEY DR

**78**

**80**

▲ Mt Hollywood

**86** **84** **85**

**79**

WESTERN CANYON RD

**82** **83**

VERMONT CANYON ROAD

SPRINGS DRIVE

**81**

observatory

5

FERN DELL DRIVE

BLVD

LOS FELIZ

VERMONT AVE

BEACHWOOD DRIVE

BRONSON

CANYON DRIVE

WESTERN AVE

FRANKLIN AVE

HILLHURST AVE

HOLLYWOOD BLVD

REFERENCE MAPS
P. 16 · 126 · 194

SUNSET BLVD

2 MILES

3 KILOMETERS

# 76. Runyan Canyon Park

**Hiking distance:** 2-mile loop
**Hiking time:** 1 hour
**Elevation gain:** 500 feet
**Maps:** U.S.G.S. Hollywood
Trails Illustrated Santa Monica Mountains Nat'l. Rec. Area

**Summary of hike:** Runyan Canyon Park, a 130-acre preserve minutes from the heart of Hollywood, was purchased by the Santa Monica Mountains Conservancy and the city of Los Angeles in 1984. This trail loops around the chaparral-clad hillsides of Runyan Canyon and crosses a broad gorge overlooking the urban canyon wilderness and Hollywood. The loop trail passes the ruins of a pool house designed by Frank Lloyd Wright and lived in for several years by Errol Flynn. Remnants of the old stone foundation and the exotic landscaping are all that remain of the ruined oasis. Runyan Canyon is a popular dog walking park.

**Driving directions:** At the intersection of Franklin Avenue and Highland Avenue in Hollywood, drive 0.3 miles west on Franklin to Fuller Avenue. Turn right and continue 0.5 miles to The Pines gate at the end of the road. Park along the street where a space is available.

**Hiking directions:** Walk through The Pines entrance gate into Runyan Canyon Park at the end of Fuller Avenue. A short distance past the entrance is a trail to the left—the beginning of the loop. Take this trail as it curves along the chaparral-covered hillside parallel to the canyon floor. At one mile, near the head of Runyan Canyon, the trail circles over to the east side of the canyon. Watch for a narrow trail to the right heading back towards the south. This trail leads to Cloud's Rest, an exceptional overlook with 360-degree panoramic views. The main trail continues to Inspiration Point and the Wright pool house ruins, then descends to the canyon floor and back to the trailhead. ■

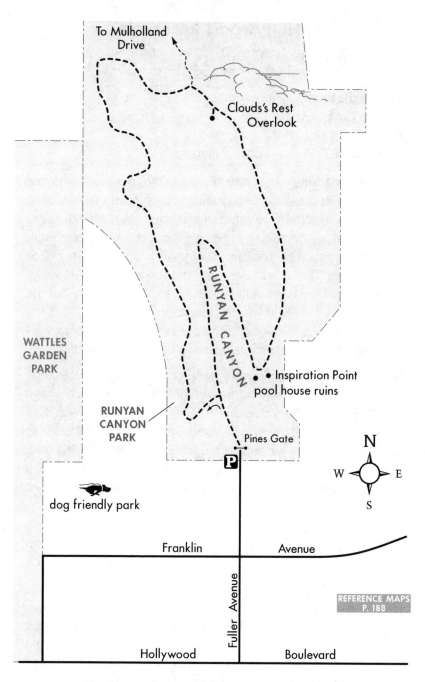

To Mulholland Drive

Clouds's Rest Overlook

RUNYAN CANYON

WATTLES GARDEN PARK

RUNYAN CANYON PARK

Inspiration Point
pool house ruins

Pines Gate

**P**

dog friendly park

N
W E
S

Franklin Avenue

Fuller Avenue

REFERENCE MAPS
P. 188

Hollywood Boulevard

# 76. Runyan Canyon Park

# 77. Hollywood Reservoir

Open weekdays 6:30 —10 a.m. and 2 —5 p.m.
Open weekends 6:30 a.m. to 5 p.m.

**Hiking distance:** 4-mile loop
**Hiking time:** 1.5 hours
**Elevation gain:** Level
**Maps:** U.S.G.S. Hollywood and Burbank

**Summary of hike:** This hike follows the perimeter of the Hollywood Reservoir on an asphalt service road that is closed to vehicles. The road, which is landscaped on both sides, is a rural retreat inside the city that is frequently used as a walking and jogging trail. The lake is fenced, preventing access to the shoreline. The tall foliage along the trail obscures full views of the reservoir except when crossing Mulholland Dam, but the dam crossing is magnificent. To the north is Mount Lee and the "Hollywood" sign overlooking the beautiful reservoir below. To the south is a view of Hollywood and the Los Angeles Basin.

**Driving directions:** From Hollywood, take Highland Avenue north past the Hollywood Bowl, curving left onto Cahuenga Boulevard West. Continue one mile to Barham Boulevard. Turn right and cross over the Hollywood Freeway. Drive 0.2 miles to Lake Hollywood Drive and turn right. Follow the winding Lake Hollywood Drive through a residential neighborhood for 0.8 miles to the Hollywood Reservoir entrance gate on the right. Park alongside the road.

From the Hollywood Freeway/Highway 101, take the Barham Boulevard Exit, and head north 0.2 miles to Lake Hollywood Drive. Turn right and drive 0.8 miles to the Hollywood Reservoir entrance gate on the right.

**Hiking directions:** The reservoir entrance is on the right (south). The paved path follows the perimeter of the reservoir through the shaded evergreen forest. At the south end of the reservoir, cross Mulholland Dam. The path then loops north to Tahoe Drive. Bear left along the road, returning to the parking area. ■

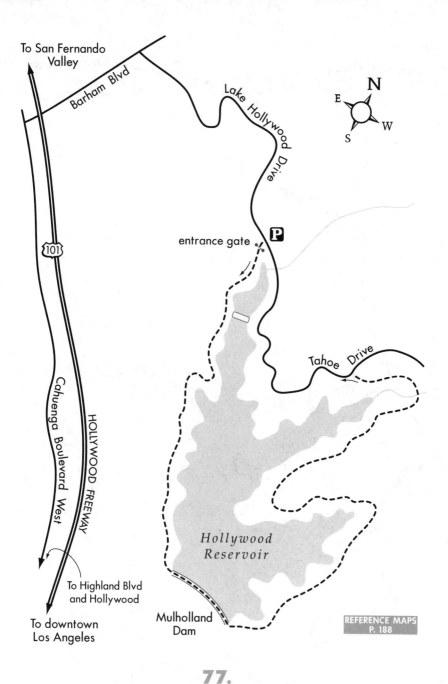

To San Fernando Valley

Barham Blvd

Lake Hollywood Drive

N
E
W
S

entrance gate

**P**

Tahoe Drive

101

Cahuenga Boulevard West

HOLLYWOOD FREEWAY

*Hollywood Reservoir*

To Highland Blvd and Hollywood

To downtown Los Angeles

Mulholland Dam

REFERENCE MAPS
P. 188

**77.**
# Hollywood Reservoir

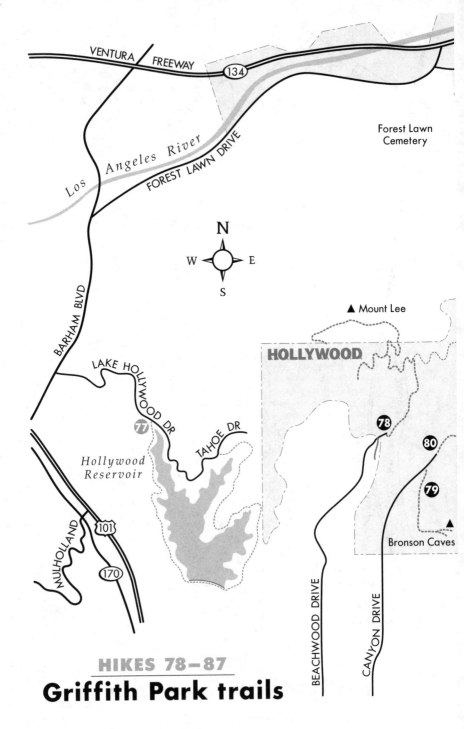

VENTURA FREEWAY

134

Forest Lawn
Cemetery

*Los Angeles River*

FOREST LAWN DRIVE

N
W   E
S

BARHAM BLVD

▲ Mount Lee

HOLLYWOOD

LAKE HOLLYWOOD DR

77

TAHOE DR

78

80

*Hollywood
Reservoir*

79

MULHOLLAND

101

170

Bronson Caves

BEACHWOOD DRIVE

CANYON DRIVE

**HIKES 78–87**
# Griffith Park trails

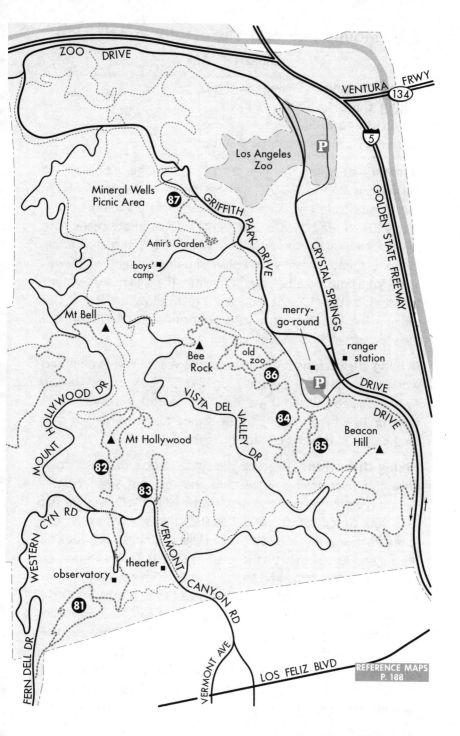

# 78. Mount Lee and the "Hollywood" sign
## GRIFFITH PARK

**Hiking distance:** 3 miles round trip
**Hiking time:** 1.5 hours
**Elevation gain:** 550 feet
**Maps:** U.S.G.S. Hollywood and Burbank

**Summary of hike:** This hike up the Hollyridge Trail leads to the famous "HOLLYWOOD" sign on the south slope of Mount Lee. The historic Los Angeles landmark was originally built in the 1920s to read "HOLLYWOODLAND" to promote real estate development in Beachwood Canyon. In 1978, entertainment celebrities donated money to replace the original sign, which was worn from time, weather, and vandalism. The sign now measures 50 feet high by 450 feet long. It sits just below the Mount Lee summit. The sign itself is fenced off from direct visitation, but the views from atop Mount Lee are superb.

**Driving directions:** At the intersection of Franklin Avenue and Western Avenue in Hollywood, drive 0.7 miles west on Franklin Avenue to Beachwood Drive. Turn right (north) and continue 1.8 miles up Beachwood Drive to the signed trailhead parking area on the right at the end of the public road.

**Hiking directions:** Head up the signed slope to a T-junction on a cliff overlooking Hollywood and the Los Angeles Basin. Behind is a picture-perfect view of the HOLLYWOOD sign. The right fork descends to the old trailhead access, which is now fenced off. Bear left and follow the ridge northeast, overlooking the Sunset Horse Ranch on the left. Continue 0.5 miles to an intersection with the unmarked Mulholland Trail. Take a sharp left up this trail as it heads west on a curvy fire road to Mount Lee Drive 0.3 miles ahead. At Mount Lee Drive, the left fork leads downhill to excellent frontal views of the sign. The right fork heads uphill to the ridge and up to the summit. The summit is above and behind the sign, overlooking Burbank, the San Fernando Valley, and the San Gabriel Mountains. Direct access to the towering whitewashed letters is prohibited. Return along the same route. ■

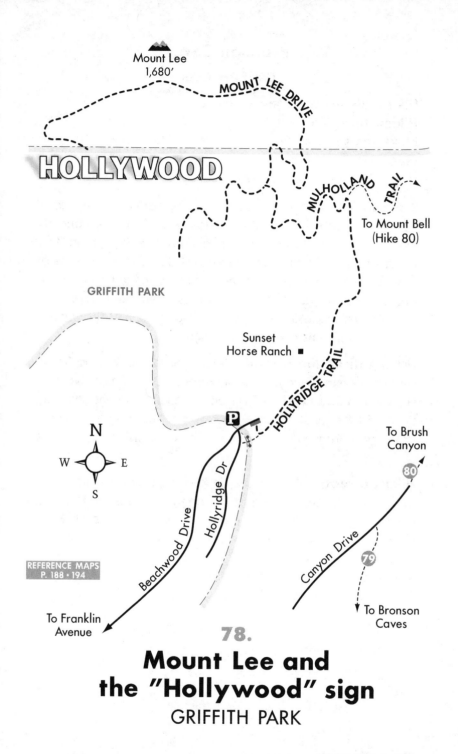

Mount Lee
1,680'

MOUNT LEE DRIVE

HOLLYWOOD

MULHOLLAND TRAIL

To Mount Bell
(Hike 80)

GRIFFITH PARK

Sunset
Horse Ranch ■

HOLLYRIDGE TRAIL

P

N
W · E
S

To Brush
Canyon

80

Beachwood Drive

Hollyridge Dr

Canyon Drive

79

REFERENCE MAPS
P. 188 · 194

To Bronson
Caves

To Franklin
Avenue

78.
**Mount Lee and
the "Hollywood" sign**
GRIFFITH PARK

# 79. Bronson Caves

## GRIFFITH PARK

**Hiking distance:** 0.6 miles round trip
**Hiking time:** 0.5 hours
**Elevation gain:** 40 feet
**Maps:** U.S.G.S. Hollywood
  Hileman's Recreational & Geological Map of Griffith Park

**Summary of hike:** At the southwest corner of Griffith Park is a short, enjoyable hike to one of Hollywood's most frequently filmed caves—the Bronson Caves. First used as a quarry in 1907, the crushed rock from the caves was used to pave the streets of a growing Hollywood. Many western and science fiction movie producers have shot on location at these man-made caves. *Star Trek, Mission Impossible, Gunsmoke, Bonanza*, and the *Batman and Robin* series have been filmed here.

**Driving directions:** At the intersection of Hollywood Boulevard and Western Avenue in Hollywood, drive 0.5 miles west on Hollywood Boulevard to Bronson Avenue. Turn right and continue 1.5 miles on Bronson Avenue (which merges with Canyon Drive) past Bronson Park to the end of the road. Park in the lot on the left.

**Hiking directions:** From the parking lot, hike back along the park road 100 feet to the trailhead on the left (east) side of the road. The trail gently climbs a quarter mile to the caves. From here you may walk through the caves and around the hill. Return along the same path.

To extend the hike, a trail heads north from the end of Canyon Drive to Brush Canyon (Hike 80). ■

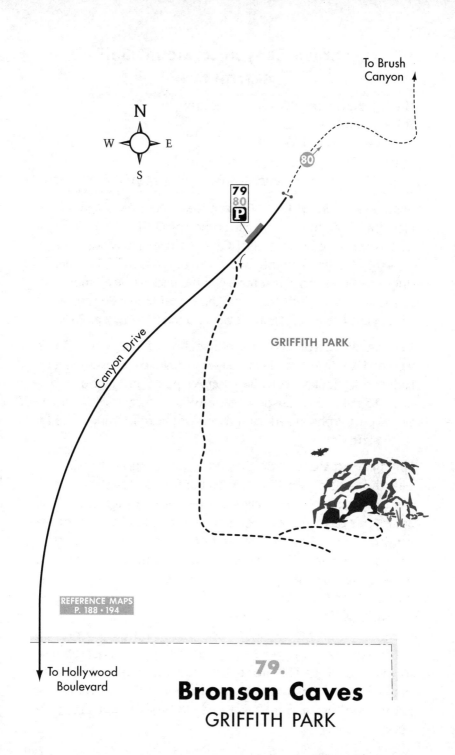

To Brush
Canyon

N
W &#9670; E
S

80

79
80
P

GRIFFITH PARK

Canyon Drive

REFERENCE MAPS
P. 188 • 194

To Hollywood
Boulevard

79.
**Bronson Caves**
GRIFFITH PARK

# 80. Brush Canyon to Mount Bell
## GRIFFITH PARK

**Hiking distance:** 2.5 miles round trip
**Hiking time:** 1.25 hours
**Elevation gain:** 750 feet
**Maps:** U.S.G.S. Hollywood and Burbank
   Hileman's Recreational & Geological Map of Griffith Park

**Summary of hike:** Brush Canyon is a beautiful yet lightly traveled trail from the southwest corner of Griffith Park. The hike begins from the north end of Canyon Drive and winds through a forest of large sycamore and oak trees. The trail climbs into a drier chaparral and shrub terrain in the undeveloped mountainous interior of Griffith Park. From the top of Mount Bell are views of secluded canyons, Hollywood, and the Los Angeles Basin.

**Driving directions:** At the intersection of Hollywood Boulevard and Western Avenue in Hollywood, drive 0.5 miles west on Hollywood Boulevard to Bronson Avenue. Turn right and continue 1.5 miles on Bronson Avenue (which merges with Canyon Drive) past Bronson Park to the end of the road. Park in the lot on the left.

**Hiking directions:** From the parking lot, hike uphill to the north past the vehicle gate. Continue on the fire road past the Pacific Electric quarry. At 0.25 miles is an expansive park and picnic area. After passing the park, the trail begins to climb out of the canyon, leaving the shade of the trees for the drought-resistant shrubs. Continue 0.75 miles to the Mulholland Trail junction. To the left, the Mulholland Trail heads west to the "Hollywood" sign on Mount Lee (Hike 78). Take the trail to the right another quarter mile to Mount Hollywood Drive.

Bear right on Mount Hollywood Drive, and quickly pick up the trail on the left to Mount Bell. The path climbs a quarter mile toward the rocky 1,587-foot summit. A few goat paths scramble up to the top, where there are more great views of the "Hollywood" sign and the San Fernando Valley Return along the same route. ■

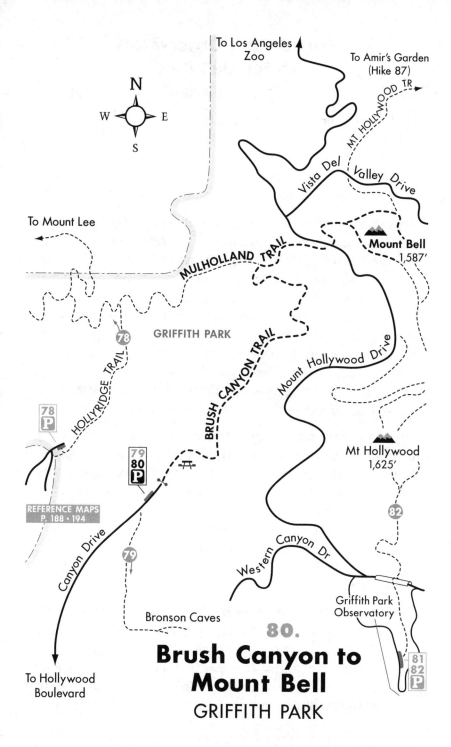

To Los Angeles Zoo

To Amir's Garden (Hike 87)

N
W    E
S

MT. HOLLYWOOD TR.

Vista Del Valley Drive

To Mount Lee

MULHOLLAND TRAIL

Mount Bell
1,587'

GRIFFITH PARK

**78**

HOLLYRIDGE TRAIL

BRUSH CANYON TRAIL

Mount Hollywood Drive

**78 P**

**79 80 P**

Mt Hollywood
1,625'

REFERENCE MAPS
P. 188 • 194

**82**

Canyon Drive

**79**

Western Canyon Dr

Bronson Caves

Griffith Park Observatory

**80.**

# Brush Canyon to Mount Bell
## GRIFFITH PARK

To Hollywood Boulevard

**81 82 P**

# 81. Griffith Park Observatory to Ferndell Park

## GRIFFITH PARK

**Hiking distance:** 2.5 miles round trip
**Hiking time:** 1.5 hours
**Elevation gain:** 500 feet
**Maps:** U.S.G.S. Hollywood
Hileman's Recreational & Geological Map of Griffith Park

**Summary of hike:** This hike in Griffith Park offers panoramic views of the Los Angeles area from the ocean to the San Gabriel Mountains. The exotic garden pathways of Ferndell Park follow the lush oasis along a tumbling brook that is lined with moss-covered rocks. Charming footbridges cross the stream.

The hike begins at the copper-domed Griffith Park Observatory perched on the slopes of Mount Hollywood. The observatory has a planetarium, laser programs, a gift shop, and various science displays. An observation deck with telescopes winds around the south side of this architectural landmark, with views across Hollywood and the expansive metropolitan area.

**Driving directions:** From Los Feliz Boulevard in Hollywood, there are two ways to arrive at the trailhead parking lot. Take Fern Dell Drive north 2.3 miles to the Griffith Park Observatory parking lot. (Fern Dell Drive becomes Western Canyon Road after the hairpin turn.)

Or, take Vermont Avenue north 1.8 miles to the observatory parking lot. (En route, Vermont Avenue curves into Vermont Canyon Road.) Both directions offer a beautiful, curving drive through Griffith Park.

**Hiking directions:** From the parking lot, walk towards the observatory. Follow the trail to the left (east) of the observatory for 0.25 miles to an overlook and trail junction. Stay to the right another 0.25 miles to the next junction. Take either the Lower Trail (the shorter route) or the Upper Trail, and continue down to Ferndell Park. Walk under large sycamore and oak trees through the picnic grounds to the brook. Stroll along the quarter-mile path, meandering along the park's year-round stream over bridges, past waterfalls and pools, and through the lush gardens and glen. To return, retrace your route, taking the Upper or Lower Trail back to the observatory. ■

REFERENCE MAPS
P. 188 • 194

## 81.
# Griffith Park
# Observatory
## Ferndell Park
### GRIFFITH PARK

# 82. Mount Hollywood and Dante's View
## GRIFFITH PARK

**Hiking distance:** 3 miles round trip
**Hiking time:** 1.5 hours
**Elevation gain:** 500 feet
**Maps:** U.S.G.S. Hollywood and Burbank
Hileman's Recreational & Geological Map of Griffith Park

**Summary of hike:** The Mount Hollywood Trail (also known as the Charlie Turner Trail) takes you to the top of Mount Hollywood at an elevation of 1,625 feet, the highest point in Griffith Park. The overlook offers commanding views of the San Fernando Valley, the Los Angeles Basin, and the San Gabriel Mountains. The trail also includes Dante's View, a terraced two-acre garden planted by Dante Orgolini in the 1960s. This south-facing garden has picnic benches and shade trees along its intertwining trail.

The hike begins just north of the Griffith Park Observatory (Hike 81). The observatory, built in 1935, has excellent science exhibits and planetarium shows.

**Driving directions:** From Los Feliz Boulevard in Hollywood, there are two ways to arrive at the trailhead parking lot. You may take Fern Dell Drive north 2.3 miles to the Griffith Park Observatory parking lot. (Fern Dell Drive becomes Western Canyon Road after the hairpin turn.)

Or, take Vermont Avenue north 1.8 miles to the observatory parking lot. (En route, Vermont Avenue curves into Vermont Canyon Road.) Both directions offer a beautiful, curving drive through Griffith Park.

**Hiking directions:** From the parking lot, hike north (opposite from the observatory) to the well-marked Charlie Turner (Mount Hollywood) trailhead. Climb the tree-lined ridge to the Berlin Forest, a friendship park between the people of Berlin and Los Angeles. There are wonderful views and benches where you can relax before continuing. At 0.75 miles, a junction indicates the beginning of the loop. The trail to the right is the shortest

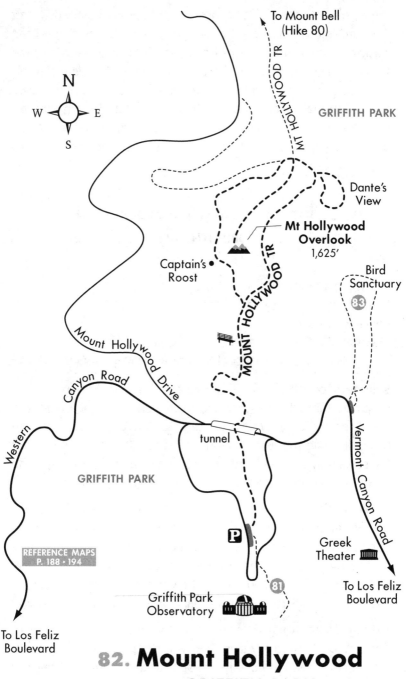

To Mount Bell
(Hike 80)

GRIFFITH PARK

MT HOLLYWOOD TR

Dante's
View

**Mt Hollywood
Overlook**
1,625'

Bird
Sanctuary

83

Captain's
Roost

MOUNT HOLLYWOOD TR

Mount Hollywood Drive

Canyon Road

Western

GRIFFITH PARK

tunnel

Vermont Canyon Road

REFERENCE MAPS
P. 188 · 194

P

Greek
Theater

81

To Los Feliz
Boulevard

Griffith Park
Observatory

To Los Feliz
Boulevard

# 82. **Mount Hollywood**
## GRIFFITH PARK

route to Dante's View. It is a joy to stroll along this path. After the garden, continue on the main trail as it curves around the hillside, opening up to views of the San Fernando Valley and the surrounding mountains. A short trail to the left leads to a lookout at the top of Mount Hollywood. After enjoying the views, go back to the main trail and continue to the left, looping around the west side of Mount Hollywood past the Captain's Roost picnic area in a grove of trees. Complete the loop and return to the parking lot. ■

# 83. Bird Sanctuary Nature Trail
## GRIFFITH PARK
2900 Vermont Canyon Road

---

**Hiking distance:** 0.5-mile loop
**Hiking time:** 0.5 hours
**Elevation gain:** Level
**Maps:** U.S.G.S. Hollywood and Burbank
       Hileman's Recreational & Geological Map of Griffith Park

---

**Summary of hike:** The Bird Sanctuary Nature Trail is a short loop hike through a pastoral wooded glen. The peaceful refuge is shaded by large eucalyptus trees and evergreens. A stream flows through the lush canyon, and a footbridge crosses over the stream by a pond. Beautiful rock walls line the pathways. The sanctuary is home to many species of indigenous birds.

**Driving directions:** At the intersection of Los Feliz Boulevard and Vermont Avenue in Hollywood, drive one mile north on Vermont Avenue past the Greek Theater to the bird sanctuary on the right side of the road. En route, Vermont Avenue becomes Vermont Canyon Road. (The Griffith Park Observatory is another 0.8 miles past the sanctuary on Vermont Canyon Road.)

**Hiking directions:** From the parking area, walk to the right past the bird sanctuary sign. The well-defined trail heads north through the sanctuary and loops back to the trailhead. A narrow footpath leads through the forest on the hillside above the east side of the sanctuary, parallel to the main path. ■

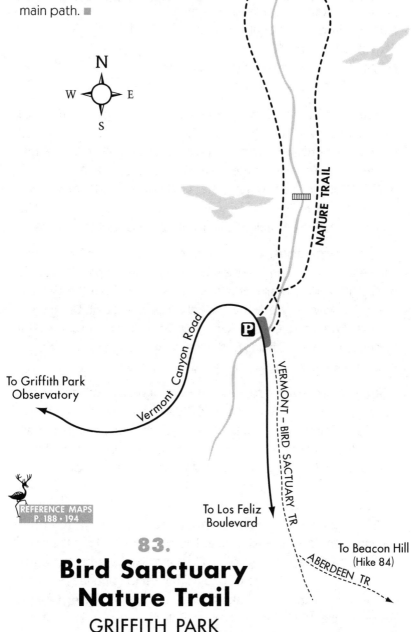

N
W · E
S

NATURE TRAIL

Vermont Canyon Road

**P**

To Griffith Park
Observatory

VERMONT – BIRD SACTUARY TR

REFERENCE MAPS
P. 188 • 194

To Los Feliz
Boulevard

To Beacon Hill
(Hike 84)

ABERDEEN TR

## 83.
# Bird Sanctuary
# Nature Trail
## GRIFFITH PARK

# 84. Beacon Hill

## GRIFFITH PARK

**Hiking distance:** 2.5 miles to 4 miles
**Hiking time:** 1.5 hours to 2 hours
**Elevation gain:** 550 feet
**Maps:** U.S.G.S. Burbank and Hollywood
   Hileman's Recreational & Geological Map of Griffith Park

**Summary of hike:** Beacon Hill is the easternmost summit of the 50-mile long Santa Monica Mountain Range. An illuminated beacon once resided on the top of Beacon Hill, warning aircraft of the mountains next to the Glendale Grand Central Airport, the main airport for Los Angeles and Hollywood during the 1910s and 1920s. From Beacon Hill you can see it all—from the Pacific Ocean to the Los Angeles Basin to the San Gabriel Mountains.

**Driving directions:** Go to the intersection of Los Feliz Boulevard and Crystal Springs Drive in Hollywood in the southeast area of Griffith Park. (To arrive at this intersection from the Golden State Freeway/I-5, take the Los Feliz Boulevard Exit. Drive west a short distance to Crystal Springs Drive.) Drive north on Crystal Springs Drive for 1.3 miles to the merry-go-round turnoff on the left. Turn left and park in the first parking lot.

**Hiking directions:** From the parking lot, walk back across the road and uphill to the right for 100 yards to a junction with the Old Zoo Trail (Hike 86). Take the trail to the left, heading uphill on the Fern Canyon Trail. Continue on the Fern Canyon Trail as it winds around the brushy hillside. At one mile, on a saddle in the hill, is a five-way trail junction and benches. The trail to the left leads up the ridge a quarter mile to the top of Beacon Hill.

After taking in the views from the domed summit, return to the junction. For a 2.5-mile round trip hike, return along the same trail back to the parking lot. To make a 4-mile loop, take the left (southeast) trail—the Coolidge Trail—and continue downhill one mile to a trail fork. Take the left fork—the Lower Beacon Trail—parallel to Griffith Park Drive. Return to the parking lot. ■

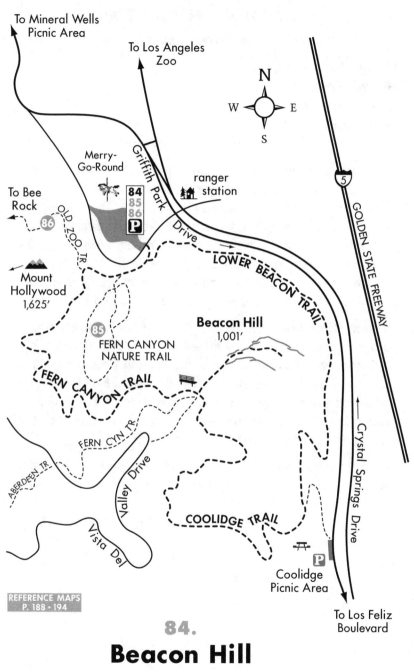

To Mineral Wells
Picnic Area

To Los Angeles
Zoo

N
W   E
S

Merry-
Go-Round

ranger
station

Griffith Park

84
85
86
P

To Bee
Rock

86

OLD ZOO TR.

Mount
Hollywood
1,625'

Drive

LOWER BEACON TRAIL

85

FERN CANYON
NATURE TRAIL

Beacon Hill
1,001'

FERN CANYON TRAIL

FERN CYN TR.

ABERDEEN TR.

Valley Drive

COOLIDGE TRAIL

Vista Del

GOLDEN STATE FREEWAY

5

Crystal Springs Drive

Coolidge
Picnic Area

P

REFERENCE MAPS
P. 188 · 194

To Los Feliz
Boulevard

84.
# Beacon Hill
## GRIFFITH PARK

# 85. Fern Canyon Nature Trail
## GRIFFITH PARK

**Hiking distance:** 0.6-mile loop
**Hiking time:** 0.5 hours
**Elevation gain:** 150 feet
**Maps:** U.S.G.S. Burbank
Hileman's Recreational & Geological Map of Griffith Park

**Summary of hike:** The Fern Canyon Nature Trail, near the eastern terminus of the Santa Monica Mountains, takes you through a forested canyon along various looping trails. The self-guided nature trails meander through dense pockets of streamside vegetation and wind through shady groves of oak, sycamore, black walnut, willow, toyon, and cedar. The path crosses footbridges and leads to a natural amphitheater. This quiet refuge is located just minutes from the merry-go-round and the Old Zoo Park.

**Driving directions:** Go to the intersection of Los Feliz Boulevard and Crystal Springs Drive in Hollywood in the southeast area of Griffith Park. (To arrive at this intersection from the Golden State Freeway/I-5, take the Los Feliz Boulevard Exit. Drive west a short distance to Crystal Springs Drive.) Drive north on Crystal Springs Drive for 1.3 miles to the merry-go-round turnoff on the left. Turn left and park in the first parking lot.

**Hiking directions:** From the parking lot, walk back across the road and uphill to the right for about 75 yards to the Fern Canyon Nature Trail, clearly marked with a large sign. (If you have reached the Fern Canyon Trail/Old Zoo Trail junction, you have gone too far.) All of the trails within this short loop interconnect and wind through the stream-fed ravine, returning back to the entrance. Choose your own path. ■

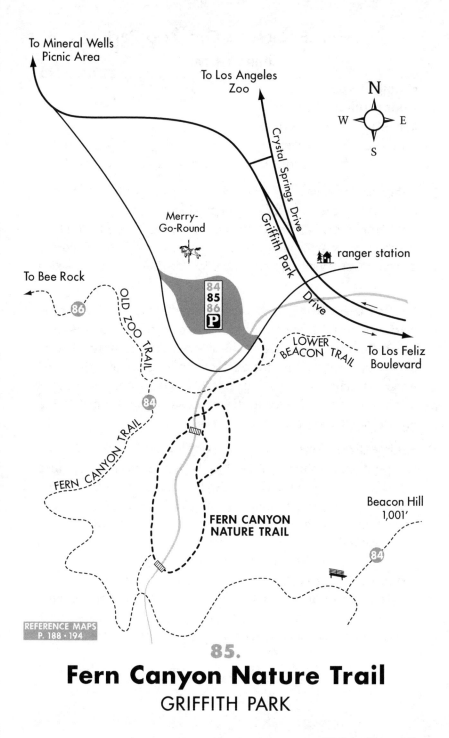

To Mineral Wells
Picnic Area

To Los Angeles
Zoo

Crystal Springs Drive

N
W E
S

Merry-
Go-Round

Griffith Park Drive

ranger station

To Bee Rock

OLD ZOO TRAIL

86

84
**85**
86
**P**

LOWER
BEACON TRAIL

To Los Feliz
Boulevard

84

FERN CANYON TRAIL

FERN CANYON
NATURE TRAIL

Beacon Hill
1,001'

84

REFERENCE MAPS
P. 188 · 194

85.
# Fern Canyon Nature Trail
## GRIFFITH PARK

# 86. Bee Rock and Old Zoo Park
## GRIFFITH PARK

**Hiking distance:** 2.2-mile loop
**Hiking time:** 1.5 hours
**Elevation gain:** 300 feet
**Maps:** U.S.G.S. Burbank
Hileman's Recreational & Geological Map of Griffith Park

**Summary of hike:** Bee Rock is a large, cavernous sandstone outcropping that is naturally sculpted into the shape of a bee-hive. From atop Bee Rock are impressive views of Griffith Park. The trail returns through the old Los Angeles Zoo, which has been converted into a park. The Old Zoo Trail includes walking paths, expansive lawns, and abandoned animal cages.

**Driving directions:** Go to the intersection of Los Feliz Boule-vard and Crystal Springs Drive in Hollywood in the southeast area of Griffith Park. (To arrive at this intersection from the Golden State Freeway/I-5, take the Los Feliz Boulevard Exit. Drive west a short distance to Crystal Springs Drive.) Drive north on Crystal Springs Drive for 1.3 miles to the merry-go-round turnoff on the left. Turn left and park in the first parking lot.

**Hiking directions:** From the parking lot, walk back across the road and uphill to the right for 100 yards to a trail junction. Take the Old Zoo Trail to the right, heading uphill into the trees. (The trail to the left goes to Beacon Hill—Hike 84.) At 0.5 miles, Bee Rock comes into view. Another quarter mile—on a ridge—is the Bee Rock Trail to the left. On the right is the return route through the old zoo. First, take the trail to Bee Rock. The final ascent up to Bee Rock is steep, but the views make it worth the effort.

After descending back to the junction, go through the gate and down along the paths of the old zoo. The paths lead back to the merry-go-round and parking lot, completing the loop. ■

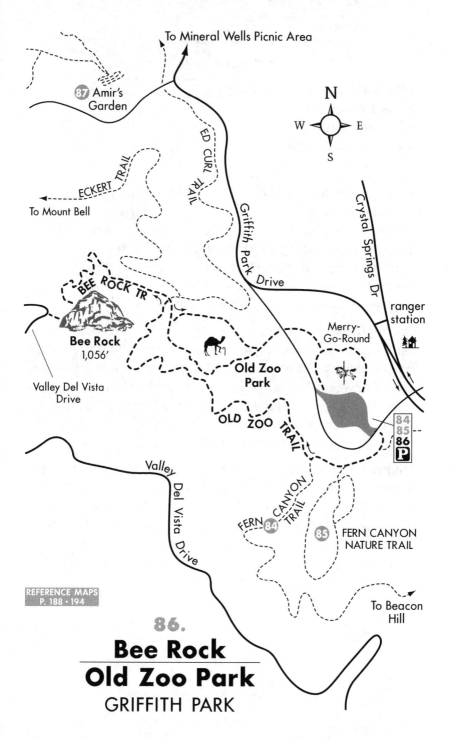

To Mineral Wells Picnic Area

**87** Amir's Garden

N
W   E
S

ED CURL TRAIL

ECKERT TRAIL

To Mount Bell

Crystal Springs Dr

Griffith Park Drive

ranger station

BEE ROCK TR

Bee Rock
1,056'

Valley Del Vista Drive

Old Zoo Park

Merry-Go-Round

OLD ZOO TRAIL

84
85
86
P

Valley Del Vista Drive

FERN CANYON TRAIL

**84**

**85** FERN CANYON NATURE TRAIL

To Beacon Hill

REFERENCE MAPS
P. 188 · 194

**86.**
# Bee Rock
# Old Zoo Park
## GRIFFITH PARK

# 87. Amir's Garden

## GRIFFITH PARK

**Hiking distance:** 1 mile round trip
**Hiking time:** 1 hour
**Elevation gain:** 300 feet
**Maps:** U.S.G.S. Burbank
Hileman's Recreational & Geological Map of Griffith Park

**Summary of hike:** Amir's Garden is a beautifully landscaped hillside with rock-lined paths, benches, and picnic tables on several layers of terraces. There is a wonderful network of trails and stairways leading through the garden. The tranquil garden oasis was created in 1971 by Amir Dialameh, who designed, planted, nurtured, and maintained this two-acre Eden on the brushy slopes above Mineral Wells Picnic Area.

**Driving directions:** Go to the intersection of Los Feliz Boulevard and Crystal Springs Drive in Hollywood in the southeast area of Griffith Park. (To arrive at this intersection from the Golden State Freeway/I-5, take the Los Feliz Boulevard Exit. Drive west a short distance to Crystal Springs Drive.) Continue 1.5 miles to Griffith Park Drive (just past the merry-go-round) and turn left. Drive 1.3 miles to the Mineral Wells Picnic Area and park.

**Hiking directions:** From the parking area at the lower south end of Mineral Wells Picnic Area, take the trail west to a 4-way junction, immediately ahead. Follow the middle fork up towards the water tank. A half mile ahead is a lookout and a sharp trail switchback. Amir's Garden is at this lookout point. The garden paths zigzag across the hillside. After strolling and enjoying the garden, return along the same path. ■

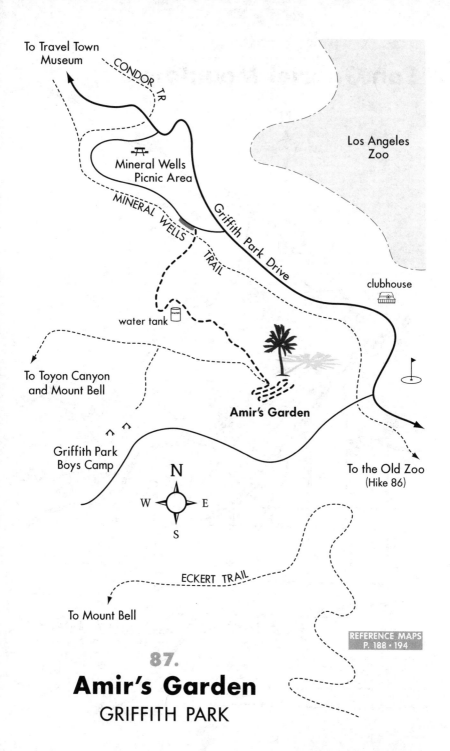

To Travel Town
Museum

CONDOR TR.

Los Angeles
Zoo

Mineral Wells
Picnic Area

MINERAL WELLS

TRAIL

Griffith Park Drive

clubhouse

water tank

To Toyon Canyon
and Mount Bell

Amir's Garden

Griffith Park
Boys Camp

To the Old Zoo
(Hike 86)

N
W      E
S

ECKERT TRAIL

To Mount Bell

REFERENCE MAPS
P. 188 • 194

**87.**
# Amir's Garden
## GRIFFITH PARK

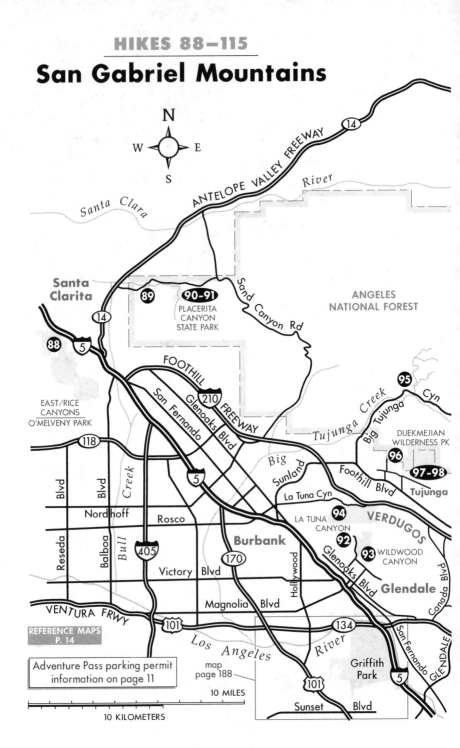

# San Gabriel Mountains

N
W · E
S

ANTELOPE VALLEY FREEWAY

14

River

Santa Clara

Santa Clarita

89

90-91
PLACERITA CANYON STATE PARK

Sand Canyon Rd

ANGELES NATIONAL FOREST

14

88

5

FOOTHILL

210 FREEWAY

San Fernando

Glenoaks Blvd

EAST/RICE CANYONS
O'MELVENY PARK

118

Creek

Blvd

Blvd

Nordhoff

Rosco

5

Big

Sunland

La Tuna Cyn

Tujunga Creek

Big Tujunga

95

Cyn

DUEKMEJIAN WILDERNESS PK

96

97-98
Tujunga

Foothill Blvd

VERDUGOS

LA TUNA CANYON

94

92

93 WILDWOOD CANYON

Burbank

170

Bull

405

Victory Blvd

Reseda

Balboa

Hollywood

Glenoaks Blvd

Glendale

Canada Blvd

Magnolia Blvd

VENTURA FRWY

101

Los Angeles River

134

San Fernando

GLENDALE

5

REFERENCE MAPS
P. 14

Adventure Pass parking permit
information on page 11

map
page 188

Griffith
Park

101

Sunset Blvd

10 MILES

10 KILOMETERS

**216** – Day Hikes Around Los Angeles

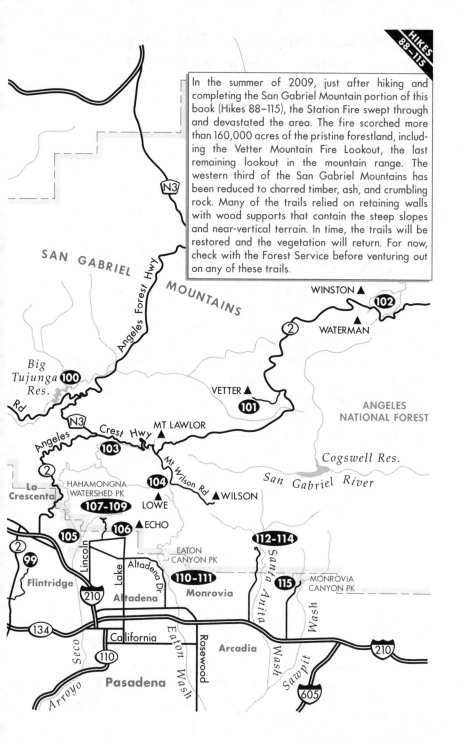

In the summer of 2009, just after hiking and completing the San Gabriel Mountain portion of this book (Hikes 88–115), the Station Fire swept through and devastated the area. The fire scorched more than 160,000 acres of the pristine forestland, including the Vetter Mountain Fire Lookout, the last remaining lookout in the mountain range. The western third of the San Gabriel Mountains has been reduced to charred timber, ash, and crumbling rock. Many of the trails relied on retaining walls with wood supports that contain the steep slopes and near-vertical terrain. In time, the trails will be restored and the vegetation will return. For now, check with the Forest Service before venturing out on any of these trails.

SAN GABRIEL MOUNTAINS

N3

Angeles Forest Hwy

WINSTON ▲
2   102
WATERMAN ▲

Big Tujunga Res. 100

VETTER ▲
101

ANGELES NATIONAL FOREST

Rd

N3   Angeles   Crest Hwy   MT LAWLOR ▲
103

Cogswell Res.

Mt Wilson Rd

San Gabriel River

2
La Crescenta

HAHAMONGNA WATERSHED PK
107-109   LOWE ▲
104   ▲WILSON

105   106 ▲ECHO

Lincoln

EATON CANYON PK

112-114

99   Flintridge

210   Altadena

Lake   Altadena Dr

110-111   Monrovia

Santa Anita Wash

115   MONROVIA CANYON PK

134

Seco   110   California

Eaton Wash

Rosewood   Arcadia   Wash

Sawpit Wash

210

Arroyo   Pasadena

605

# 88. East Canyon and Rice Canyon
## SANTA CLARITA WOODLANDS PARK
24255 The Old Road · Newhall

**Hiking distance:** 5.6 miles round trip
**Hiking time:** 3 hours
**Elevation gain:** 1,100 feet
**Maps:** U.S.G.S. Oat Mountain

**Summary of hike:** East Canyon and Rice Canyon sit on the north-facing slope of the Santa Susana Mountains in Santa Clarita. The canyons are included in the 4,000-acre Santa Clarita Woodlands Park, managed by the Santa Monica Mountains Conservancy. The East Canyon Trail is a dirt fire road that climbs through forested pockets of coast live oak, bay laurel, black walnut, big leaf maple, toyon, and Douglas fir. The hiking, biking, and equestrian trail leads nearly four miles to the Weldon Canyon Motorway, straddling the ridgeline. This hike leads to an overlook (shy of the ridge), with magnificent views across Santa Clarita Valley. Rice Canyon, an adjoining drainage, diverts from East Canyon and follows seasonal Rice Creek up the canyon bottom to a grassy knoll with an overlook of the canyon and surrounding mountains. The Rice Canyon Trail, for hikers only, winds through the forested canyon at an easy grade, gaining only 300 feet to the plateau dotted with oaks above the canyon floor. En route, the trail leads through open pastoral meadows and groves of oaks, sycamores, cottonwoods, and willows.

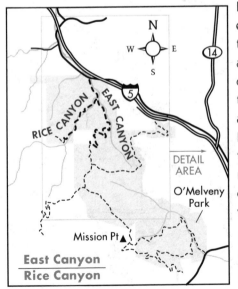

**East Canyon**
**Rice Canyon**

**Driving directions:**
From the Golden State Freeway (Interstate 5) in

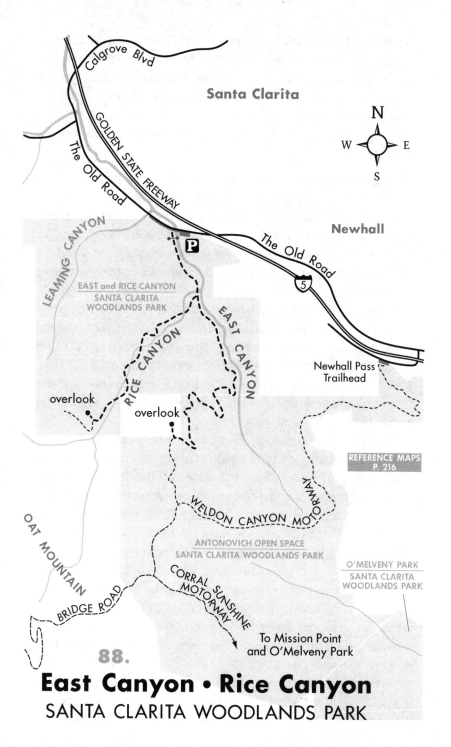

Calgrove Blvd

Santa Clarita

GOLDEN STATE FREEWAY

The Old Road

N
W · E
S

Newhall

The Old Road

5

LEAMING CANYON

P

EAST and RICE CANYON
SANTA CLARITA
WOODLANDS PARK

RICE CANYON

EAST CANYON

overlook

overlook

Newhall Pass
Trailhead

REFERENCE MAPS
P. 216

OAT MOUNTAIN

WELDON CANYON MOTORWAY

ANTONOVICH OPEN SPACE
SANTA CLARITA WOODLANDS PARK

O'MELVENY PARK
SANTA CLARITA
WOODLANDS PARK

BRIDGE ROAD

CORRAL SUNSHINE MOTORWAY

To Mission Point
and O'Melveny Park

## 88.
# East Canyon · Rice Canyon
## SANTA CLARITA WOODLANDS PARK

Santa Clarita, exit on Calgrove Boulevard. Head south on Calgrove Boulevard, which quickly becomes The Old Road. Follow the frontage road one mile to the signed trailhead on the right (located just before The Old Road goes under I-5.) Park along the right side of the road for free, or pull into the trailhead parking lot on the right for a fee. An Adventure Pass is required for parking.

**Hiking directions:** Walk east on the side road, parallel to The Old Road, to the signed trailhead just shy of the pay-parking lot. Bear right, head past the botanical garden and vehicle gate, and enter the mouth of the East Canyon. Follow the west side of ephemeral East Canyon Creek. At 0.3 miles is a signed trail fork. The right fork heads up Rice Canyon. For now, continue straight, staying in East Canyon while gently climbing past oak groves. The canyon narrows at 0.7 miles and the vegetation thickens. Climb out of the canyon bottom, and wind up the west canyon slope with far-reaching vistas. At 1.8 miles is a short, steep climb. As the path curves left, take the unsigned footpath to the right. Walk 100 yards to a lone majestic oak on a knoll overlooking the fir and pine forest deep in Rice Canyon. Enjoy the great views across the Santa Clarita Valley.

To extend the hike along this route, the East Canyon Trail continues less than a mile to the Weldon Canyon Motorway atop the ridge. The left fork traverses the ridge and descends the mountain into Weldon Canyon. The right fork stays on the 3.8-mile East Canyon Trail to its terminus at a trail split. To the right, Bridge Road follows the ridge to Oat Mountain. To the left, Corral Sunshine Motorway leads to Mission Point and O'Melveny Park.

Return down the mountain to the junction at the foot of Rice Canyon. Veer left into Rice Canyon and stroll through the open meadow as the canyon narrows. Enter the shade of the oaks and cross the seasonal drainage. Pass through a small oak-rimmed meadow, then duck back into the forest. Cross the stream four more times, weaving up thr canyon. Ascend the west canyon wall to an unsigned Y-fork one mile from the junction. The right fork leads 25 yards to a knoll with a stately oak and a vista of the forested canyon. The left fork heads steeply up the mountain. ∎

# 89. Placerita Canyon Trail
## PLACERITA CANYON STATE PARK and NATURAL AREA
19152 Placerita Canyon Road · Newhall

**Hiking distance:** 4 miles round trip
**Hiking time:** 2 hours
**Elevation gain:** 250 feet
**Maps:** U.S.G.S. Mint Canyon
Harrison: Angeles Front Country Trail Map
Placerita Canyon Natural Area Map

*map
page 224*

**Summary of hike:** Placerita Canyon State Park is a designated state historic landmark. The canyon is the site of the original gold discovery in California, dating back to 1842, six years prior to the famous discovery of gold by John Marshall at Sutter's Mill in the northern town of Coloma. This 350-acre natural area is located on the north slope of the San Gabriel Mountains, over-looking the Santa Clarita Valley. The park sits in a transition zone between the San Gabriel Mountains and the Mohave Desert. The east-west running canyon links the Angeles National Forest with the Santa Susana Mountains, the Simi Hills, and the Santa Monica Mountains. Placerita Canyon contains sandstone forma-tions, seasonal streams, and riparian woodlands with stands of oaks, sycamores, cottonwoods, and willows.

This hike begins at the nature center and follows the pictur-esque canyon and meandering creek east into the Walker Ranch Campground. The camp is named for Frank Walker, who built his home on the historic ranch in the 1920s.

**Driving directions:** From the Golden State Freeway (I-5) in Newhall, take the Antelope Valley Freeway (H-14) east. Continue 3 miles and exit on Placerita Canyon Road. Turn right and drive 1.4 miles to the signed Placerita Canyon State Park on the right. Turn right and continue 0.1 mile to the nature center. Park in the spaces on the left. An Adventure Pass is required for parking.

**Hiking directions:** From the nature center, cross the drainage to a junction. The Hillside Trail climbs the hill to the south. Stay in

Placerita Canyon and continue up canyon to the east. Follow the rock-lined path on the south edge of the seasonal creek under oaks, willows, cottonwoods, alders, and sycamores. The rock-walled drainage narrows to a gorge, and the footpath crosses the transient drainage four times. Pass through a beautiful oak grove and a seasonal drainage on the right by a 10-foot ephemeral waterfall at one mile. The canyon widens out and the grade remains relatively level. Climb a short slope and curve left by signpost 19 at a bubbling spring with a mixture of oil and water (known as *white oil*) on the right. At two miles enter the Walker Ranch Campground on a grassy flat covered in majestic oaks, reaching a signed junction with Los Pinetos Trail (Hike 91) and the Placerita Waterfall Trail (Hike 90).

To extend the hike, continue with Hike 90 to Placerita Falls or Hike 91 to the crest of the San Gabriel Mountains, overlooking the San Fernando Valley. ■

## 90. Placerita Waterfall Trail
### PLACERITA CANYON STATE PARK and NATURAL AREA

**Hiking distance:** 1.5 miles round trip
**Hiking time:** 1 hours
**Elevation gain:** 250 feet

*map
page 225*

**Maps:** U.S.G.S. Mint Canyon and San Fernando
       Harrison: Angeles Front Country Trail Map
       Placerita Canyon Natural Area Map

**Summary of hike:** Placerita Falls is a 25-foot seasonal waterfall (generally active between January and May) tucked into a cool, rock-enclosed grotto in Placerita Canyon State Park. The easy hike into narrow Los Pinetos Canyon follows Placerita Creek through the shaded gorge under a canopy of live oak, big leaf maple, and big cone spruce trees. An understory of moist ferns surrounds the path. The trail begins at the Walker Ranch Campground by historic remnants of a settler's cottage built in the early 1900s. The cement foundation and chimney are still intact. En route, the trail meanders along the waterway, crossing the ephemeral creek seven times. The path scrambles over water-polished metamorphic rock to the trail's end in a steep-walled box canyon, where the creek slides over the rock wall.

**Driving directions:** From the Golden State Freeway (I-5) in Newhall, take the Antelope Valley Freeway (H-14) east. Continue 3 miles and exit on Placerita Canyon Road. Turn right and drive 3.1 miles to the signed Walker Ranch Trailhead parking area on the right. An Adventure Pass is required for parking.

**Hiking directions:** Pass through the vehicle gate and walk down the dirt road. Descend and cross the seasonal stream into the Walker Ranch Campground to the Placerita Canyon Trail (Hike 89). Veer right a few yards to the Placerita Waterfall Trail on the left. Pass a small rock wall and head up the oak-dotted canyon on the west side of the transient creek. The Los Pinetos Trail (Hike 91) can be seen perched on the west canyon wall. Climb steps and traverse the oak-covered hillside just above the canyon floor. The canyon narrows and follows the edge of the seasonal stream to a rock grotto and pool. Curve left and cross the stream for the first of seven crossings. At the fifth crossing, the canyon bends left. The trail ends in a box canyon with vertical rock walls. The vernal falls drops down the face of the cliff. ■

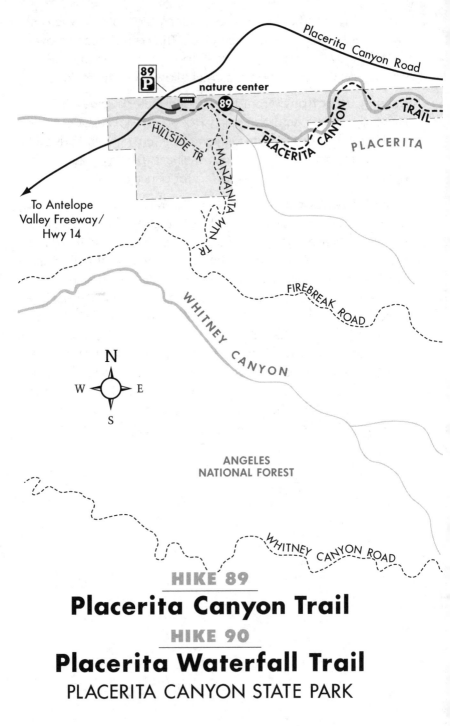

# HIKE 89
# Placerita Canyon Trail
## HIKE 90
# Placerita Waterfall Trail
## PLACERITA CANYON STATE PARK

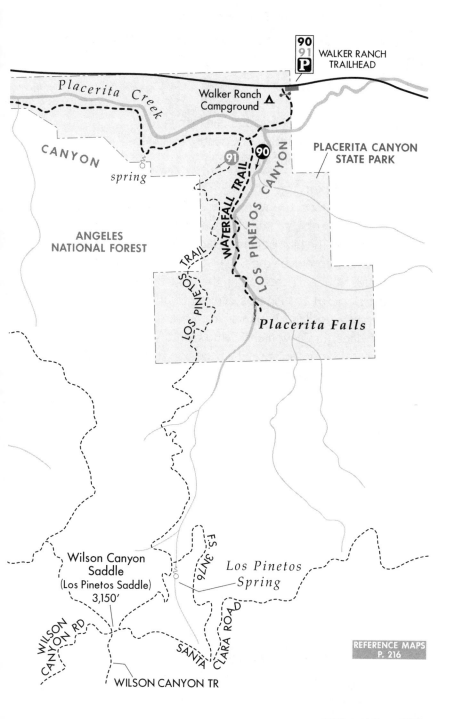

## 91. Los Pinetos Trail

### PLACERITA CANYON STATE PARK and NATURAL AREA

**Hiking distance:** 4.7 miles round trip
**Hiking time:** 3 hours
**Elevation gain:** 1,300 feet
**Maps:** U.S.G.S. Mint Canyon and San Fernando
Harrison: Angeles Front Country Trail Map
Placerita Canyon Natural Area Map

**Summary of hike:** Los Pinetos Trail is a moderately steep trail that climbs from the Walker Ranch Campground in Placerita Canyon to the crest of the San Gabriel Mountains at Wilson Canyon Saddle. The hike begins in Placerita Canyon State Park, on the northwest corner of the San Gabriel Mountains, and enters the Angeles National Forest along the way. The route weaves up the west slope of Los Pinetos Canyon through riparian, chaparral, and oak woodland habitats. From the summit are northern views of Placerita Canyon and Santa Clarita Valley and southern vistas across the urban sprawl of the San Fernando Valley and downtown Los Angeles.

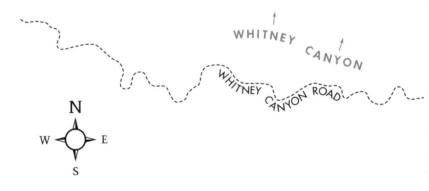

## 91.
# Los Pinetos Trail
## PLACERITA CANYON STATE PARK

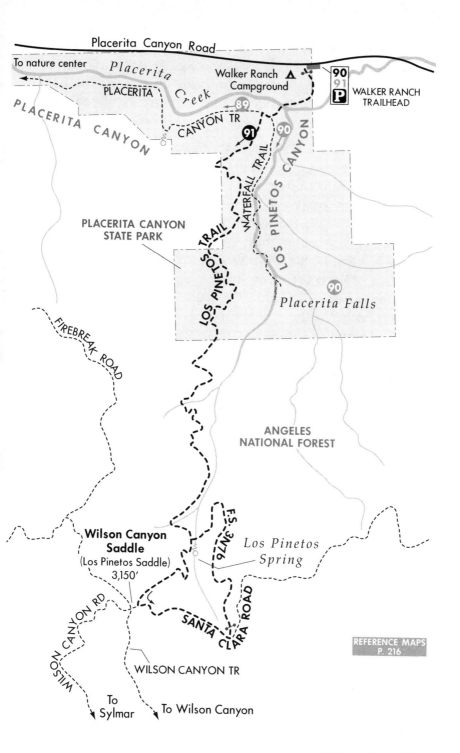

**Driving directions:** From the Golden State Freeway (I-5) in Newhall, take the Antelope Valley Freeway (H-14) east. Continue 3 miles and exit on Placerita Canyon Road. Turn right and drive 3.1 miles to the signed Walker Ranch. The trailhead parking area is on the right. An Adventure Pass is required for parking.

**Hiking directions:** Pass through the vehicle gate and walk down the dirt road. Descend and cross the seasonal stream into the Walker Ranch Campground to the Placerita Canyon Trail (Hike 89). Veer right, passing the Placerita Waterfall Trail on the left (Hike 90) to the posted Los Pinetos Trail, also on the left. Bear left through a grove of coast live oaks and head up the foothill. Begin climbing the west flank of Los Pinetos Canyon to an overlook of Placerita Canyon, the oak-dotted campground, and forested Los Pinetos Canyon. Continue climbing at a steady incline, curving in and out of the mountain contours from sunny, exposed chaparral to forested pockets with manzanita and oak. At 1.5 miles, leave the state park and enter the Angeles National Forest. Descend a short distance through the forest, then begin climbing again. Loop around and cross a drainage to a trail split by Los Pinetos Spring and a cement water tank, nestled in a shaded glen with spruce and oak.

Begin the small loop by veering right, staying on the Los Pinetos Trail. Head up the hill, reaching the crest of the San Gabriel Mountains on Wilson Canyon Saddle (also called Los Pinetos Saddle) at a three-way dirt road junction. The right fork follows Whitney Canyon Road to Whitney Canyon and a junction with the Firebreak Road. (This route can also be taken as an 8-mile loop, returning to the Placerita Canyon Nature Center via the Firebreak Trail and Manzanita Mountain Trail.) Straight ahead, across the road, the Wilson Canyon Road descends into Wilson Canyon and leads to the city of Sylmar. For this hike, go to the left on the Santa Clara Road and head east, parallel to the ridge on its north side. Continue 0.3 miles on the dirt road to a left bend at an overlook with far-reaching views across the San Fernando Valley. On the bend is gated Forest Service Road 3N76. Bear left on the side road and weave downhill, completing the loop at Los Pinetos Spring. Retrace your steps to the right. ■

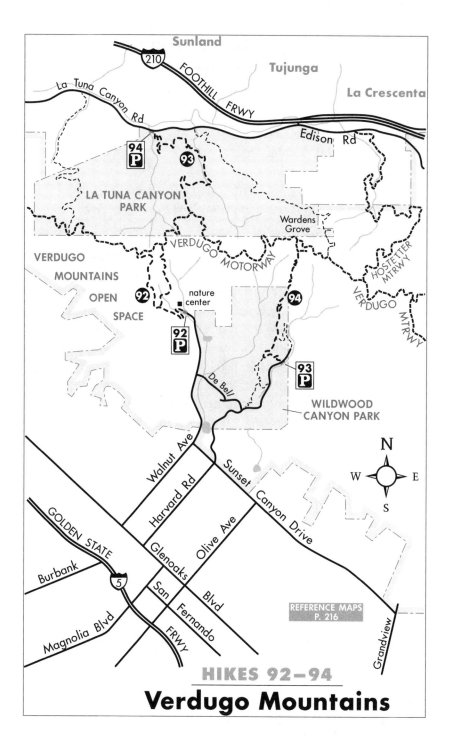

Sunland

210

Tujunga

La Crescenta

FOOTHILL FRWY

La Tuna Canyon Rd

Edison Rd

94 P

93

LA TUNA CANYON PARK

Wardens Grove

VERDUGO MOTORWAY

HOSTETTER MTRWY

VERDUGO

MOUNTAINS

OPEN

92

nature center

94

VERDUGO MTRWY

SPACE

92 P

93 P

De Bell

WILDWOOD CANYON PARK

N
W      E
S

Walnut Ave

Harvard Rd

Sunset Canyon Drive

GOLDEN STATE

Olive Ave

Glenoaks

Burbank

5

San Fernando

Blvd

FRWY

Magnolia Blvd

REFERENCE MAPS
P. 216

Grandview

**HIKES 92–94**
# Verdugo Mountains

# 92. Stough Canyon Loop
## VERDUGO MOUNTAINS
### 2300 Walnut Avenue · Burbank

**Hiking distance:** 2.3-mile loop
**Hiking time:** 1.5 hours
**Elevation gain:** 650 feet
**Maps:** U.S.G.S. Burbank
Harrison: Angeles Front Country Trail Map
Harrison: Verdugo Mountains Trail Map

**Summary of hike:** Stough Canyon sits on the southern slope of the Verdugo Mountains, an urban mountain range rising above the northern edge of Burbank and Glendale. Stough Canyon is named after Oliver J. Stough, who purchased the land in 1883 and deeded it to the city of Burbank in 1916 as a gift to be used as public parkland. This hike begins at the Stough Canyon Nature Center, a beautiful facility opened in 1991 with exhibits and interpretive displays that highlight the natural history, native plants, and Native Americans. This loop hike follows a sun-baked dirt road up the brushy slopes of the canyon to the Verdugo Motorway, a well-maintained fire road that follows the ridge of the mountain range. From the crest are dramatic vistas of the San Fernando Valley, Los Angeles, Griffith Park, the Santa Monica Mountains, and the San Gabriel Mountains.

**Driving directions:** From the Golden State Freeway (I-5) in Burbank, exit on Olive Avenue. Wind back to Olive Avenue, following the signs. Head 1.2 miles north on Olive Avenue to Sunset Canyon Drive. Turn left and drive 0.7 miles to Walnut Avenue. Turn right and continue 1.1 mile, passing the DeBell Golf Course, to the Stough Canyon Nature Center parking lot at the end of the road. An Adventure Pass is required for parking.

**Hiking directions:** Walk past the trailhead kiosk and gate, heading up the wide, sandy road. Wind up the west wall of Stough Canyon, with a view of the ridge towering over Wildwood Canyon (Hike 93). Steadily climb to a posted junction at 0.4 miles. Begin the loop to the left, leaving the Stough Canyon Motorway

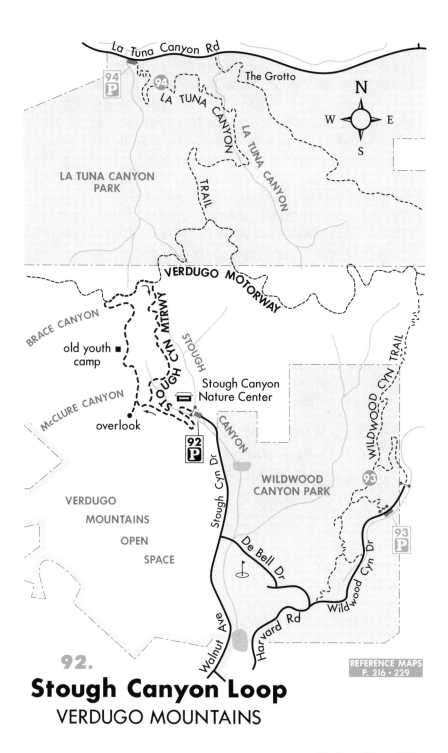

# 92.
# Stough Canyon Loop
## VERDUGO MOUNTAINS

and hiking the loop clockwise. Follow the wide trail to another junction. Detour ninety yards to the left to an overlook with a bench. The vistas extend across Glendale, the Los Angeles Basin, and the entire San Fernando Valley. Continue on the main trail among scrub oak, sage, toyon, and lemonade berry while overlooking McClure Canyon and Stough Canyon as the trail narrows to a footpath. On a flat is an old house foundation on the left with a 30-foot brick chimney, remnants of a youth camp from the 1920s. Cross the flat and start climbing again. Follow the trail signs toward Verdugo Motorway, the fire road atop the ridge. Top the slope to northern views of the San Gabriel Mountains above Tujunga. Veer left and gently descend to the Verdugo Motorway in a saddle at the head of Brace Canyon at 1.1 miles.

Take the road to the right, and head 0.3 miles downhill to the top of Stough Canyon and a junction. The ridge road continues a half mile to the La Tuna Canyon Trail (Hike 94) and 2 miles to the Wildwood Park Trail by the radio towers (Hike 93). Bear right on the Stough Canyon Motorway, and descend along the west canyon wall, completing the loop at 1.9 miles. Retrace your steps to the nature center. ■

# 93. Wildwood Canyon Trail to Wardens Grove

## VERDUGO MOUNTAINS: WILDWOOD CANYON PARK
1701 Wildwood Canyon Drive · Burbank

**Hiking distance:** 4 miles round trip
**Hiking time:** 2.5 hours
**Elevation gain:** 1,300 feet
**Maps:** U.S.G.S. Burbank
Harrison: Angeles Front Country Trail Map
Harrison: Verdugo Mountains Trail Map

**Summary of hike:** The Verdugo Mountains are a small, three-mile-wide mountain range running parallel to the western end of the San Gabriel Mountains, forming part of the eastern boundary of the San Fernando Valley. The Verdugo Range stretches for eight miles above the cities of Burbank and Glendale (on the southwest) and Sunland, Tujunga, and La Crescenta (on the northeast). Wildwood Canyon, located in Burbank on the south-facing slope, is a 500-acre park with an open grassland, picnic areas, and this two-mile trail.

Wildwood Canyon Trail is a steep, spine-climbing trail. The hike gains 1,300 feet from the lower foothills to the 2,900-foot ridge, located less than a mile west of 3,126-foot Verdugo Peak, the highest point in the range. Atop the ridgeline, the Verdugo Motorway, an unpaved, vehicle-restricted fire road, leads

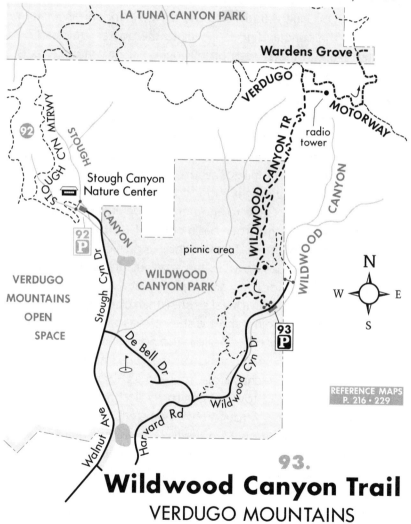

**93.**
# Wildwood Canyon Trail
## VERDUGO MOUNTAINS

to fenced radio towers and Wardens Grove, a pine forest on the mountain's crest. Throughout the shadeless, aerobic climb are spectacular vistas of Los Angeles, the San Fernando Valley, Griffith Park, the Santa Monica Mountains, and the San Gabriel Mountains.

**Driving directions:** From the Golden State Freeway (I-5) in Burbank, exit on Olive Avenue. Wind back to Olive Avenue, following the signs. Head 1.2 miles north on Olive Avenue to Sunset Canyon Drive. Turn left and drive 0.4 miles to Harvard Road. Turn right and continue 0.6 miles to the signed park entrance. Turn right into the park, and go 0.6 miles to the posted trailhead on the left. Park in the spaces on the right. An Adventure Pass is required for parking.

**Hiking directions:** Pass the trailhead gate (located by the restrooms) and bend left. Follow the unpaved fire road and curve around the water tanks to the footpath. Loop around the contour of the mountain on a steep uphill grade to the ridge and a T-junction at 0.2 miles. The left fork descends south to the lower trailheads. Bear right and follow the narrow ridge above Wildwood Canyon. Climb to another junction at 0.4 miles. Savor the great views of the urban basin below, Griffith Park, and the Santa Monica Mountains. To the right is a picnic area and overlook, which continues down to the terminus of the park road.

Veer left on the footpath and zigzag up at a very steep grade. Cross a narrow spine on a level stretch, then climb again to a trail split. Both routes rejoin a short distance ahead; the right fork is the longer but easier route. Follow the ridge and climb a series of short but steep switchbacks on the sun-drenched chaparral slope. The trail reaches a dirt road on a U-bend at 1.4 miles. To the right is a radio tower. Veer to the left and go downhill to a road split at the Verdugo Motorway, with north and west vistas. The left fork leads 1.5 miles to La Tuna Canyon (Hike 94) and 2 miles to Stough Canyon (Hike 92). The right fork meanders through Wardens Grove, a partially burned pine grove atop the ridge that was planted by the Los Angeles County Department of Forestry in the 1930s. Return along the same route. ∎

# 94. La Tuna Canyon Trail
## VERDUGO MOUNTAINS

8000 block of La Tuna Canyon Rd · Los Angeles (near Sunland)

**Hiking distance:** 4.4 miles round trip
**Hiking time:** 2.5 hours
**Elevation gain:** 1,100 feet
**Maps:** U.S.G.S. Burbank

**map
page 236**

       Harrison: Angeles Front Country Trail Map
       Harrison: Verdugo Mountains Trail Map

**Summary of hike:** The Verdugo Mountains, an offshoot range of the San Gabriel Mountains, were named for the Jose Verdugo family, owners of the land during the late 1700s. The two mountain ranges are separated by the Crescenta Valley, containing the communities of Sunland, Tujunga, and La Crescenta. A network of trails weave though the Verdugos, with a fire road bisecting the ridge. La Tuna Canyon Park, located on the north slope of the Verdugo Mountains, encompasses 1,100 acres. The undeveloped park provides access up the steep canyon to the Verdugo Motorway atop the crest of the range. The 2.2-mile-long trail climbs through the quiet, tree-lined canyon among mature coast live oaks, bay laurels, big leaf maples, and sycamores to the chaparral and scrub-covered slope at the summit. From the ridge are sweeping views of the San Gabriel Mountains, downtown Los Angeles, and the San Fernando Valley.

**Driving directions:** From the Foothill Freeway (Interstate 210) in Tujunga, exit on La Tuna Canyon Road. Drive 1.1 mile west to the signed trailhead on the left. Park in the signed pullout by the trailhead. An Adventure Pass is required for parking.

**Hiking directions:** From the east end of the parking pullout, take the signed trail into an unnamed canyon. Drop down along the east side of the drainage among oaks and sycamores. Zigzag up the canyon wall on five switchbacks, then traverse the mountain. Follow the contours on a steady uphill grade. At 0.8 miles, the trail levels out on the north-facing slope and crosses into La Tuna Canyon. Descend into the forested canyon and cross the seasonal drainage. Ascend the east canyon slope and return to the streambed. Follow the drainage under the shaded canopy and cross the stream. Climb the west canyon slope, winding to a ridge. Make a horseshoe left bend and follow the ridge south, reaching the Verdugo Motorway at 2.2 miles. To the left (east), the dirt fire road leads 1.5 miles to Wardens Grove and the Wildwood Canyon Trail (Hike 93). To the right (west), the road leads 0.5 miles to the head of Stough Canyon (Hike 92). Return by retracing your route. ■

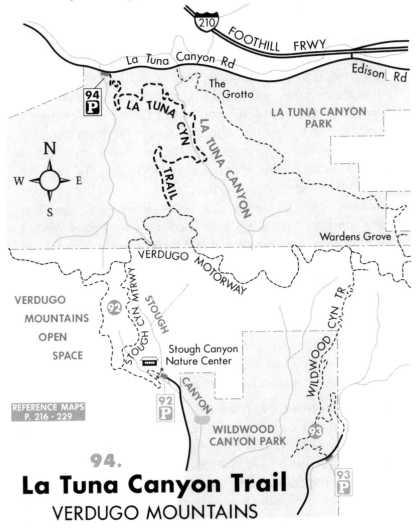

## 94.
# La Tuna Canyon Trail
## VERDUGO MOUNTAINS

# 95. Trail Canyon Falls

**Hiking distance:** 3 miles round trip
**Hiking time:** 1.5 hours
**Elevation gain:** 700 feet
**Maps:** U.S.G.S. Sunland
    Harrison: Angeles Front Country Trail Map

map
page 239

**Summary of hike:** Trail Canyon Creek forms on the southern slope of Iron Mountain in the San Gabriel Mountains. The creek drops five miles down the steep, rocky canyon before joining Big Tujunga Creek. On its downward journey, Trail Canyon Falls freefalls 40 feet off a granite precipice into a pool etched into the metamorphic rock. This hike begins in Big Tujunga Canyon and follows the creek up Trail Canyon to the crest of the falls. The trail starts on a closed fire road that passes through a cluster of private cabins that date back to the 1920s. The diverse hike leads through streamside vegetation with sycamores, alders, and cottonwoods, then traverses an exposed chaparral-covered canyon wall to the falls.

**Driving directions:** From the Foothill Freeway (Interstate 210) in Sunland, exit on Sunland Boulevard. Drive 0.7 miles east on Foothill Boulevard to Oro Vista Avenue and turn left. Continue 0.8 miles to Big Tujunga Canyon Road and curve right. Drive 4.4 miles to a dirt road on the left, directly across the road from a "Delta Flats" sign. (If you reach Ottie Road, you have gone 0.1 mile too far.) Turn left on Trail Canyon Road (Forest Service Road 3N34), and wind 0.4 miles on the narrow dirt road to the trailhead parking area at the end of the road. An Adventure Pass is required for parking. An Adventure Pass is required for parking.

**Hiking directions:** From the trailhead kiosk, take the gated fire road. Pass a group of privately owned cabins, and follow the winding road on the east wall of Trail Canyon. Pass a small waterfall on the left, and drop into the canopy of oaks, alders, and cottonwoods. Cross a tributary and climb over an exposed scrub-covered slope. Leave the road at a sharp left bend, and veer right on a footpath. Cross Trail Canyon Creek and stroll up the shaded canyon floor along the west side of the creek. Cross the boulder-filled creek four more times, then leave the canyon bottom. Climb up the open chaparral-clad hillside to great views up and down Trail Canyon. Traverse the canyon wall on an upward slope. As the path levels out, bend left to an overlook of Trail Canyon Falls, dropping off a rounded granite rock lip. Continue on a sweeping curve, and pass a couple of steep paths with loose gravel on the right that descend to the base of the falls and pool. A short distance ahead, another side path on the right leads to an overlook from the brink of the falls. Return by retracing your steps.

To extend the hike, the trail follows the creek two miles to Tom Lucas Camp on a grassy flat with lush vegetation along the banks of Trail Canyon Creek. Beyond the camp, the trail continues up the east flank of Iron Mountain. ▪

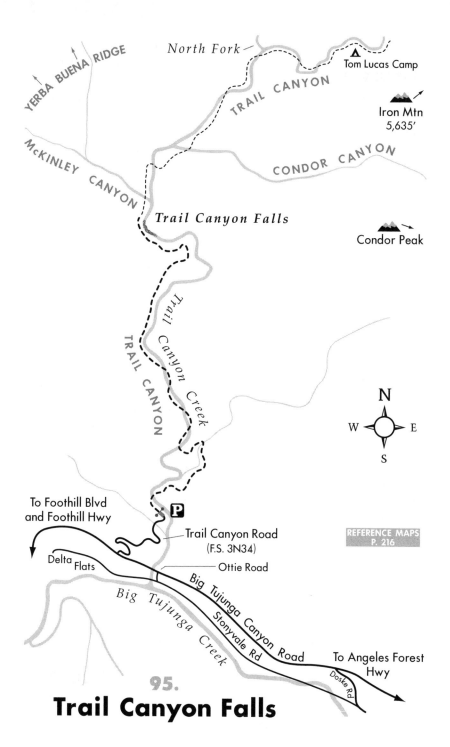

YERBA BUENA RIDGE

*North Fork*

TRAIL CANYON

▲ Tom Lucas Camp

🌲 Iron Mtn
5,635'

McKINLEY CANYON

CONDOR CANYON

*Trail Canyon Falls*

🌲 Condor Peak

Trail Canyon Creek

TRAIL CANYON

N
W    E
S

To Foothill Blvd
and Foothill Hwy

🅿 ✗

Trail Canyon Road
(F.S. 3N34)

REFERENCE MAPS
P. 216

Delta Flats

Ottie Road

Big Tujunga Canyon Road

Big Tujunga Creek

Stonyvale Rd

To Angeles Forest
Hwy

Doske Rd

95.
# Trail Canyon Falls

# 96. Haines Canyon

**map page 242**

**Hiking distance:** 3 miles round trip
**Hiking time:** 1.5 hours
**Elevation gain:** 1,000 feet
**Maps:** U.S.G.S. Sunland
Harrison: Angeles Front Country Trail Map

**Summary of hike:** Haines Creek forms on the west slope of Mount Lukens on the western end of the San Gabriel Mountains. The creek flows through the canyon, emptying into the Haines Canyon Reservoir on the northeast corner of Tujunga. The basin is a catch-all for rocks and brush washed down the drainage. The Haines Canyon Trail begins at the dam and catch basin, following the waterway up canyon. The trail is an often-used route to the summit of Mount Lukens, the highest peak in Los Angeles. Instead of climbing up the 5,074-foot mountain, this hike follows the canyon bottom through a jungle of riparian habitat to a lush spring with ferns.

**Driving directions:** Heading westbound on the Foothill Freeway (Interstate 210) in La Crescenta, exit on Lowell Avenue. Drive 0.3 miles straight ahead on Honolulu Avenue to Tujunga Canyon Boulevard. Veer right on Tujunga Canyon Boulevard, and go 1.3 miles to Haines Canyon Avenue. Turn right and continue 0.2 miles to Day Street. Turn right and go one block, returning to Haines Canyon Avenue. Turn left and drive 0.6 miles to the end of the road at the trailhead gate. An Adventure Pass is required for parking.

Heading eastbound on the Foothill Freeway (Interstate 210) in La Crescenta, exit on La Tuna Canyon Road. Turn left under the freeway and drive 1.3 miles to Tujunga Canyon Boulevard. Turn left and continue with the directions above.

**Hiking directions:** Head up the dirt fire road and pass the vehicle gate, following the left side of the Blanchard debris dam and the Haines Canyon Reservoir. Stay on the main road, passing a dirt road coming in from the left and another from the right.

Steadily climb along the west edge of Haines Canyon under oaks and sycamores. The road levels out at one mile, and the canyon bends left at a trail split. Haines Canyon Road (also known as Mount Lukens Road) veers to the right, passing another vehicle gate. The fire road climbs the south-facing slope to the summit of 5,074-foot Mount Lukens. For this hike, take the left fork, staying in Haines Canyon. The forested canyon quickly narrows, and the dirt road becomes a footpath. Pass a cement water tank on the right, and cross Haines Creek under a lush canopy. Continue up canyon, curving right along the drainage to a signed fork at a fern-filled spring. The left fork follows the Sister Elsie Trail to the Stone Canyon Trail. The right fork continues one mile to the Haines Canyon Road. Choose your own turn around spot. ■

## 97. Rim of the Valley Trail
### DEUKMEJIAN WILDERNESS PARK
3429 Markridge Road · La Crescenta

**Hiking distance:** 3.5 miles round trip
**Hiking time:** 2 hours
**Elevation gain:** 1,200 feet
**Maps:** U.S.G.S. Sunland and Condor Peak
      Harrison: Angeles Front Country Trail Map
      Deukmejian Wilderness Park Trail Map

*map page 243*

**Summary of hike:** Deukmejian Wilderness Park is a rugged 702-acre park on the north edge of Glendale in the foothills of the San Gabriel Mountains. The park is named for George Deukmejian, the former governor of California. The wilderness park is home to Cooks Canyon and Dunsmore Canyon, two stream-fed drainages with riparian woodland habitats and steep chaparral-covered slopes. The Rim of the Valley Trail passes through lush Cooks Canyon, teaming with native plants. The path crosses bridges over gorges to the arid upper slopes and Haines Canyon Road, a narrow dirt fire road that weaves up to 5,074-foot Mount Lukens, the highest peak in Los Angeles. From the upper foothills are great vistas across the San Fernando Valley.

# 96.
# Haines Canyon
## 97.
# Rim of the Valley Trail
## DEUKMEJIAN WILDERNESS PARK

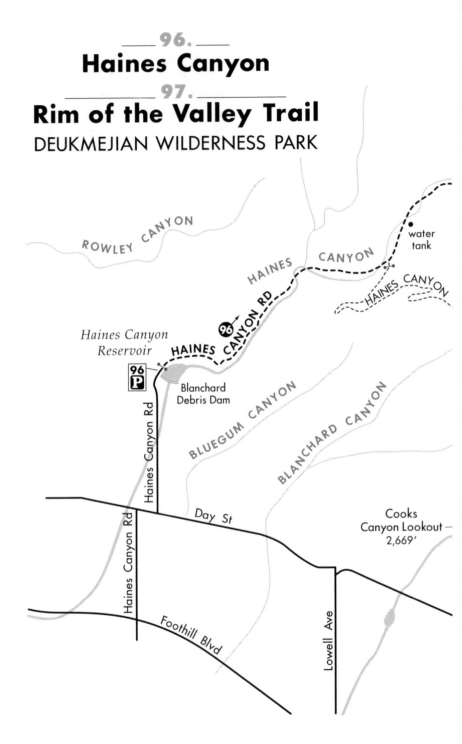

ROWLEY CANYON

HAINES CANYON

water tank

HAINES CANYON

Haines Canyon Reservoir

HAINES CANYON RD

96

96
P

Haines Canyon Rd

Blanchard Debris Dam

BLUEGUM CANYON

BLANCHARD CANYON

Day St

Cooks Canyon Lookout – 2,669'

Haines Canyon Rd

Foothill Blvd

Lowell Ave

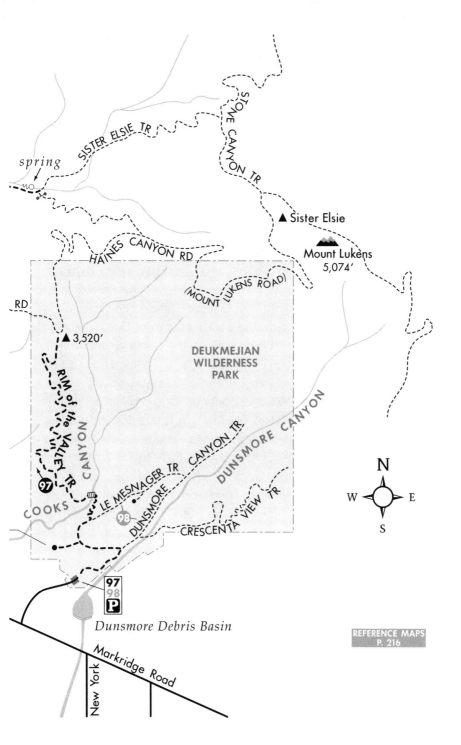

spring

SISTER ELSIE TR

STONE CANYON TR

▲ Sister Elsie

Mount Lukens
5,074'

HAINES CANYON RD

(MOUNT LUKENS ROAD)

RD

▲ 3,520'

DEUKMEJIAN
WILDERNESS
PARK

RIM of the VALLEY TR

DUNSMORE CANYON

COOKS CANYON

LE MESNAGER TR

DUNSMORE CANYON TR

CRESCENTA VIEW TR

**97**

**98**

N
W    E
S

**97**
**98**
**P**

Dunsmore Debris Basin

REFERENCE MAPS
P. 216

Markridge Road

New York

**Driving directions:** From the Foothill Freeway (Interstate 210) in La Crescenta, exit on Pennsylvania Avenue. Drive 0.4 miles north to Foothill Boulevard. Turn left and go 0.3 miles to New York Avenue. Turn right and continue 0.9 miles to Markridge Road. Turn left and drive 0.1 mile to the park entrance on the right. Turn right, enter the park, and go 0.2 miles uphill to the trailhead parking lots on both sides of the road. An Adventure Pass is required for parking.

**Hiking directions:** From the far north end of the parking lot, take the graveled path through the landscaped grounds to the map kiosk. Head up the canyon on the Dunsmore Canyon Trail, staying on the west side of the drainage to a posted junction. Leave the Dunsmore Canyon Trail, and bear left on the Rim of the Valley Trail. Ascend the west canyon wall to a signed Y-fork with the Cooks Canyon Lookout Trail. Detour to the left, and follow a narrow ridge 265 yards on the southeast rim of Cooks Canyon. The side path ends at an overlook of the Verdugo Mountains, the San Gabriel Mountains, the San Gabriel Valley, and the San Fernando Valley.

Return to the main trail, and continue 130 yards to a junction with the Le Mesnager Loop Trail. Bear left, staying on the Rim of the Valley Trail. Descend into Cooks Canyon to the forested canyon floor. Follow the narrow, stream-fed canyon bottom and cross the stream. Climb wooden steps to a bridge, and cross over the steep-walled ravine. Traverse the west wall of Cooks Canyon, zigzagging up the hillside. Steadily gain elevation to magnificent views. The pines of Wardens Grove can be spotted atop Verdugo Ridge (Hike 93). Near the top, cross a ridge to views across the entire San Fernando Valley, from the Santa Susana Mountains to the Santa Monica Mountains. Follow the ridge between Blanchard Canyon and Cooks Canyon. Zipper up two more switchbacks, arriving at Haines Canyon Road, a narrow dirt road at the upper end of the trail at 3,520 feet. ■

# 98. Dunsmore Canyon
# —Le Mesnager Loop

## DEUKMEJIAN WILDERNESS PARK

3429 Markridge Road · La Crescenta

**Hiking distance:** 2 miles round trip
**Hiking time:** 1 hour
**Elevation gain:** 700 feet

**map
page 247**

**Maps:** U.S.G.S. Sunland and Condor Peak
Harrison: Angeles Front Country Trail Map
Deukmejian Wilderness Park Trail Map

**Summary of hike:** Dunsmore Canyon is the main drainage in Deukmejian Wilderness Park. The canyon is tucked into the mountains above the Crescenta Valley and is bordered by the Angeles National Forest. The elevations range from 2,159 feet at the park's southern end to 4,775 feet in the northeast corner. Aside from the lower 12 acres, the rustic terrain is relatively undisturbed.

This hike makes a loop up Dunsmore Canyon and returns on Le Mesnager Trail, stopping at a couple of overlooks. It is a popular hiking, biking, and equestrian route. The Dunsmore Canyon Trail parallels the creek for nearly one mile on an easy uphill grade. The trail passes a series of low dams used to control the flow of water and contain sediments. The Le Mesnager Trail winds along the east-facing hillside through native chaparral, connecting with short spur trails to Le Mesnager Lookout and Cooks Canyon Lookout. The lookouts sit atop knolls that overlook the Verdugo Mountains, Glendale, the San Fernando Valley, the Los Angeles basin, and the San Gabriel Valley.

The Le Mesnager Trail is named for George Le Mesnager, an immigrant and World War 1 vet who originally purchased the land in 1898 and began a wine growing operation. The old two-story granite stone building at the trailhead was built in 1914 and used for the storage of Le Mesnager's equipment and grapes. Later it was converted into the ranch house. The ranch was purchased by the city of Glendale in 1988.

**Driving directions:** From the Foothill Freeway (Interstate 210) in La Crescenta, exit on Pennsylvania Avenue. Drive 0.4 miles north to Foothill Boulevard. Turn left and go 0.3 miles to New York Avenue. Turn right and continue 0.9 miles to Markridge Road. Turn left and drive 0.1 mile to the park entrance on the right. Turn right, enter the park, and go 0.2 miles uphill to the trailhead parking lots on both sides of the road. An Adventure Pass is required for parking.

**Hiking directions:** From the far north end of the parking lot, take the graveled path through the landscaped grounds to the map kiosk. Head up the canyon 300 yards on the Dunsmore Canyon Trail (a fire road), staying on the west side of the drainage to a posted junction. The Rim of the Valley Trail goes to the left. Stay to the right on the Dunsmore Canyon Trail another 70 yards to a second signed junction. The Crescenta View Trail veers off to the right. Stay left, following the west side of the drainage to Le Mesnager Loop Trail on the left—our return route. Continue climbing straight ahead as the canyon narrows. The trail ends by the seasonal stream under the shade of oaks and alders by a concrete weir.

Descend back to Le Mesnager Loop Trail, losing 325 feet in elevation. Bear right and head up the slope on the west wall of the canyon. Climb the chaparral-cloaked hillside, topping a rise to great views of the Verdugo Mountains and the pocket communities of La Crescenta and Tujunga. Detour left on Le Mesnager Lookout Trail for 40 yards to a knoll with a bench and expansive vistas of Dunsmore Canyon, the urban basins, and the surrounding mountain ranges. Return to the main trail and head downhill. Pass the Rim of the Valley Trail heading off to the right (Hike 97), and continue to Cooks Canyon Lookout Trail, also on the right. Detour to the right and follow a narrow ridge 265 yards on the southeast rim of Cooks Canyon to an overlook. From this spot are additional vast views of the cities and mountains. The main trail drops back down into Dunsmore Canyon, completing the loop. Return to the trailhead on the right. ■

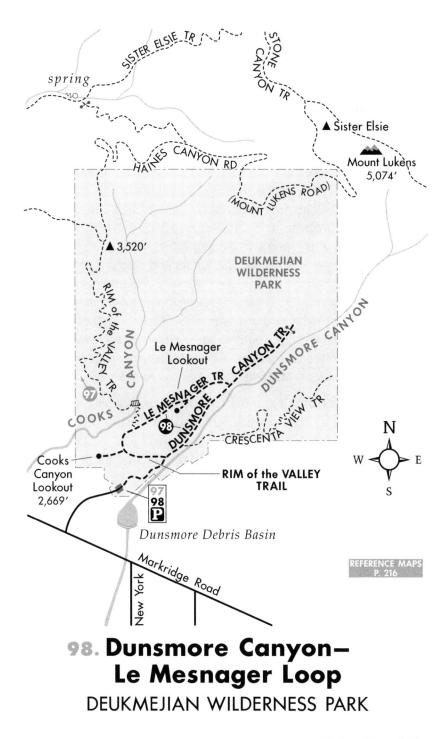

# 98. Dunsmore Canyon–
# Le Mesnager Loop
## DEUKMEJIAN WILDERNESS PARK

# 99. Cerro Negro (Black Hill)
## SAN RAFAEL HILLS

**Hiking distance:** 1.5 miles round trip
**Hiking time:** 45 minutes
**Elevation gain:** 200 feet
**Maps:** U.S.G.S. Pasadena

**Summary of hike:** The San Rafael Hills are a small mountain rise on the eastern flank of the Verdugo Mountains at the east end of Glendale. The hills are bordered by the Verdugo Canyon, the Arroyo Seco Drainage, and La Crescenta Valley. A network of fire road trails weave through the San Rafael Hills.

This hike begins off Camino San Rafael and climbs through native chaparral habitat to an out-of-service fire lookout tower atop Cerro Negro. Cerro Negro, Spanish for *black hills*, is the second highest peak in the hills at 1,887 feet, two feet shorter than Flint Peak to its south. From the summit are sweeping 360-degree vistas of the San Gabriel Mountains, the Verdugo Mountains, La Crescenta Valley, and the Los Angeles Basin.

**Driving directions:** From the Glendale Freeway (Highway 2) in Glendale, exit on Mountain Street. Drive east on Mountain Street, which becomes Camino San Rafael en route. At 1.9 miles, the road tops a ridge by two gated fire roads on the left. The northern (right) road is the trail. Park along the side of the road. An Adventure Pass is required for parking.

**Hiking directions:** Walk past the vehicle gate, and head up the paved road 100 yards to the end of the pavement. Continue up the dirt road to westward views of Glendale, La Crescenta, Tujunga, the San Gabriel Mountains, and the east face of the Verdugo Mountains. Top the slope to a Y-fork. Stay left and gently descend to a view of the fire lookout tower. Drop down to the edge of the subdivision, passing another trail access at the north end of Camino San Rafael. Skirt the west flank of the homes along the back side of Flintridge Drive. Ascend the hill to a junction and veer right, staying on the Ridge Motorway. Pass the lookout tower above to an overlook and bench, with vistas east along the San Gabriel Range and across Pasadena. The road continues to the right up to the fenced lookout tower, with views of Hollywood and the Los Angeles Basin. ■

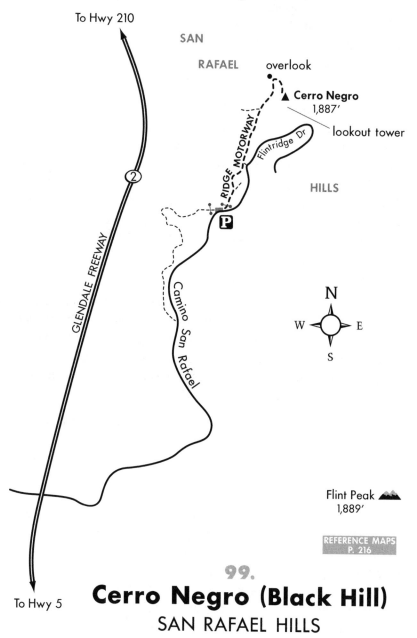

To Hwy 210

SAN

RAFAEL          overlook

▲ **Cerro Negro**
1,887'

lookout tower

RIDGE MOTORWAY

Flintridge Dr

HILLS

(2)

GLENDALE FREEWAY

P

Camino San Rafael

**N**

W ✦ E

**S**

Flint Peak
1,889'

REFERENCE MAPS
P. 216

To Hwy 5

## 99.
# Cerro Negro (Black Hill)
## SAN RAFAEL HILLS

# 100. Fall Creek Falls

**Hiking distance:** 4 miles round trip
**Hiking time:** 2 hours
**Elevation gain:** 600 feet
**Maps:** U.S.G.S. Condor Peak
Harrison: Angeles Front Country Trail Map
Harrison: Mt. Wilson Trail Map

**Summary of hike:** Fall Creek Falls is a four-tiered waterfall that tumbles down the cliff walls for more than 250 feet. The waterfall is located on Fall Creek in Big Tujunga Canyon, just above its confluence with Big Tujunga Creek. All four drops have a pool at their base. The Fall Creek Trail descends on a dirt fire road into Big Tujunga Canyon, a mile upstream from Big Tujunga Reservoir. The road/trail drops 700 feet down the south canyon wall to the creek. En route is a spectacular view of Big Tujunga Canyon and an overlook of the waterfall, seen across the scenic canyon. To see Fall Creek Falls in its glory, it is best to go after a rain.

**Driving directions:** From the Foothill Freeway (Interstate 210) in La Canada, exit on the Angeles Crest Highway (Highway 2). Drive 9.4 miles north to the signed Angeles Forest Highway. Turn left and continue 3.8 miles to Big Tujunga Canyon Road. Turn left and go 0.6 miles to a wide parking pullout on the right. An Adventure Pass is not necessary.

**Hiking directions:** Pass the vehicle gate and head down the old dirt road (Forest Service Road 3N27). Curve right to the spectacular view of Big Tujunga Canyon from a perch 600 feet above. Steadily descend on the serpentine road at an easy grade. Follow the contours of the mountain beneath the eroding rock wall. At 1.7 miles, the road lies directly across the canyon from Fall Creek and Fall Creek Falls. This is the best vantage point to view portions of the four-tier cataract. Parts of the waterfall are obscured by a dense pocket of alder trees.

Continue down the road to the canyon floor and Big Tujunga Creek. At the creek is very primitive Fall Creek Camp, precariously tucked within the boulders and brush. To reach the base of the lower 80-foot falls, rock-hop and bushwack a quarter mile downstream, carving out your own route. To view the upper falls, climb less than a half mile up Fall Creek Road (on the north wall of the canyon) to views of all four tiers. Return by retracing your steps. ■

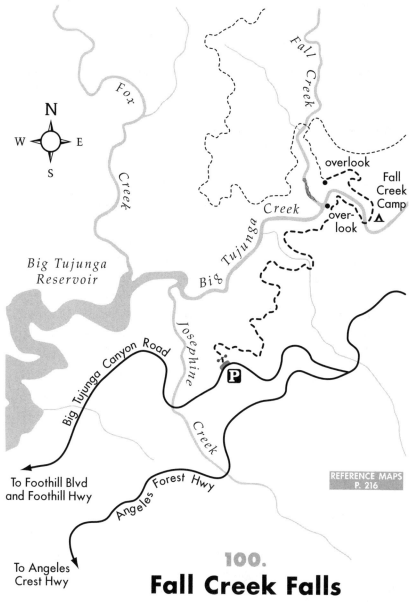

# 101. Vetter Mountain Fire Lookout

**Hiking distance:** 1.8-mile loop
**Hiking time:** 1 hour
**Elevation gain:** 400 feet
**Maps:** U.S.G.S. Chilao Flat
Harrison: Angeles Front Country Trail Map
Harrison: Mt. Wilson Trail Map

**Summary of hike:** Vetter Mountain, formerly called Pine Mountain, rises 5,908 feet in the front range of the San Gabriel Mountains. The mountain sits between the hot and dry Chaparral Zone to the south and the Montaine Forest Zone to the north, home to big cone spruce, Jeffrey pine, sugar pine, white fir, incense cedar, and canyon oak. Perched atop the summit is an active fire lookout built by the U.S. Forest Service in 1937. The historic Vetter Lookout offers spectacular 360-degree panoramas that include San Gabriel Peak, Mount Wilson, Fox Mountain, Condor Peak, Mount Gleason, Mount Waterman, and Mount Baldy. On the east flank of the summit is Charlton Flat, a forested picnic area. The Vetter Mountain Trail, a 1.5-mile-long trail, leads from the picnic area to the fire lookout. This hike includes just the upper section of the trail through a shallow draw, utilizing a gated dirt road to form a loop. The trail winds through chaparral and a stately conifer forest, exploring both ecological zones.

**Driving directions:** From the Foothill Freeway (Interstate 210) in La Canada, exit on the Angeles Crest Highway (Highway 2). Drive 23.2 miles north to the Charlton Flat Picnic Area turnoff (Forest Service Road 3N16) on the left. Turn left and continue 1.3 miles, staying left at the junctions, to a Y-fork and gated dirt road. Park on the side of the road. An Adventure Pass is required for parking.

**Hiking directions:** At the Y-fork, Forest Service Road 3N16 divides into 3N16A on the right—our return route—and 3N16B on the left. Begin the loop on the left fork, passing the vehicle gate. Follow the dirt road parallel to the north side of the ridge. The gentle uphill slope gains 300 feet in 0.7 miles to the Vetter

Mountain Lookout. Just before reaching the lookout, pass the posted Vetter Mountain Trail on the right, our return route. Veer left, then right, forming an S pattern to the active lookout with its sweeping 360-degree vistas. Inside the tower are photos identifying the surrounding peaks and valleys. After savoring the views, return to the Vetter Mountain Trail. Leave the road and zigzag down eleven switchbacks on the footpath. Stroll down a seasonal drainage through chaparral and under oaks to F.S. Road 3N16A. The trail continues across the road and leads 0.7 miles to the lower Charlton Flat Picnic Area. For this hike, bear right on the dirt road. Head up the serpentine road among oaks and pines, completing the loop at the Y-fork. ■

Vetter Mtn
5,908'

fire
lookout

VETTER MOUNTAIN TR

F.S. 3N16B

F.S. 3N16A

SILVER
MOCCASIN
TRAIL

P

SILVER MOCCASIN TR

CHARLTON

FLAT

2

Angeles Crest Hwy

W
S — N
E

REFERENCE MAPS
P. 216

F.S. 3N16

**101.**

# Vetter Mountain
# Fire Lookout

To La Canada and Foothill Freeway

# 102. Cooper Canyon Falls via Burkhart Trail

**Hiking distance:** 3.6 miles round trip
**Hiking time:** 2 hours
**Elevation gain:** 750 feet
**Maps:** U.S.G.S. Waterman Mountain
Harrison: Angeles High Country Trail Map

**Summary of hike:** Cooper Canyon Falls drops 30 feet off a moss-covered rock wall into a lush grotto with a pool. The cataract is set within the San Gabriel Wilderness in a deep canyon northeast of Waterman Mountain. The pristine, 6,000-foot-high landscape is rich with a fragrant forest of towering incense cedar, Jeffrey and sugar pine, fir, oak, alder, and perennial cascading waters. The Burkhart Trail descends through Buckhorn Canyon to Cooper Canyon and follows Cooper Creek to the waterfall, where the trail joins with the Pacific Crest Trail.

**Driving directions:** From the Foothill Freeway (Interstate 210) in La Canada, exit on the Angeles Crest Highway (Highway 2). Drive 34 miles north to the signed Buckhorn Campground on the left. Turn left and wind one mile down the narrow paved road to the day use trailhead parking area. An Adventure Pass is required for parking.

**Hiking directions:** From the far end of the parking area, head northeast on the signed trail. Follow the sandy footpath on the west side of the forested canyon high above Buckhorn Creek. Steadily descend among the towering cedars, pines, firs, and pockets of ferns. Pass overlooks of the stream-fed Buckhorn Canyon with views of beautiful outcrops. When the outcrops on the east canyon wall come into view, three spur trails on the right descend to the stream by small falls and pools. The Burkhart Trail veers left into Cooper Canyon, then switchbacks to the right. Traverse the south canyon wall, and parallel Cooper Creek to the base of Buckhorn Canyon by majestic cedar trees with multiple trunks grown together. Rock hop over Buckhorn Creek above its confluence with Cooper Canyon Creek. Continue downstream to the east, passing more cedars. At 1.7 miles is a T-junction with the Pacific Crest Trail. The left fork leads 1.1 mile to Cooper Canyon Camp. Go to the right and walk 100 yards to the top of Cooper Canyon Falls on the left. Continue 30 yards to an unsigned fork. (If you reach the crossing of Little Rock Creek, you have gone 0.2 miles past the fork.) The short, steep spur trail on the left descends to the base of the falls in a vertical rock bowl. If descending to the base, use caution, as this path has loose rock and is steep. ■

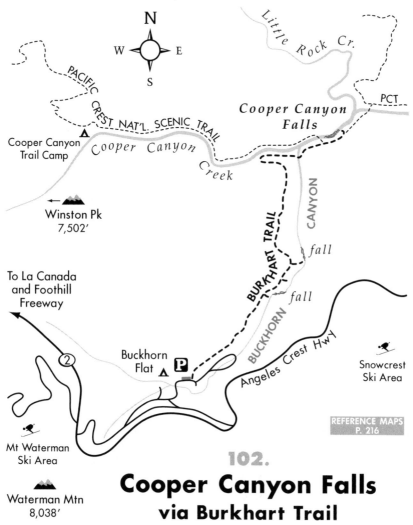

**102.**
# Cooper Canyon Falls
## via Burkhart Trail

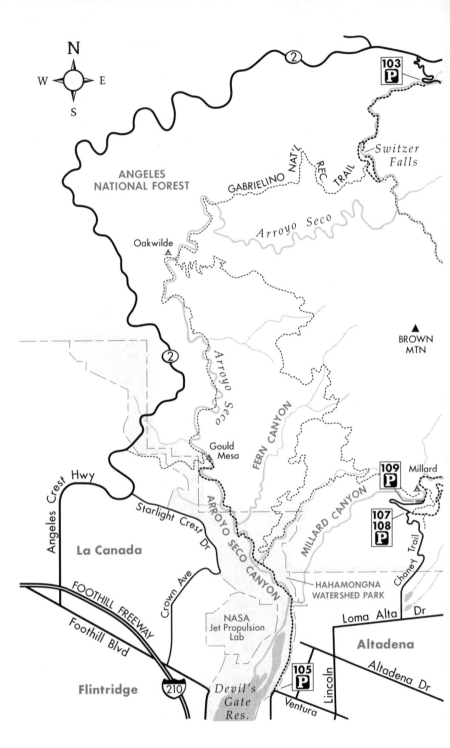

N
W E
S

2

103
P

ANGELES
NATIONAL FOREST

GABRIELINO NAT'L REC. TRAIL

*Switzer Falls*

*Arroyo Seco*

Oakwilde

BROWN
MTN

2

*Arroyo Seco*

FERN CANYON

Gould
Mesa

109
P  Millard

107
108
P

Chaney Trail

Angeles Crest Hwy

Starlight Crest Dr

ARROYO SECO CANYON

MILLARD CANYON

La Canada

HAHAMONGNA
WATERSHED PARK

FOOTHILL FREEWAY

Crown Ave

Loma Alta Dr

Altadena

NASA
Jet Propulsion
Lab

Foothill Blvd

210

Flintridge

*Devil's
Gate
Res.*

105
P

Ventura

Lincoln

Altadena Dr

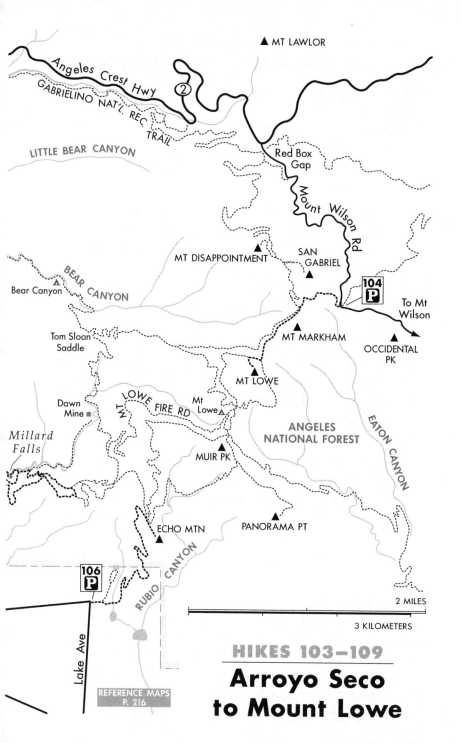

MT LAWLOR

Angeles Crest Hwy ②

GABRIELINO NAT'L. REC. TRAIL

LITTLE BEAR CANYON

Red Box Gap

Mount Wilson Rd

MT DISAPPOINTMENT

SAN GABRIEL

BEAR CANYON

Bear Canyon

**104** P

To Mt Wilson

Tom Sloan Saddle

MT MARKHAM

OCCIDENTAL PK

MT LOWE

Dawn Mine

MT LOWE FIRE RD

Mt Lowe

ANGELES NATIONAL FOREST

EATON CANYON

*Millard Falls*

MUIR PK

PANORAMA PT

ECHO MTN

RUBIO CANYON

**106** P

Lake Ave

2 MILES

3 KILOMETERS

REFERENCE MAPS P. 216

## HIKES 103–109

# Arroyo Seco to Mount Lowe

# 103. Switzer Falls
## GABRIELINO NATIONAL RECREATION TRAIL

**Hiking distance:** 4.6 miles round trip
**Hiking time:** 2.5 hours
**Elevation gain:** 600 feet
**Maps:** U.S.G.S. Condor Peak
Harrison: Angeles Front Country Trail Map
Harrison: Mt. Wilson Trail Map

**Summary of hike:** Switzer Falls is a gorgeous 50-foot, two-tiered waterfall deep in Arroyo Seco Canyon. The upper fall drops through a narrow gorge into a pool naturally carved into the rock. The 15-foot lower fall is tucked into a steep-walled rock grotto with a small pool. The trailhead is located off of the Angeles Crest Highway (Highway 2) at the mouth of the canyon by Switzer Picnic Area. The hike to Switzer Falls follows Arroyo Seco Creek through intimate creekside habitat with granite boulders, numerous pools, and the shade of alder, oak, maple, spruce and willow trees. The trail leads to primitive Commodore Switzer Camp, traverses sheer rock walls, passes overlooks of the upper falls, and doubles back along the creek to the base of the lower falls.

**Driving directions:** From the Foothill Freeway (Interstate 210) in La Canada, exit on the Angeles Crest Highway (Highway 2). Drive 9.9 miles north to the signed Switzer Picnic Area turnoff on the right. (The turnoff is located 0.5 miles past the Angeles Forest Highway.) Turn right and wind a half mile down the paved road to the parking lot at the end of the road. An Adventure Pass is required for parking.

**Hiking directions:** Walk across the oak-covered picnic area, and cross the footbridge over Arroyo Seco Creek. Follow the paved path downhill, parallel to the south side of the creek through the cool wooded glades. Pass pools along the rock-filled creek as the paved path turns to a dirt path. Cross the creek, passing more pools carved into the bedrock. Stay on the canyon floor, crossing the creek five more times. After the sixth

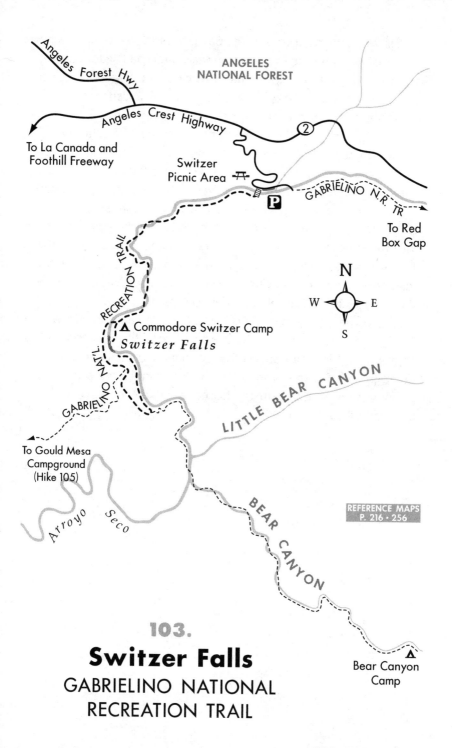

ANGELES
NATIONAL FOREST

Angeles Forest Hwy

Angeles Crest Highway

2

To La Canada and
Foothill Freeway

Switzer
Picnic Area

P

GABRIELINO N.R. TR

To Red
Box Gap

N
W   E
S

RECREATION TRAIL

▲ Commodore Switzer Camp
*Switzer Falls*

GABRIELINO NAT'L

LITTLE BEAR CANYON

To Gould Mesa
Campground
(Hike 105)

Arroyo Seco

BEAR CANYON

REFERENCE MAPS
P. 216 · 256

103.
# Switzer Falls
GABRIELINO NATIONAL
RECREATION TRAIL

Bear Canyon
Camp

crossing is Commodore Switzer Camp, a primitive camp on the banks of Arroyo Seco Creek. An undesignated path leads straight ahead through the camp to the brink of upper Switzer Falls on the edge of steep, rocky walls. This overlook is dangerous with unstable, slippery rock. It has been the scene of numerous falling deaths and is an ill-advised route. If you go, use caution!

Bear right at the signed Gabrielino National Recreation Trail sign, and cross Arroyo Seco Creek. Head up the exposed west canyon wall, leaving the riparian vegetation behind. Pass overlooks of the narrow, rock-walled chasm with bird's-eye views of the 50-foot upper tier of Switzer Falls and the pool etched into the rock. At 1.4 miles is a Y-fork with the Bear Canyon Trail. The Gabrielino National Recreation Trail continues to the right, leading 3.7 miles to Oakwilde Camp and 6.5 miles to Gould Mesa Camp (Hike 105). Take the Bear Canyon Trail to the left, perched on the vertical canyon wall. Descend 0.7 miles and reunite with Arroyo Seco Creek under the shade of oaks to a posted fork. To the right, the Bear Canyon Trail continues to the Bear Canyon Campground. For this hike, go to the left and follow the rocky creek 0.2 miles upstream to the gorge at the base of lower Switzer Falls. ■

# 104. Mount Lowe Summit from Eaton Saddle

**Hiking distance:** 3 miles round trip
**Hiking time:** 1.5 hours
**Elevation gain:** 500 feet
**Maps:** U.S.G.S. Mount Wilson
Harrison: Angeles Front Country Trail Map
Harrison: Mt. Wilson Trail Map

**map
page 263**

**Summary of hike:** Mount Lowe is located 1.5 miles west of Mount Wilson. The mountain was named for Thaddeus Lowe by his friends on their first horseback ride to the summit on September 24, 1892. Known as Oak Mountain until that time, he built the Mount Lowe Railway from Echo Mountain to the foot of Mount Lowe, a thousand feet shy of the summit. The trolley offered access to the Mount Lowe Alpine Tavern, a Swiss-style hotel. The historic site, located south of the peak at the current location of the Mount Lowe Trail Camp, operated from 1893 through 1935. The railway enabled guests to ride from Altadena to Mount Lowe via a tram up Rubio Canyon to the Echo Mountain Resort (Hike 106). The trolley took guests a few miles farther, from Echo Mountain to the Mount Lowe Tavern. The tavern burned down in 1936. Several foundations and rock wall ruins remain, along with interpretive panels describing the tavern and its history.

The scenic 5,603-foot summit of Mount Lowe also has interpretive panels and viewing scopes of Mount Disappointment, Mount Markham, Mount Baldy, San Gabriel Peak, Mount Wilson, and Mount Harvard. This hike begins off of Mount Wilson Road on Eaton Saddle, tucked between San Gabriel Peak and Occidental Peak. The trail passes through a tunnel built in 1942 to Markham Saddle between Mount Markham and Mount Disappointment. Atop Mount Lowe are comprehensive views of the urban basins below and sighting tubes which identify the surrounding peaks.

**Driving directions:** From the Foothill Freeway (Interstate 210) in La Canada, exit on the Angeles Crest Highway (Highway 2). Drive 14 miles north to the signed Mount Wilson Road turnoff on the right. Turn right and continue 2.3 miles to Eaton Saddle by a metal vehicle gate on the right. Park in the dirt pullouts on either side of the road. An Adventure Pass is required for parking.

**Hiking directions:** Walk around the trailhead gate to a close-up view of Mount Markham and San Gabriel Peak. Follow Mount Lowe Fire Road, an old gravel road perched on a vertical south cliff of San Gabriel Peak. Along the road are great vistas, from the head of Eaton Canyon to the San Gabriel Valley. At 0.3 miles, walk through Mueller Tunnel, carved through the southern base of San Gabriel Peak in 1942. At a half mile, the historic road reaches Markham Saddle and a posted junction. To the right, the trail leads 0.8 miles to Mount Disappointment and 1.1 mile to San Gabriel Peak. Straight ahead, the fire road descends and circles Mount Lowe counterclockwise to Mount Lowe Trail Camp, nestled in a grove of oaks and big cone spruce.

Take the footpath to the left, and enter a shaded oak canopy and a chaparral landscape. Traverse the west slope of Mount Markham at a level grade, directly toward Mount Lowe to a saddle between the two mountains. Continue 220 yards through a pocket of oaks to an unsigned fork. The Mount Lowe East Trail goes straight ahead to Mount Lowe Trail Camp. Go sharply right on the Mount Lowe West Trail, and climb 0.3 miles to a signed fork. The right fork descends and also leads to Mount Lowe Trail Camp. Veer left less than 0.1 mile to the exposed Mount Lowe summit. From the 5,603-foot peak are metal sighting tubes directed at the surrounding mountains and views across the San Gabriel Valley, the Verdugo Mountains, Griffith Park, downtown Los Angeles, and the San Fernando Valley. Return by retracing your steps. ■

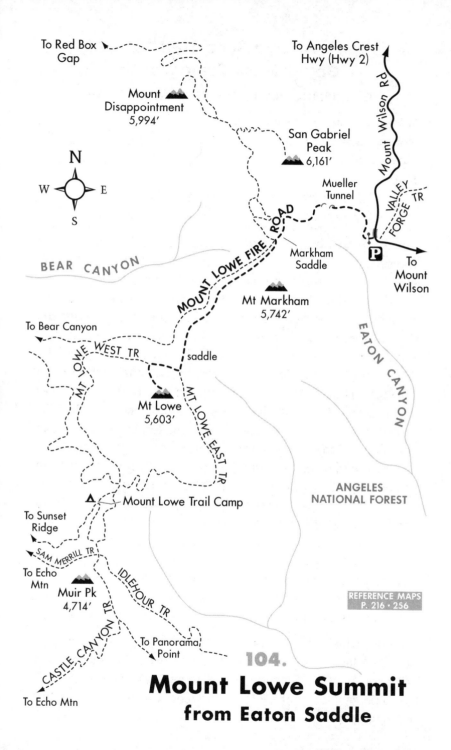

To Red Box Gap

Mount Disappointment 5,994'

San Gabriel Peak 6,161'

To Angeles Crest Hwy (Hwy 2)

Mount Wilson Rd

Mueller Tunnel

N
W    E
S

BEAR CANYON

MOUNT LOWE FIRE ROAD

Markham Saddle

Mt Markham 5,742'

VALLEY FORGE TR

P

To Mount Wilson

To Bear Canyon

MT LOWE WEST TR

saddle

EATON CANYON

Mt Lowe 5,603'

MT LOWE EAST TR

Mount Lowe Trail Camp

ANGELES NATIONAL FOREST

To Sunset Ridge

SAM MERRILL TR

To Echo Mtn

Muir Pk 4,714'

IDLEHOUR TR

REFERENCE MAPS
P. 216 · 256

CASTLE CANYON TR

To Panorama Point

104.

To Echo Mtn

# Mount Lowe Summit
## from Eaton Saddle

# 105. Arroyo Seco Trail to Gould Mesa Campground

## GABRIELINO NATIONAL RECREATION TRAIL

**Hiking distance:** 4.8 miles round trip
**Hiking time:** 2.5 hours
**Elevation gain:** 230 feet
**Maps:** U.S.G.S. Pasadena
Harrison: Angeles Front Country Trail Map
Harrison: Mt. Wilson Trail Map

**Summary of hike:** Arroyo Seco Creek forms from three stream forks near Red Box Gap on the south flank of Mount Lawlor. The scenic creek weaves through the deeply cut canyon from the upper San Gabriel Mountains. The perennial waterway flows through the communities of La Canada, Altadena, Pasadena, South Pasadena, and northeast Los Angeles to its terminus at the Los Angeles River, just north of downtown Los Angeles. The Gabrielino National Recreation Trail follows the Arroyo Seco through the canyon, from the foothills on the northwest corner of Pasadena to the headwaters at Red Box Gap. The 28-mile-long Gabrielino Trail continues east from Red Box Gap through Santa Anita Canyon to Chandry Flat north of Arcadia (Hike 112).

This hike follows the lower portion of the Gabrielino Trail from Hahamongna Watershed Park, a 1,300-acre park with oak groves, picnic areas, and walking paths (formerly called Oak Grove Park). The trail passes the NASA Jet Propulsion Laboratory, then enters the gorgeous stream-fed canyon. The trail was originally a road from the 1920s that provided access into the canyon to resorts and rustic cabins. Now the multi-use trail follows this historic route along the creek through dense groves of big leaf maples, white alders, sycamores, Douglas firs, and live oaks.

**Driving directions:** From the Foothill Freeway (Interstate 210) in Altadena, exit on Windsor Ave. Drive 0.9 miles north on Windsor Ave to its junction with Ventura Street. Park in the trailhead parking lot on the left. An Adventure Pass is required for parking.

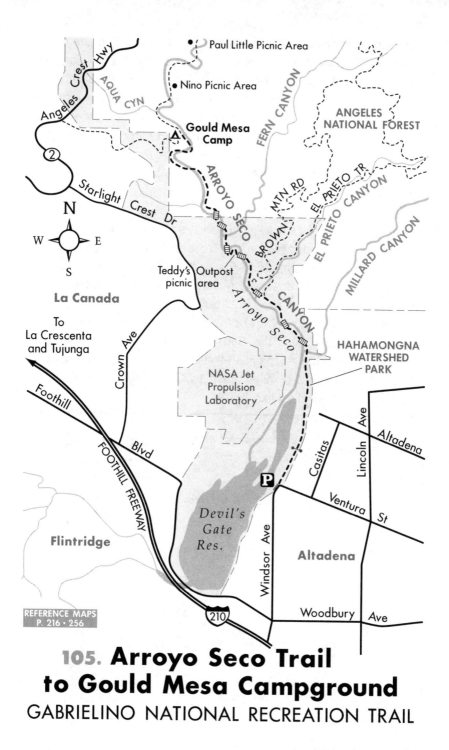

Paul Little Picnic Area

Nino Picnic Area

**Gould Mesa Camp**

FERN CANYON

ANGELES
NATIONAL FOREST

Angeles Crest Hwy

AQUA CYN

2

ARROYO SECO

BROWN MTN RD

EL PRIETO TR

EL PRIETO CANYON

MILLARD CANYON

N
W — E
S

Starlight Crest Dr

Teddy's Outpost
picnic area

Arroyo Seco

CANYON

Arroyo Seco

HAHAMONGNA
WATERSHED
PARK

La Canada

To
La Crescenta
and Tujunga

Crown Ave

NASA Jet
Propulsion
Laboratory

Altadena Ave

Lincoln Ave

Casitas

Foothill

Blvd

FOOTHILL FREEWAY

P

Ventura St

Flintridge

Windsor Ave

*Devil's
Gate
Res.*

**Altadena**

210

Woodbury Ave

REFERENCE MAPS
P. 216 · 256

# 105. Arroyo Seco Trail
# to Gould Mesa Campground
## GABRIELINO NATIONAL RECREATION TRAIL

**Hiking directions:** Walk to the posted trailhead at the north end of Windsor Avenue. Head north along the east edge of Hahamongna Watershed Natural Park. Take the signed Gabrielino Trail, and follow the gated, paved road parallel to the jet propulsion laboratory. At a half mile, enter the mouth of Arroyo Seco Canyon. Cross a bridge over the creek into an oak grove. Cross a second bridge to a signed Y-fork with the Lower Brown Mountain Road on the right at one mile. Stay left on the trail closest to the creek, passing Forest Service residences on the right. The unpaved road follows the canyon bottom as the canyon narrows. Cross a bridge to Teddy's Outpost Picnic Area on the left at just under two miles. Cross three more bridges, then rock-hop over Arroyo Seco Creek three times. Round a bend to the left, and enter Gould Mesa Campground, a developed backcountry camp. A road/trail on the left leads 1.3 miles up to a trailhead on the lower end of the Angeles Crest Highway.

To extend the hike, the Gabrielino National Recreation Trail continues 0.6 miles to the Nino Picnic Area, 1.6 miles to the Paul Little Picnic Area, 2.6 miles north to Oakwilde Camp, and 4.3 miles to Switzer Falls (Hike 103). ■

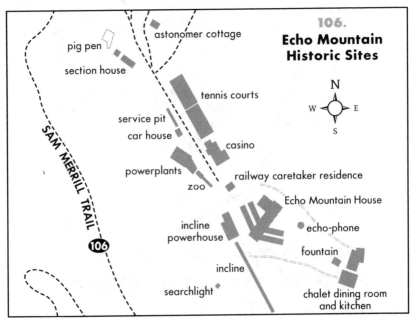

## 106. Echo Mountain
## via the Sam Merrill Trail

**Hiking distance:** 5.8 miles round trip
**Hiking time:** 2.5 hours
**Elevation gain:** 1,400 feet
**Maps:** U.S.G.S. Pasadena and Mount Wilson
        Harrison: Angeles Front Country Trail Map
        Harrison: Mt. Wilson Trail Map

map
page 269

**Summary of hike:** Echo Mountain, jutting southward between Las Flores Canyon and Rubio Canyon, is a 3,250-foot promontory overlooking the city of Altadena. The name Echo Mountain was derived from the echoing sound of one's voice when yelling into Castle Canyon, which descends from the mountain's northeast. Ground-mounted megaphones, known as *echo-phones,* were strategically placed to amplify the sound. A usable replica is mounted at the top of Castle Canyon.

Echo Mountain is listed on the National Register of Historic Places. It was the site of White City, an active mountaintop resort from 1893 through 1936. The ruins of White City still remain, creating a museum-like atmosphere. Atop the promontory are rock foundations, old retaining walls, rusting Pacific Electric railroad parts, iron tracks, abandoned gears, and ballwheels. Interpretive panels with historic photos are mounted in the exact spot they were originally taken. The photos highlight the Echo Mountain House, a four-story, 70-room Victorian hotel; the 40-room Echo Chalet; as well as dormitories, the powerhouse, a car barn, an observatory, casino, dance hall, and zoo. The Mount Lowe Railway shuttled guests seven miles and 1,300 feet up Rubio Canyon, from Altadena to the top of the Echo Mountain promontory. The trip continued to the base of Mount Lowe via 18 trestles and 127 hairpin curves. The multi-stage trip included electric trolleys, cable cars, and open-air railway cars. For four decades, the tourist attraction thrived. In 1900, a fire destroyed the Echo Mountain House. Another fire and a windstorm in 1905 burned additional structures and the trestles. In the late 1930s, flash floods and gale force winds wiped out the remaining buildings. The railway was abandoned in 1938.

The Sam Merrill Trail, located at the top of Lake Avenue in Altadena, is a major hiking route to Echo Mountain. The historic site can also be accessed from the Sunset Ridge Trail (Hike 107), which is a longer (3.7-mile) route. The Sam Merrill Trail zigzags 2.5 miles up the scrub-covered, southwest mountain slope to the ruins atop Echo Mountain. En route are grand vistas of the rugged canyons, the surrounding mountains, Los Angeles, and the San Gabriel Valley.

**Driving directions:** From the Foothill Freeway (Interstate 210) in Altadena, exit on Lake Avenue. Drive 3.6 miles north on Lake Avenue to its end at Loma Alta Drive. Park along the side of the road. An Adventure Pass is required for parking.

**Hiking directions:** From the corner of Loma Alta Drive and Lake Avenue, pass through the stone-pillared gate of the former Cobb Estate, now part of the Angeles National Forest. Follow the rutted road 100 yards east to a left bend, and veer right at the "trail" sign to the posted Sam Merrill Trailhead at the base of Las Flores Canyon. Cross the dry riverbed and zigzag up the southwest slope of Echo Mountain. Steadily climb the east canyon wall, overlooking the seasonal watershed with a network of walking paths leading to an enclosed reservoir. Continue up the serpentine, cliff-hugging path cut into the steep cliffs to the upper reaches of the canyon. The amazing views extend across the San Gabriel Valley and Los Angeles Basin to the Pacific Ocean. Curve through a small pocket of oaks, reaching a junction at 2.7 miles. The Echo Mountain Trail cuts sharply left and leads to Mount Lowe Road and Sunset Ridge Trail. Stay to the right on the south-heading Echo Mountain Trail. Pass the Sam Merrill Trail on the left in about 65 yards, which leads 3 miles to the Mount Lowe Trail Camp (see Hike 104). Ten yards farther is the Castle Canyon Trail, also on the left, which leads 2 miles to Inspiration Point and 2.5 miles to Mount Lowe Trail Camp. Continue descending south to the historic promontory of Echo Mountain, passing a picnic area on the left. Explore the ruins and overlooks, choosing your own route. ∎

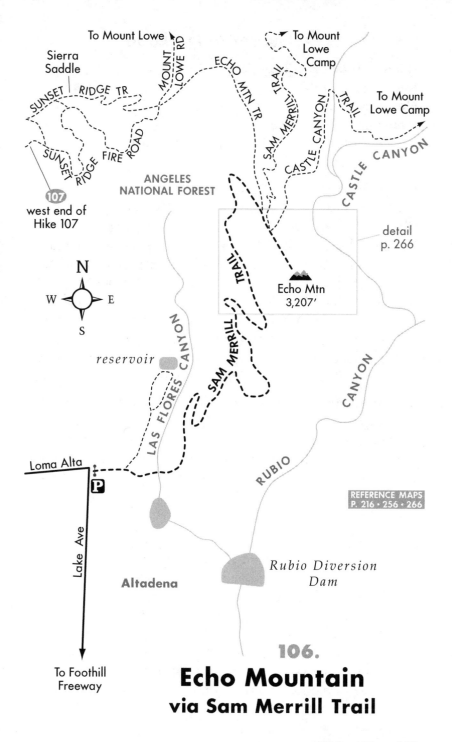

To Mount Lowe

Sierra Saddle

SUNSET RIDGE TR

MOUNT LOWE RD

ECHO MTN TR

SAM MERRILL TRAIL

To Mount Lowe Camp

To Mount Lowe Camp

CASTLE CANYON TRAIL

CASTLE CANYON

SUNSET RIDGE FIRE ROAD

107 west end of Hike 107

ANGELES NATIONAL FOREST

detail p. 266

TRAIL

Echo Mtn 3,207'

N
W   E
S

SAM MERRILL TRAIL

reservoir

LAS FLORES CANYON

CANYON

Loma Alta

P

RUBIO

REFERENCE MAPS
P. 216 • 256 • 266

Lake Ave

Altadena

Rubio Diversion Dam

To Foothill Freeway

**106.**

# Echo Mountain
## via Sam Merrill Trail

# 107. Sunset Ridge Loop

**Hiking distance:** 3.3-mile loop
**Hiking time:** 1:45 hours
**Elevation gain:** 1,000 feet
**Maps:** U.S.G.S. Pasadena
      Harrison: Angeles Front Country Trail Map
      Harrison: Mt. Wilson Trail Map

**map
page 272**

**Summary of hike:** The Sunset Ridge Trail contours the upper, south-facing slope of Millard Canyon. The trail parallels the Sunset Ridge Fire Road, a historic route to the ruins at the Mount Lowe Trail Camp. Historical markers along the road tell the story of the Mount Lowe Railway, the resorts atop Echo Mountain and Mount Lowe, and about the fire and floods that destroyed the resorts (see Hikes 104 and 106). This hike combines the fire road with the trail to form a loop. The hike offers a mix of pine forests; brushy slopes blanketed with sage, scrub oak, toyon, and lemonade berry; deep canyon views; and sweeping vistas across the San Gabriel and Los Angeles basins.

**Driving directions:** From the Foothill Freeway (Interstate 210) in Altadena, exit on Lake Avenue. Drive 3.6 miles north on Lake Avenue to its end. Turn left on Loma Alta Drive, and go one mile to Chaney Trail. Turn right and continue 1.1 mile, staying left at a fork, to a sharp left bend in the road and a vehicle gate on the right. Park along the side of the road. An Adventure Pass is re-quired for parking.

**Hiking directions:** Walk past the vehicle gate and follow the Sunset Ridge Fire Road, a narrow, paved road. Pass an access trail on the left, leading to the Millard Campground. Stay on the road, which overlooks Millard Canyon and the San Gabriel Mountains on the left and Altadena, Pasadena, and Los Angeles on the right. At 0.4 miles is a fork. Leave the Sunset Ridge Fire Road—our return route—and veer left on the Sunset Ridge Trail. Skirt the upper slope of Millard Canyon, weaving along the contours of the hills to a signed junction at 0.9 miles. The left fork crosses an old bridge and leads to the brink of Millard Falls (Hike 108).

Stay on the Sunset Ridge Trail to the right, and ascend the mountain with the aid of fourteen switchbacks. At the ninth switchback is a view up Saucer Branch Canyon. Zigzag under tall oaks and Coulter pines past beautiful fern-covered rock walls, steadily climbing to views of Glendale and the Verdugo Mountains. At 1.6 miles, the trail emerges at the Sierra Saddle by a junction with a short connector to Sunset Ridge Road. On the right is a picnic area. The Sunset Ridge Trail continues one mile, connecting again with the Sunset Ridge Fire Road just a mile shy of Echo Mountain. Take the short connector road to the paved Sunset Ridge Road.

To make a much longer hike, the left fork continues one mile uphill to a junction. The Mount Lowe Road veers left and winds 3.5 miles up to Mount Lowe Trail Camp, nestled in a grove of oaks and big cone spruce (Hike 104). The right fork, the Echo Mountain Trail, leads 0.8 miles on the old railway bed to the historic ruins atop Echo Mountain (Hike 106).

For this much shorter loop hike, head downhill (west) on the Sunset Ridge Fire Road along the exposed, south-facing slope. The spectacular vistas span across the urban basin as far as the haze will allow. Follow the upper south wall of Millard Canyon, completing the loop back at the junction with the Sunset Ridge Trail. Return a quarter mile to the trailhead. ∎

## 108. Brink of Millard Falls

**Hiking distance:** 2.2 miles round trip
**Hiking time:** 1 hour
**Elevation gain:** 300 feet
**Maps:** U.S.G.S. Pasadena
      Harrison: Angeles Front Country Trail Map
      Harrison: Mt. Wilson Trail Map

*map
page 275*

**Summary of hike:** Millard Canyon, tucked between Sunset Ridge and Brown Mountain, is filled with a lush forest of oaks, alders, maples and Douglas firs. Millard Creek flows through the mossy, boulder-strewn canyon. Millard Falls tumbles 50 feet

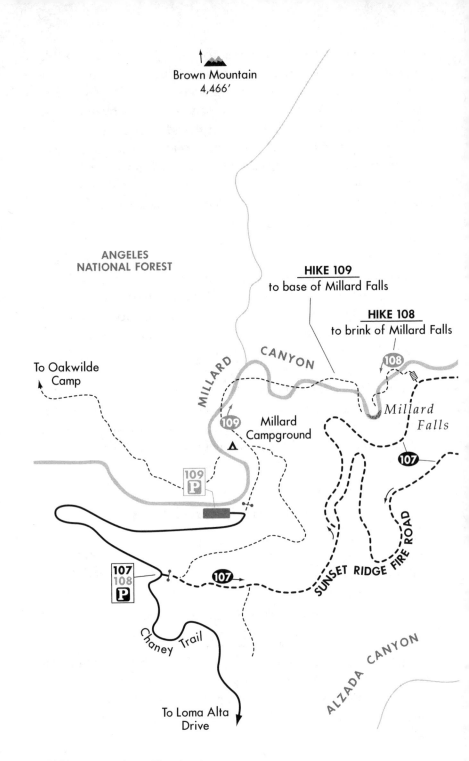

Brown Mountain
4,466'

ANGELES
NATIONAL FOREST

**HIKE 109**
to base of Millard Falls

**HIKE 108**
to brink of Millard Falls

108

To Oakwilde
Camp

MILLARD    CANYON

109

Millard
Campground

*Millard
Falls*

107

109
**P**

SUNSET RIDGE FIRE ROAD

107
108
**P**

107

Chaney Trail

ALZADA CANYON

To Loma Alta
Drive

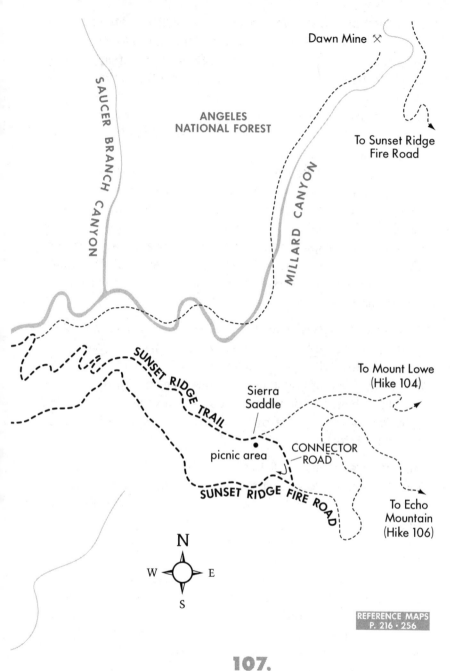

Dawn Mine ✕

ANGELES
NATIONAL FOREST

SAUCER BRANCH CANYON

MILLARD CANYON

To Sunset Ridge
Fire Road

SUNSET RIDGE TRAIL

Sierra
Saddle

To Mount Lowe
(Hike 104)

picnic area

CONNECTOR
ROAD

SUNSET RIDGE FIRE ROAD

To Echo
Mountain
(Hike 106)

N
W · E
S

REFERENCE MAPS
P. 216 · 256

## 107.
# Sunset Ridge Loop

through chockstones wedged into the vertical cleft to a pool surrounded by boulders. The water filters through the gaps in the boulders to the box canyon below. By carefully peering over the sheer rock wall, people can be spotted in the boulder-strewn grotto below (accessed from Hike 109). This trail begins on Sunset Ridge along the upper south slope of Millard Canyon. A footpath descends to the serene, shaded canyon floor and downstream to the brink of the falls.

To extend the hike, an old trail weaves up canyon along the creek to Dawn Mine. The abandoned gold mine, perched on the west canyon slope, was active from 1895 until the 1950s. This 1.5-mile path entails a considerable amount of hopping over boulders, crossing the creek, and climbing over down logs. The path is partially washed away and fades in and out. The rough but atmospheric route passes cascades, pools, old mining machinery, and assorted rusting parts.

**Driving directions:** From the Foothill Freeway (Interstate 210) in Altadena, exit on Lake Avenue. Drive 3.6 miles north on Lake Avenue to its end. Turn left on Loma Alta Drive, and go one mile to Chaney Trail. Turn right and continue 1.1 mile, staying left at a fork, to a sharp left bend in the road and a vehicle gate on the right. Park along the side of the road. An Adventure Pass is required for parking.

**Hiking directions:** Walk past the vehicle gate and follow the Sunset Ridge Fire Road, a narrow, paved road. Pass an access trail on the left, leading to the Millard Campground. Stay on the road, which overlooks Millard Canyon and the San Gabriel Mountains on the left and Altadena, Pasadena and Los Angeles on the right. At 0.4 miles is a fork. Leave the Sunset Ridge Fire Road, and veer left on the Sunset Ridge Trail. Skirt the upper slope of Millard Canyon, weaving along the contours of the hills to a signed junction at 0.9 miles. The right fork stays on the Sunset Ridge Trail and climbs the hillside to Sierra Saddle, reconnecting with the Sunset Ridge Fire Road (Hike 107). For this hike, stay left and cross an old metal bridge. Pass a cabin on the right, and descend through the lush forest thick with ferns, mosses, and live oak trees to Millard

Creek on the canyon floor. Bear left and head downstream along the south side of the creek. Pass rock-formed pools, crossing the creek three times in the shady, rock-walled canyon. The trail ends at a jumble of huge boulders at the brink of the falls. ▪

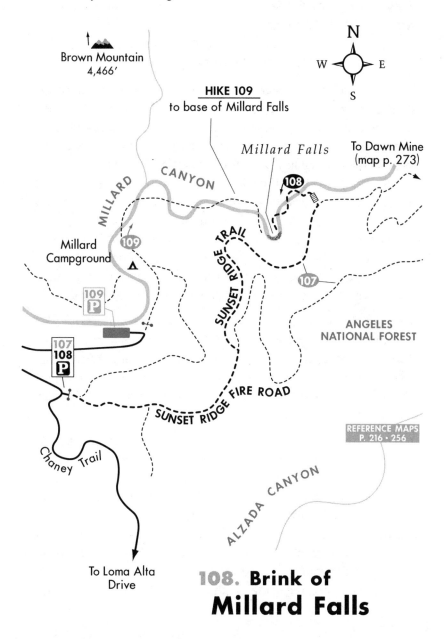

Brown Mountain
4,466'

**HIKE 109**
to base of Millard Falls

N

W    E

S

*Millard Falls*

To Dawn Mine
(map p. 273)

108

*MILLARD*    CANYON

Millard
Campground

109

107

SUNSET RIDGE TRAIL

109
P

ANGELES
NATIONAL FOREST

107
108
P

SUNSET RIDGE FIRE ROAD

REFERENCE MAPS
P. 216 · 256

Chaney Trail

ALZADA CANYON

To Loma Alta
Drive

**108. Brink of
Millard Falls**

# 109. Base of Millard Falls

**Hiking distance:** 1.5 miles round trip
**Hiking time:** 1 hour
**Elevation gain:** 150 feet
**Maps:** U.S.G.S. Pasadena
      Harrison: Angeles Front Country Trail Map
      Harrison: Mt. Wilson Trail Map

**Summary of hike:** Millard Falls is a 50-foot cataract that drops over a moss-covered vertical rock face. The waterfall braids through a jumble of huge boulders, wedged into the V-shaped notch, to a pool in a narrow box canyon. This hike leads to the base of the falls, while Hike 108 leads to the brink of the falls from the Sunset Ridge Trail. The hike begins near Millard Campground in a small tree-shaded flat. The trail follows Millard Creek up a narrow boulder-strewn canyon under towering alders, oaks, sycamores, and willow trees to the falls in a cool, lush grotto. Millard Canyon was originally known as Church Canyon. The canyon was renamed for Henry Millard, a beekeeper who homesteaded in the mouth of the canyon with his family in 1862.

**Driving directions:** From the Foothill Freeway (Interstate 210) in Altadena, exit on Lake Avenue. Drive 3.6 miles north on Lake Avenue to its end. Turn left on Loma Alta Drive and go one mile to Chaney Trail. Turn right and continue 1.7 miles to a parking lot at the end of the road by Millard Campground. An Adventure Pass is required for parking.

**Hiking directions:** Walk to the upper (front) end of the parking lot by the kiosk. Take the gated dirt road under the shaded forest canopy. Follow the serpentine course of Millard Creek into Millard Campground. Veer right on the footpath, staying close to the creek. Pass pools and small waterfalls as the steep-walled canyon narrows. Weave among the boulders under a canopy of alders. Pass a cabin on the right, and follow the course of the stream up canyon. Cross the creek six times, reaching the falls from the south (right) side of the creek. The trail ends at the base of the falls in a box canyon with moss and ferns growing from the vertical rock walls. ∎

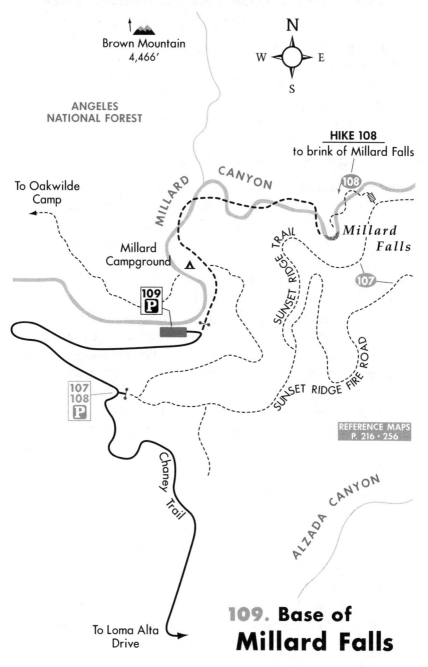

Brown Mountain
4,466'

ANGELES
NATIONAL FOREST

To Oakwilde
Camp

MILLARD CANYON

HIKE 108
to brink of Millard Falls

108

Millard
Falls

Millard
Campground

SUNSET RIDGE TRAIL

109
P

107

107
108
P

SUNSET RIDGE FIRE ROAD

REFERENCE MAPS
P. 216 · 256

Chaney Trail

ALZADA CANYON

To Loma Alta
Drive

## 109. Base of
# Millard Falls

# 110. Eaton Canyon Falls

## EATON CANYON COUNTY PARK and NATURAL AREA

### 1750 N. Altadena Drive · Pasadena

**Hiking distance:** 3 miles round trip
**Hiking time:** 1.5 hours
**Elevation gain:** 400 feet
**Maps:** U.S.G.S. Mount Wilson
      Harrison: Angeles Front Country Trail Map
      Harrison: Mt. Wilson Trail Map
      Eaton Canyon Natural Area County Park map

**Summary of hike:** Eaton Canyon is a major drainage that stretches from the upper mountain slopes at Eaton Saddle, between Mount Markham and Occidental Peak, to the mouth of the canyon at Eaton Canyon County Park. Eaton Creek flows through the canyon, emerging from the foothills, and continues south through Eaton Wash and Pasadena to the Los Angeles River. Eaton Canyon County Park, located on the north end of Altadena, encompasses 190 acres in the foothills of the San Gabriel Mountains. The popular park includes a nature center and picnic areas. It is a staging area for hikes into Eaton Canyon and the gateway to Henninger Flats, Idlehour Campground, and Mount Wilson via the Mount Wilson Toll Road. This hike winds through the natural area along Eaton Wash and enters the canyon to Eaton Canyon Falls, upstream from the Mount Wilson Toll Road. Eaton Canyon Falls drops 40 feet off the rock cliffs through a jagged, V-shaped notch in the bedrock into the pool below.

**Driving directions:** From the Foothill Freeway (Interstate 210) in Pasadena, exit on Altadena Drive. Drive 1.6 miles north on Altadena Drive to the signed Eaton Canyon County Park on the right. Turn right into the park and park 0.2 miles ahead by the nature center. Parking is free.

An alternative trailhead pullout is also located 0.5 miles past the turnoff into Eaton Canyon Park. It is on the right, directly across from Roosevelt Avenue and Midwick Drive. This trailhead will shorten the hike by one mile round trip.

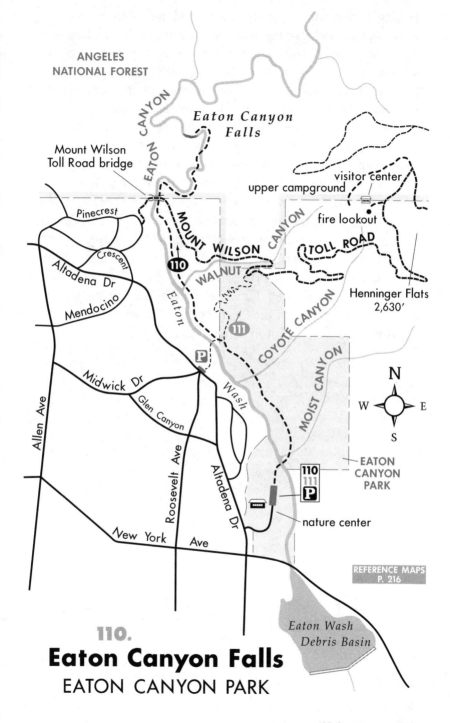

ANGELES
NATIONAL FOREST

*Eaton Canyon
Falls*

EATON CANYON

Mount Wilson
Toll Road bridge

visitor center
upper campground

Pinecrest

MOUNT WILSON CANYON

fire lookout

**110**

Crescent

TOLL ROAD

WALNUT

Altadena Dr

Eaton

Henninger Flats
2,630'

Mendocino

COYOTE CANYON

**111**

**P**

MOIST CANYON

Midwick Dr

Allen Ave

Glen Canyon

Wash

N

W        E

S

Roosevelt Ave

Altadena Dr

EATON
CANYON
PARK

**110**
**111**
**P**

nature center

New York    Ave

REFERENCE MAPS
P. 216

*Eaton Wash
Debris Basin*

**110.**
# Eaton Canyon Falls
## EATON CANYON PARK

**Hiking directions:** From the far (north) end of the parking lot, pass the gate and take the wide dirt path north. Follow the west edge of Eaton Wash towards the mountains, passing a picnic area on the left. Cross the rocky wash and enter an oak grove. Continue north, following the terrace above Eaton Wash through chaparral, cactus, scattered maples, willows and oaks. At a half mile is a posted Y-fork at the mouth of Walnut Canyon. The right fork leads 2.9 miles to Henninger Flats (Hike 111). Veer left, passing Walnut Canyon, and continue up the Eaton Creek drainage to a posted fork on the left at one mile. (The junction is located 200 yards shy of the Mount Wilson Toll Road bridge.) Take the fork to the left, and drop down into the wash to Eaton Creek. Follow the creek under the Mount Wilson Toll Road bridge, and enter the forested canyon under oaks and alders. Pass pools, cascades, and small waterfalls, crossing the creek two times. The rock-embedded path curves along the floor of the narrow, serpentine canyon with vertical rock cliffs. Curve left into a box canyon at the base of Eaton Canyon Falls. ■

# 111. Mount Wilson Toll Road
## Eaton Canyon to Henninger Flats
### EATON CANYON COUNTY PARK and NATURAL AREA
1750 N. Altadena Drive · Pasadena

**Hiking distance:** 7 miles round trip
**Hiking time:** 3.5 hours
**Elevation gain:** 1,600 feet
**Maps:** U.S.G.S. Mount Wilson
Harrison: Angeles Front Country Trail Map
Harrison: Mt. Wilson Trail Map

*map*
*page 283*

**Summary of hike:** The Mount Wilson Toll Road is a historic wagon road that begins in the foothills of Altadena and ascends nine miles to the summit of Mount Wilson. The road, active from 1891 through 1936, was closed to vehicles when the Angeles Crest Highway was completed. The old road was turned over to the U.S. Forest Service and became a hiking, biking, and equestrian route. The Mount Wilson Toll Road climbs the exposed, chaparral-covered slopes to Henninger Flats, a forested flat above Altadena with incense cedar, sequoia, cypress, and a variety of pines. William Henninger settled on the mesa above Altadena in the early 1880s. He built a home and planted fruits, vegetables, grasses, and nut trees. He also started an experimental reforestation project at Henninger Flats. After his death, the flat was used as a high-elevation forest nursery.

The hike to Henninger Flats follows the exposed dirt fire road, with exceptional vistas of Los Angeles and the San Gabriel Valley. Set amid the trees on the 2,600-foot bench is a nature center, picnic area, campground, and a historic fire lookout, relocated here from Castro Peak in the Santa Monica Mountains.

In the past, the toll road has been closed intermitently for repairs. Call ahead to the nature center to verify: (626) 398-5420.

**Driving directions:** From the Foothill Freeway (Interstate 210) in Pasadena, exit on Altadena Drive. Drive 1.6 miles north on Altadena Drive to the signed Eaton Canyon County Park on the right. Turn right into the park and park 0.2 miles ahead by the nature center. Parking is free.

An alternative trailhead pullout is also located 0.5 miles past the turnoff into Eaton Canyon Park. It is on the right, directly across from Roosevelt Avenue and Midwick Drive. This trailhead will shorten the hike by a mile round trip.

**Hiking directions:** From the far (north) end of the parking lot, take the wide dirt path north. Follow the west edge of Eaton Wash towards the mountains. Cross the rocky wash and enter an oak grove. Continue north, following the rim of Eaton Wash through chaparral, cactus, scattered maples, willows and oaks. At a half mile is a posted Y-fork at the mouth of Walnut Canyon. The left fork continues up Eaton Canyon to Eaton Canyon Falls (Hike 110). Stay to the right and head up the north wall of Walnut Canyon. Zigzag a half mile up the mountain to Mount Wilson Toll Road, a narrow dirt road on a U-bend. En route, pass two overlooks of Eaton Canyon, Altadena, Pasadena, and the San Gabriel Valley. The left fork descends 0.8 miles to the toll road bridge that crosses Eaton Wash at the mouth of Eaton Canyon.

Bear right on the one-lane dirt road, which frequently narrows to a footpath due to erosion. Head uphill at a moderate grade. The views span from the Verdugo Mountains and the San Rafael Hills to the Los Angeles basin. At 3.3 miles, enter the shade of the forested Lower Henninger Flats Campground and a trail split. On the left is the visitor center and the old Castro Peak Fire Lookout from the Santa Monica Mountains, in service from 1925 through 1971. Continue up the slope on the Mount Wilson Toll Road to a signed fork. The main road curves right and continues 6 miles to Mount Wilson at 5,710 feet. For this hike, go to the left and loop back above the visitor center. Walk a half mile to the upper campground, perched on the end of a 2,600-foot forested ridge with spectacular vistas. ■

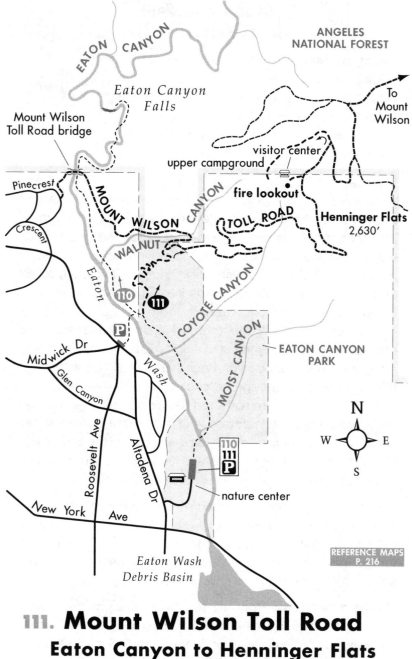

ANGELES
NATIONAL FOREST

EATON CANYON

Eaton Canyon
Falls

Mount Wilson
Toll Road bridge

To
Mount
Wilson

visitor center
upper campground

Pinecrest

MOUNT WILSON CANYON

fire lookout

Crescent

TOLL ROAD

Henninger Flats
2,630'

Eaton

WALNUT

110

111

COYOTE CANYON

MOIST CANYON

EATON CANYON
PARK

Midwick Dr

Glen Canyon

Wash

N

W   E

S

Roosevelt Ave

Altadena Dr

110
111
P

nature center

New York Ave

Eaton Wash
Debris Basin

REFERENCE MAPS
P. 216

# 111. Mount Wilson Toll Road
## Eaton Canyon to Henninger Flats
### EATON CANYON PARK

# 112. Sturtevant Falls

## SANTA ANITA CANYON

**Hiking distance:** 4.3 miles round trip
**Hiking time:** 2.5 hours
**Elevation gain:** 650 feet
**Maps:** U.S.G.S. Mount Wilson
Harrison: Angeles Front Country Trail Map
Harrison: Mt. Wilson Trail Map

map
page 286

**Summary of hike:** Sturtevant Falls is a beautiful 50-foot waterfall tucked into a lush gulch with colorful moss-covered cliffs in Santa Anita Canyon. The creek freefalls over a vertical limestone precipice into a natural rock bowl. This popular hike begins at Chantry Flat, north of Arcadia, and follows the eastern portion of the Gabrielino National Recreation Trail to Sturtevant Falls. The trail immediately drops into Santa Anita Canyon at Roberts Camp, a historic vacation lodge nestled along Santa Anita Creek. Built in 1912, the stone lodge, dining hall, store, rustic cabins, and tents remained active until 1931. The trail meanders along the stream-fed canyon floor in a jungle-like environment, thick with oaks, alders, spruce, cedars, willows, ferns and vines. Old charming cabins are scattered beside the trail. The path parallels Santa Anita Creek, dotted with large granite boulders and occasional flood control dams. The dams, built in the early 1960s, are overgrown with moss, ferns, and leafy vegetation. Waterfalls and pools have formed around the structures.

**Driving directions:** From the Foothill Freeway (Interstate 210) in Arcadia, exit on Santa Anita Avenue. Turn left and head 4.8 miles north to the end of the road and the Chantry Flat parking lots on the right. En route, the road becomes Santa Anita Canyon Road. An Adventure Pass is required for parking.

**Hiking directions:** From the top (front end) of the parking lot, take the signed trail downhill. Follow the winding, paved fire road on the west wall of Santa Anita Canyon to Roberts Camp on the canyon floor at 0.6 miles. Cross a metal bridge over Winter Creek, just above its confluence with Santa Anita Creek, to a 4-way junction. The right fork follows the creek down canyon past a group of turn-of-the-century cabins to Hermit Falls (Hike 114), located just above Santa Anita Dam. The Winter Creek Trail (Hike 113) bears left, following the creek.

Continue straight ahead in the lush riparian scenery, staying in Santa Anita Canyon on the Gabrielino National Recreation Trail. Stroll through the shade of the forest along the boulder–filled creek, passing rustic cabins with beautiful rock walls and chimneys. Flood control dams along the creek form 20-foot waterfalls and pools. At 1.5 miles is a signed junction at Fern Lodge Junction. The Gabrielino National Recreation Trail goes to the left 0.3 miles to the top of Sturtevant Falls.

For now, stay to the right and cross Santa Anita Creek at Fiddler's Crossing. Cross the creek two more times. Scramble over river rock to the base of Sturtevant Falls and a rock-lined pool in a vertical-walled box canyon. After enjoying the falls, return to Fern Lodge Junction. Bear right and wind up the hillside on the west canyon wall. Traverse the slope, perched on a precipitous cliff, to various views of Sturtevant Falls. Return to the trailhead by retracing your steps.

From the Fern Lodge Junction, the Gabrielino National Recreation Trail continues another 2.25 miles to Spruce Grove Campground, 4.5 miles to Newcomb Pass, and 5.5 miles to Mount Wilson. ■

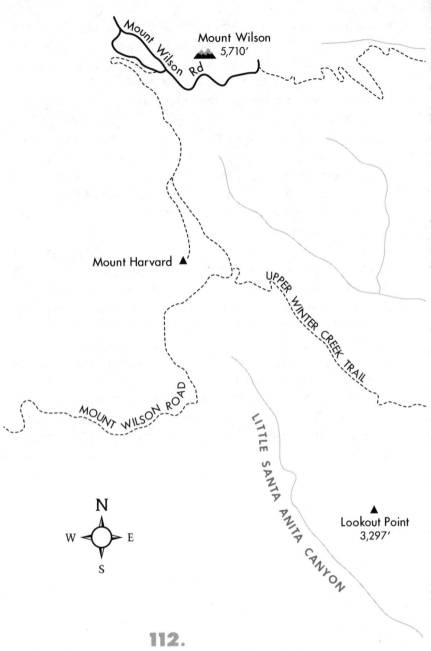

Mount Wilson Rd

Mount Wilson
5,710'

Mount Harvard ▲

UPPER WINTER CREEK TRAIL

MOUNT WILSON ROAD

LITTLE SANTA ANITA CANYON

Lookout Point
3,297' ▲

N
W ✦ E
S

**112.**
# Sturtevant Falls
## SANTA ANITA CANYON

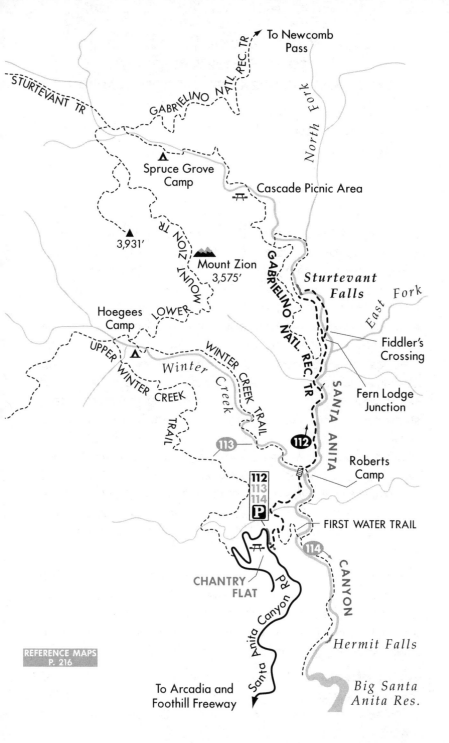

To Newcomb Pass

STURTEVANT TR

GABRIELINO NATL. REC. TR

North Fork

Spruce Grove Camp

Cascade Picnic Area

MOUNT ZION TR

3,931'

Mount Zion
3,575'

GABRIELINO NATL. REC. TR

*Sturtevant Falls*

East Fork

Hoegees Camp

LOWER

Fiddler's Crossing

UPPER WINTER CREEK

WINTER CREEK TRAIL

*Winter* Creek

Fern Lodge Junction

TRAIL

SANTA ANITA

113

112

FIRST WATER TRAIL

112
113
114
P

Roberts Camp

114

CANYON

CHANTRY FLAT

Santa Anita Canyon Rd

*Hermit Falls*

REFERENCE MAPS P. 216

To Arcadia and Foothill Freeway

*Big Santa Anita Res.*

# 113. Winter Creek Canyon to Hoegees Camp

## SANTA ANITA CANYON • WINTER CREEK CANYON

**Hiking distance:** 6-mile loop
**Hiking time:** 3 hours
**Elevation gain:** 950 feet
**Maps:** U.S.G.S. Mount Wilson
Harrison: Angeles Front Country Trail Map
Harrison: Mt. Wilson Trail Map

**Summary of hike:** Winter Creek, a major tributary of Santa Anita Creek, forms on the upper south slope of Mount Wilson. Winter Canyon, a shady, deeply cut canyon, is an arboreal haven with stately alders, three varieties of oaks, California bays, big leaf maples, sycamores, willows, and a lush understory of giant ferns and ivy. This hike begins on the lower (south) end of the 28-mile Gabrielino National Recreation Trail at Chantry Flat. The trail descends into bucolic Santa Anita Canyon, then veers up perennial Winter Creek. The route passes historic stone and wood cottages built in the early 1900s; huge granite boulders; stacked, log-shaped concrete dams that form 20-foot cascades; and rock-scoured pools. At the upper end of this loop hike, the Winter Creek Trail passes through rustic Hoegees Camp, a deep, wooded trail camp on the south bank of the creek. It is named for Arie Hoegee, who built and operated a resort camp at the site from 1908 to 1938. The resort buildings were ruined in the floods of 1938 and burned during the Monrovia Peak Fire of 1953.

**Driving directions:** From the Foothill Freeway (Interstate 210) in Arcadia, exit on Santa Anita Avenue. Turn left and head 4.8 miles north to the end of the road and the Chantry Flat parking lots on the right. En route, the road becomes Santa Anita Canyon Road. An Adventure Pass is required for parking.

**Hiking directions:** From the top (front end) of the parking lot, take the signed trail downhill. Follow the winding, paved fire road on the west wall of Santa Anita Canyon to the historic

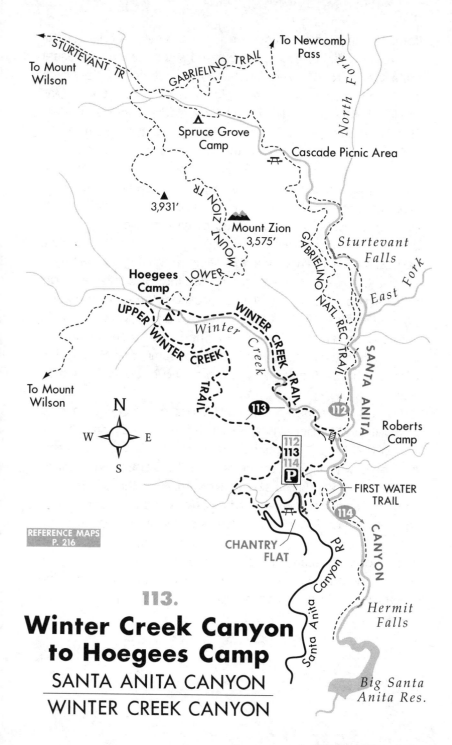

STURTEVANT TR

To Mount
Wilson

GABRIELINO TRAIL

To Newcomb
Pass

North Fork

△ Spruce Grove
Camp

Cascade Picnic Area

3,931'

MOUNT ZION TR

▲ Mount Zion
3,575'

Sturtevant
Falls

East Fork

GABRIELINO NATL REC TRAIL

**Hoegees
Camp**

LOWER

Winter

Creek

WINTER CREEK TRAIL

UPPER WINTER CREEK TRAIL

SANTA ANITA

To Mount
Wilson

N
W   E
S

113

112

Roberts
Camp

112
113
114
P

FIRST WATER
TRAIL

114

CANYON

REFERENCE MAPS
P. 216

CHANTRY
FLAT

Santa Anita Canyon Rd

Hermit
Falls

## 113.
# Winter Creek Canyon
# to Hoegees Camp
## SANTA ANITA CANYON
## WINTER CREEK CANYON

Big Santa
Anita Res.

Roberts Camp on the canyon floor at 0.6 miles. Cross a metal bridge over Winter Creek, just above its confluence with Santa Anita Creek, to a 4-way junction. The right fork follows the creek down canyon past a group of turn-of-the-century cabins to Hermit Falls (Hike 114), located just above Santa Anita Dam. Sturtevant Falls (Hike 112) is straight ahead another 1.25 miles.

For this hike, bear left on the Winter Creek Trail, and enter the narrow, scenic canyon. Cross the creek and head upstream, passing pools under a mix of alder, willow, bay and oak trees. Cross the creek at the base of a flood control dam and head up the hillside, passing a small group of cabins. Climb the hillside, passing a small waterfall and a deep pool on the left beneath a vertical rock wall. Pass through a camp, following the trail signs. Cross the creek and ascend the hillside into Hoegees Camp beneath big cone spruce at 2.1 miles. Meander through the shaded camp, and cross Winter Creek to a posted junction on the right with the Lower Mount Zion Trail. The Lower Mount Zion Trail leads 1.25 miles north to the 3,575-foot summit of Mount Zion, then another 1.25 miles to the Gabrielino National Recreation Trail.

Instead, continue straight and cross the creek to a junction with the Upper Winter Creek Trail—the return route. The Winter Creek Trail continues to the right 4.5 miles to the summit of Mount Wilson. Stay to the left on the Upper Winter Creek Trail, and loop around a side canyon. Traverse the upper south canyon wall under a canopy of bay trees and an understory of ferns and vines. Follow the contours of the steep mountainside, weaving in and out of shady side canyons and exposed chaparral. Slowly descend, overlooking Chantry Flat. The footpath ends at the paved access road. Bear left on the road and wind downhill into Chantry Flat, completing the loop at the parking lot. ▪

# 114. Hermit Falls
## SANTA ANITA CANYON

**Hiking distance:** 3 miles round trip
**Hiking time:** 2 hours
**Elevation gain:** 600 feet
**Maps:** U.S.G.S. Mount Wilson
       Harrison: Angeles Front Country Trail Map
       Harrison: Mt. Wilson Trail Map

map
page 292

**Summary of hike:** Hermit Falls is tucked away in Santa Anita Canyon, downstream from well-known Sturtevant Falls. The 30-foot falls sits among huge rock formations with overhangs and caves. The cataract spills out of water chutes in the rock, joined by a series of four descending pools etched into the water-polished granite. It is an amazing spot. The hike begins on the southern end of the 28-mile Gabrielino National Recreation Trail at Chantry Flat, the same trail to Sturtevant Falls (Hike 112) and Winter Creek (Hike 113). While most hikers are headed to popular Sturtevant Falls, the trip to Hermit Falls avoids the crowds in a quiet forest, thick with foliage along perennial Santa Anita Creek.

**Driving directions:** From the Foothill Freeway (Interstate 210) in Arcadia, exit on Santa Anita Avenue. Turn left and head 4.8 miles north to the end of the road and the Chantry Flat parking lots on the right. En route, the road becomes Santa Anita Canyon Road. An Adventure Pass is required for parking.

**Hiking directions:** From the top (front end) of the parking lot, take the signed trail downhill on the west wall of Santa Anita Canyon. Follow the winding, paved fire road a quarter mile to the posted First Water Trail on the right. Take the footpath, perched on the cliff covered with chaparral and yucca, and weave downhill along the mountain contours. At the canyon floor is a flood control dam, forming a pool and a manmade waterfall in a lush riparian canopy of alders and oaks. Boulder-hop over Santa Anita Creek to a posted T-junction at 0.75 miles. The left fork follows the creek 0.75 miles up canyon past a group of turn-of-the-century cabins to the historic Roberts Camp and a 4-way junction (Hikes 112 and 113).

Go to the right and descend past another flood control dam. Stroll through the quiet of the shaded forest among giant sword, chain, and maidenhair ferns to a stream crossing. Cross the creek and head up the west canyon hillside. Traverse the slope, slowly descending to a Y-fork among gorgeous rock formations and pools. Take the left branch down to Hermit Falls. Explore the area, choosing your own route. ■

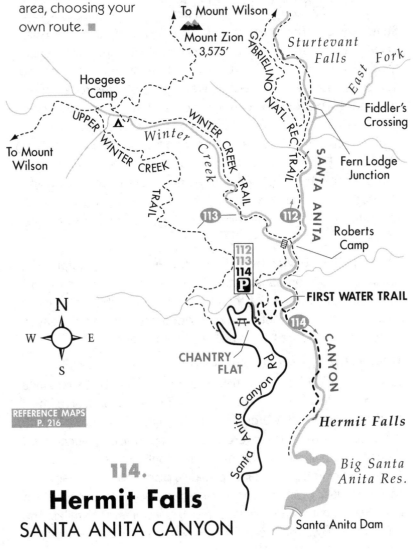

**114.**
# Hermit Falls
## SANTA ANITA CANYON

# 115. Monrovia Canyon Falls

## MONROVIA CANYON PARK

1200 North Canyon Boulevard · Monrovia

**Hiking distance:** 2 miles round trip
**Hiking time:** 1 hour
**Elevation gain:** 350 feet
**Maps:** U.S.G.S. Azusa
      Monrovia Canyon Park Trail Guide
      Harrison: Angeles High Country Trail Map

**map page 294**

**Summary of hike:** Monrovia Canyon Falls is a 40-foot, two-tiered cataract fed by year-round springs from the upper slopes of Clamshell Peak and Rankin Peak. The perennial fall cascades off a granite ledge in a verdant box canyon, fronted by a pool and large, smooth boulders. The picturesque cataract is located in 80-acre Monrovia Canyon Park in the foothills above the city of Monrovia. The popular park contains shady picnic areas, a nature center, a lush canyon with check dams to control the power of the stream, hiking trails, and the boulder-flanked waterfall.

Three different trailheads offer access to the waterfall. From the lower (south) end of the park by the entrance station, the Bill Cull Trail forms a 3.4-mile round-trip hike. The shortest route, a 1.5-mile round-trip hike, begins by the nature center at the upper end of the park road. This hike begins between the two, mid-way up the park road by a picnic area, where the Bill Cull Trail connects with the Falls Trail. The Falls Trail stays close to Monrovia Creek through rich oak woodland and riparian habitat under a lush canopy of coast live oak, big leaf maple, white alder, sycamores and ferns. The path leads up narrow Monrovia Canyon and dead-ends by the pool at the base of the falls.

**Driving directions:** From the Foothill Freeway (Interstate 210) in Monrovia, exit on Myrtle Avenue. Turn left and drive 0.8 miles to Foothill Boulevard. Turn right (west) and go 0.25 miles to Canyon Boulevard. Turn left and continue 1.2 miles north. Veer to the right, staying on Canyon Boulevard for one mile and following signs to the park entrance. Drive 0.3 miles to the middle

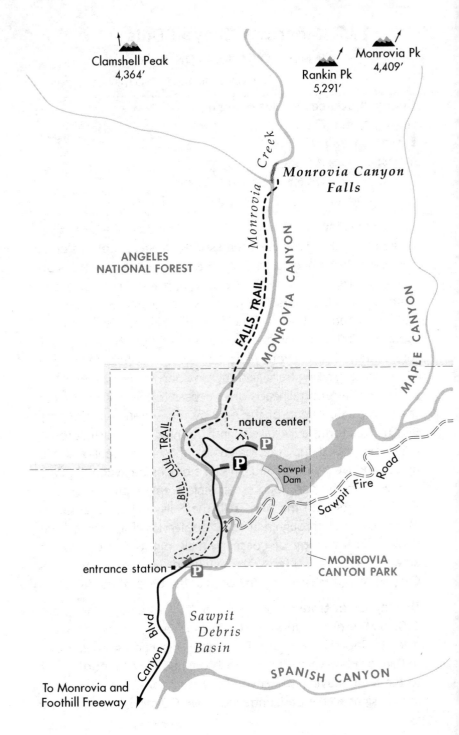

Clamshell Peak
4,364'

Rankin Pk
5,291'

Monrovia Pk
4,409'

Monrovia Creek

*Monrovia Canyon
Falls*

ANGELES
NATIONAL FOREST

**FALLS TRAIL**

MONROVIA CANYON

MAPLE CANYON

BILL CULL TRAIL

nature center

P

P

Sawpit
Dam

Sawpit Fire Road

MONROVIA
CANYON PARK

entrance station

P

Canyon Blvd

*Sawpit
Debris
Basin*

SPANISH CANYON

To Monrovia and
Foothill Freeway

parking area, just after crossing over a bridge. Parking spaces are on the right to the east of the restroom building. A parking fee is required.

**Hiking directions:** Walk fifty yards up the road. As the road veers right, take the signed footpath straight ahead, veering left. Enter the dense forest under the shade of alders, bays, sycamores and oaks. Follow the east side of the canyon, and pass a junction on the right, which leads up the hill among pines and oak to the nature center and picnic area. Gently wind up canyon and cross the creek just above a manmade waterfall. Traverse the west canyon wall above the stream, weaving past rock formations and through a tunnel of vegetation. Return to the stream and follow the canyon floor. Pass a couple more flood control dams with waterfalls. At just under one mile, cross the stream and boulder hop a short distance to Monrovia Falls and a pool in the rock-walled grotto at the end of the trail. ∎

To Deer Park

To White Saddle

SAWPIT CANYON

BEN OVERTURFF TR

VASSAR CANYON

Ben Overturff Trailhead

N

W    E

S

REFERENCE MAPS
P. 216

**115.**

# Monrovia Canyon Falls
## MONROVIA CANYON PARK

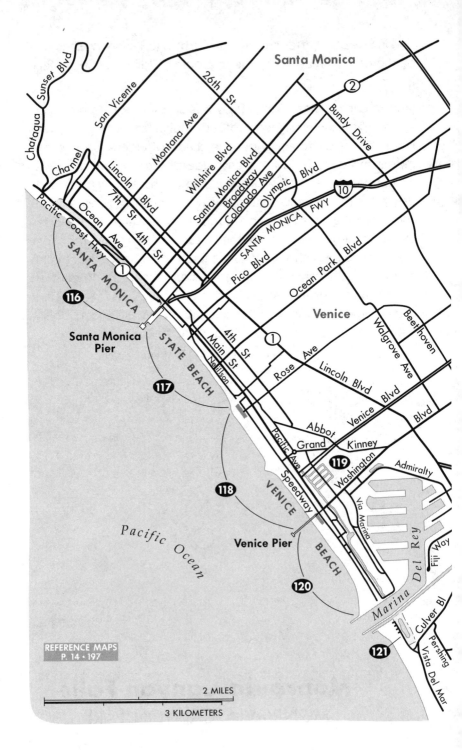

Santa Monica

Chataqua
Sunset Blvd
San Vicente
26th St
Bundy Drive
2
Channel
Montana Ave
Wilshire Blvd
Santa Monica Blvd
Broadway
Colorado Ave
Olympic Blvd
10
Lincoln Blvd
7th St
4th St
Ocean Ave
Pacific Coast Hwy
SANTA MONICA FWY
1
116
SANTA MONICA
Pico Blvd
Ocean Park Blvd

**Santa Monica Pier**

Venice

STATE BEACH
117
4th St
Main St
Neilson
1
Walgrove Ave
Beethoven
Rose Ave
Lincoln Blvd
Venice Blvd
Blvd

118
Pacific Ave
Speedway
Abbot
Grand
Kinney
Washington
119
Admiralty

VENICE BEACH

*Pacific Ocean*

**Venice Pier**
120

Via Marina

Marina Del Rey

Fiji Way

Culver Bl
Pershing
Vista Del Mar
121

REFERENCE MAPS
P. 14 • 197

2 MILES

3 KILOMETERS

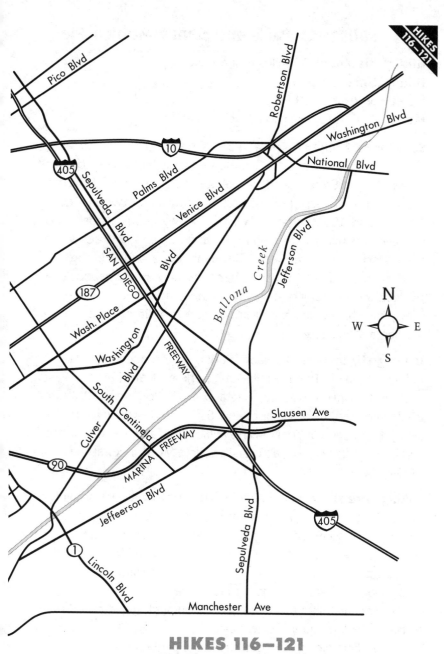

Pico Blvd

Robertson Blvd

Washington Blvd

10

405

National Blvd

Sepulveda Blvd

Palms Blvd

Venice Blvd

Washington Blvd

Ballona Creek

Jefferson Blvd

SAN DIEGO

187

Blvd

N

W ✦ E

S

Wash. Place

FREEWAY

Washington Blvd

South Centinela

Slausen Ave

Culver

90

MARINA FREEWAY

Jeffeerson Blvd

Sepulveda Blvd

405

1

Lincoln Blvd

Manchester Ave

## HIKES 116–121

# Santa Monica to
# Marina Del Rey

# 116. Palisades Park and Santa Monica Pier

**Hiking distance:** 3.5 miles round trip
**Hiking time:** 2 hours
**Elevation gain:** 100 feet
**Maps:** U.S.G.S. Topanga and Beverly Hills

**Summary of hike:** Palisades Park is perched on the eroding 100-foot bluffs above the Pacific Coast Highway, overlooking Santa Monica State Beach, the Santa Monica Pier, and the entire bay. The 26-acre park stretches 1.6 miles between Ocean Avenue and the sandstone cliffs. The gorgeous landscaped grounds are filled with palm, oak, and eucalyptus trees lining the paved and natural paths. Throughout the park are gardens with exotic and native plants, benches, and a few gazebos. A pedestrian bridge and stairway connect the park to the wide, sandy beach. The south end of the park has direct access onto the Santa Monica Pier.

**Driving directions:** Palisades Park is on the oceanfront bluffs in Santa Monica. The 1.6-mile-long park is located at the west end of Colorado Avenue, Santa Monica Boulevard, Wilshire Boulevard, Montana Avenue, and San Vicente Boulevard. Park along the oceanfront park in an available metered parking space. Parking may also be available on the Santa Monica Pier at the end of Colorado Avenue.

**Hiking directions:** Begin the hike by strolling along the bluffs on the parallel paths, enjoying the vistas, people, and landscaping. From the south end of the park—at Colorado Avenue—bear right and head out onto the Santa Monica Pier. To return, descend steps on the north side of the pier, and follow the paved boardwalk 400 yards to the bridge crossing over the PCH. Cross the bridge and climb the eroding cliffs on brick steps, reentering Palisades Park by the historic cannon.

To continue along the coast from the Santa Monica Pier, hike south on the Santa Monica Beach Promenade (Hike 117). ■

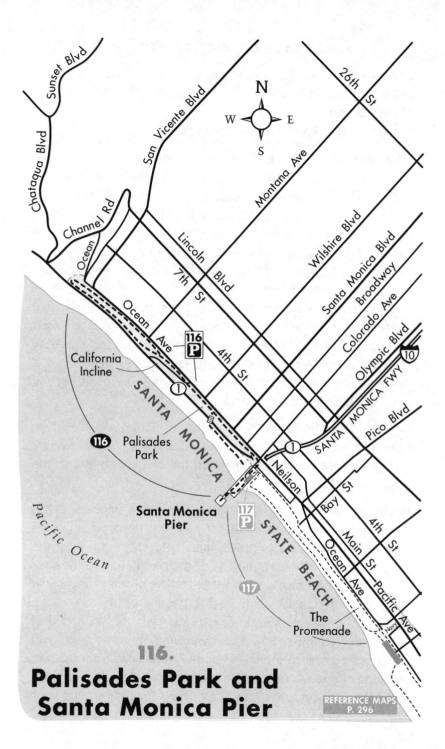

# 116.
# Palisades Park and
# Santa Monica Pier

# 117. Santa Monica Pier to Venice Beach

**Hiking distance:** 2.5 miles round trip
**Hiking time:** 1.5 hours
**Elevation gain:** Level
**Maps:** U.S.G.S. Beverly Hills and Venice

**Summary of hike:** The Santa Monica Pier sits beneath sandstone bluffs at the foot of Colorado Avenue in downtown Santa Monica. The landmark pier dates back to the early 1900s as a privately owned amusement center. It is still an amusement park, with an historic turn-of-the-century carousel, a ferris wheel, arcades, souvenir shops, food vendors, and pier fishing. Stairways from the north, south, and east sides of the pier descend onto Santa Monica State Beach.

Santa Monica State Beach is a broad stretch of white sand that stretches 3 miles from Chautauqua Boulevard to Venice Beach. Along the backside of the beach are a bicycle trail and a walking path. The South Bay Bicycle Trail extends over 20 miles, from Will Rogers State Beach south to Redondo Beach (Hike 122) at the base of Palos Verdes.

**Driving directions:** From downtown Santa Monica, take Colorado Avenue west to Ocean Avenue. Cross Ocean Avenue onto the Santa Monica Pier. Park on the pier in the lots to the left.

**Hiking directions:** Before hiking the Santa Monica Beach Promenade, walk out on the pier past the ferris wheel, roller coaster, bumper cars, arcades, and curio shops to view the ocean and coastline from the end of the pier. Return to the parking lot, and descend the wood steps to the promenade. Follow the wide, paved path south (right), passing old historic buildings and the original Muscle Beach. Just past the west end of Pico Boulevard at Bay Street, the walking path curves right and continues parallel to the biking path. At 1.2 miles from the pier, the promenade connects with Ocean Front Walk at the north end of the Venice Beach Boardwalk. This is the turn-around spot.

Return by retracing your route, or walk to the shoreline and return along the water.

For extended hiking, continue south through Venice Beach (Hike 118) or north through Palisades Park (Hike 116). ▪

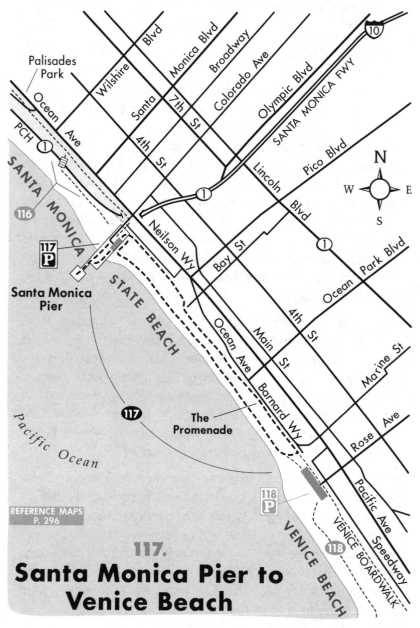

## 117.
# Santa Monica Pier to Venice Beach

# 118. Venice Beach

**Hiking distance:** 3 miles round trip
**Hiking time:** 2 hours
**Elevation gain:** Level
**Maps:** U.S.G.S. Venice

map
page 304

**Summary of hike:** Venice Beach is a unique wedge of Los Angeles between Ocean Park (in Santa Monica) and the Marina Del Rey Harbor Channel. The famous Venice Beach Boardwalk is on Ocean Front Walk, an asphalt walkway that runs parallel to the back end of the wide, sandy beach. It extends south from Navy Street to the Venice Pier at the foot of Washington Boulevard. The 1.5-mile promenade, built in 1905, is lined with beachfront businesses, cafes, hawkers, vendors, bodybuilders, musicians, comedians, artists, jugglers, fortune-tellers, dancers, drunks, hiking book publishers, panhandlers, spectators, and a vast array of other unique characters. The calm of the ocean is only steps away from the endless parade of people. Winding through the sand between the boardwalk and the water is the 20-mile South Bay Bicycle Trail.

**Driving directions:** Venice Beach can be accessed from numerous east–west streets, including Washington Boulevard, Venice Boulevard, Windward Avenue, and Rose Avenue. This hike begins from the north end of Venice Beach off of Rose Avenue.

From the Santa Monica (10) Freeway in Santa Monica, exit on Lincoln Boulevard. Head 1.4 miles south to Rose Avenue. Turn right and follow Rose Avenue 0.9 miles into the Venice Beach oceanfront parking lot. A parking fee is required.

**Hiking directions:** From the north end of Venice Beach, walk south along the boardwalk, passing cafes and beautiful old brick buildings. Stroll through the parade of humanity, marveling at the diverse circus. At 1 mile is the Venice Pavilion and outdoor roller skating area on the right. To the left is Windward Avenue, show-casing massive murals and charming Italian-style buildings with colonnades, dating back to 1905. Just past Windward Avenue are paddle tennis courts, basketball courts, and an outdoor weight-lifting arena known as Muscle Beach (named after the historical Muscle Beach south of the Santa Monica Pier). The active, theatrical portion of the boardwalk ends at 1.5 miles by Venice Pier, a 1,100-foot pier at the west end of Washington Boulevard. This is the turn-around spot. Return along the boardwalk or go to the shoreline and return along the ocean.

To extend the hike, continue south to the mouth of the Marina Del Rey Harbor Channel 1.1 miles ahead (Hike 120), north along Ocean Front Walk (Hike 117), or 2 blocks inland to the Venice Canals (Hike 119). ▪

## 119. The Venice Canals

**Hiking distance:** 1 mile or more
**Hiking time:** Variable
**Elevation gain:** Level
**Maps:** U.S.G.S. Venice
       City of Venice map

map
page 305

**Summary of hike:** The Venice Canals are located between Venice Boulevard and Washington Boulevard, two blocks inland from Venice Beach. In 1904, Abbott Kinney purchased 160 acres of coastal marshland, part of the Ballona Creek wetlands, to develop a new cultural center. He dreamed of and developed "Venice in America," a seaside resort recreating the canals of Venice, Italy. The area was embellished with lagoons, arched Venetian-style bridges, gondolas imported from Italy, and a network of 16 interconnected canals. What remains are six interwoven water canals flowing through a charming seaside community with landscaped walkways, diverse architecture, and 14 bridges. Canoes, paddle boats, and ducks grace the waterways, adding to an enchanting and unique experience.

**Driving directions:** From the San Diego Freeway / Interstate 405 in Culver City, take the Washington Boulevard exit, and drive 3.5 miles west towards the ocean to Dell Avenue.

The Venice Canals are located near the Pacific Coast between Washington Boulevard and Venice Boulevard, two blocks east of Pacific Avenue, which parallels the ocean. Dell Avenue crosses over the canals via four arched bridges. Park on Dell Avenue anywhere along the residential street.

**Hiking directions:** Walking paths border the canals on each side. Fourteen bridges span the canals, connecting all the walkways. Choose your

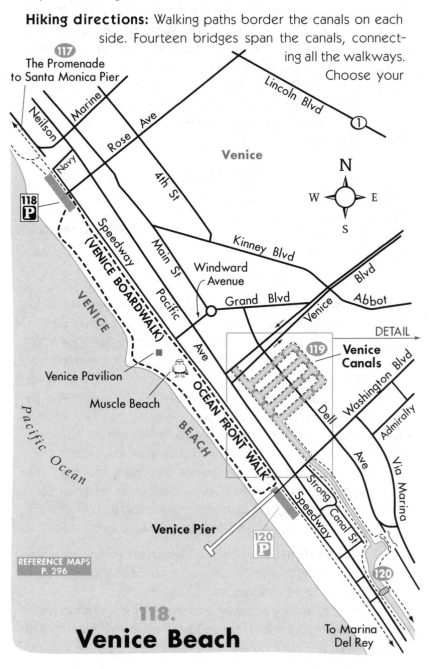

own path. The Grand Canal continues south across Washington Boulevard a little over one mile to the Marina Del Rey harbor channel (Hike 120)

One block west of the Grand Canal is Venice Beach and the Venice Boardwalk. The boardwalk parallels the oceanfront, from Washington Boulevard for 2.5 miles north to the Santa Monica Pier (Hike 118). ■

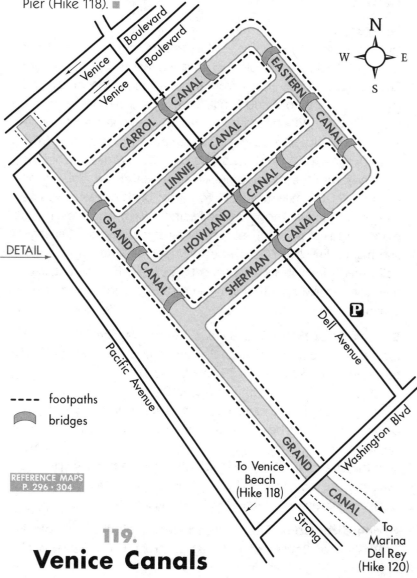

---- footpaths

🌉 bridges

REFERENCE MAPS
P. 296 · 304

119.
**Venice Canals**

# 120. Ballona Lagoon Marine Preserve
## GRAND CANAL to MARINA DEL REY HARBOR CHANNEL

**Hiking distance:** 2.4-mile loop
**Hiking time:** 1.5 hours
**Elevation gain:** Level
**Maps:** U.S.G.S. Venice

map
page 309

**Summary of hike:** The Ballona Lagoon Marine Preserve is a 16.3-acre natural saltwater estuary between Hurricane Street (south of Washington Boulevard) and the Marina Del Rey Harbor Channel, one block inland from Venice Beach. The ocean-fed lagoon connects to Grand Canal, the main channel of the Venice Canals (Hike 119). Ballona Lagoon was originally part of the once-extensive 1,700-acre Ballona Creek wetlands, extending from Playa Del Rey to Santa Monica. The lagoon was cut off from the wetlands with the development of Marina Del Rey. The lagoon is on the 2,000-mile migratory route for birds between Alaska and Latin America, known as the Pacific Flyway. The preserve is a protected habitat for hundreds of birds, native plants, animals, and marine life. It is one of the last tidal wetlands in southern California, with high and low tides twice daily. This route utilizes natural and paved paths, making a loop on the north side of the channel.

**Driving directions:** The Ballona Lagoon Marine Preserve is located between Washington Boulevard and the north side of the Marina Del Rey Harbor Channel, one block east of Pacific Avenue in Venice. From the 405 (San Diego) Freeway, take the Washington Boulevard exit, and drive 3.5 miles west towards the ocean. The trail can be accessed from several locations. This hike begins on the 300 block of Washington Boulevard. Park alongside the street or on the side streets where a parking space is available. At the west end of Washington Boulevard, 2 blocks past the lagoon, is an oceanfront parking lot for a fee.

**Hiking directions:** The trailhead begins on the 300 block of Washington Boulevard, just east of Strong Drive. Head south along the east bank of the Grand Canal on the narrow footpath. Under a canopy of lush foliage, the natural path changes to a paved path between the canal and homes. At 0.4 miles, near the end of the path, curve left to Via Dolce. Cross over the wetlands on the bridge to the right. Take the rail-fenced walkway to the right, and enter the Ballona Lagoon Marine Preserve.

Continue southeast through the preserve. Pass a cement bridge over the lagoon that leads to Pacific Avenue by Lighthouse Street. At the far south end of the path, just before Via Marina by the harbor channel, a boardwalk leads to an observation deck with interpretive panels about the preserve. Across Via Marina is Austin Park, a narrow, landscaped park fronting the north edge of the Marina Del Rey Harbor Channel that is a great place to view boats entering and leaving the marina. Continue to the right along the sidewalk on the west side of the street to Topsail Street. Cross the street to the dirt path along the lagoon, passing the Lighthouse Street Bridge to Jib Street. Curve right, leaving Pacific Avenue while staying close to the lagoon. A paved path follows the west bank of Grand Canal and returns parallel to Strong Drive back to Washington Boulevard. ∎

# 121. Del Rey Lagoon and Ballona Creek

**Hiking distance:** 2.8 miles round trip
**Hiking time:** 1.5 hours
**Elevation gain:** Level
**Maps:** U.S.G.S. Venice

map
page 309

**Summary of hike:** The Del Rey Lagoon in Playa Del Rey, near the Marina Del Rey Harbor Channel, is tucked between the north end of Dockweiler Beach and Ballona Creek. The 13-acre lagoon is surrounded by a grassy park with geese and ducks. It is a remnant of the original 1,700-acre Ballona Creek wetlands, stretching from Playa Del Rey to Santa Monica. Ballona Creek borders the south edge of the harbor channel and heads 9 miles inland through Culver City to the north side of the Santa Monica Freeway.

This hike begins at Del Rey Lagoon and follows Ballona Creek seaward to the mouth of the harbor and inland along the creek. A section of the path follows the boulder levee that forms the south side of the harbor channel, utilizing a paved walking and biking path over the boulders.

**Driving directions:** From the south side of Marina Del Rey at the intersection of Lincoln Boulevard and Culver Boulevard in Marina Del Rey, head 1.5 miles southwest on Culver Boulevard (towards the ocean) to Vista Del Mar at a traffic light. Stay to the right on Culver Boulevard 2 blocks to Pacific Avenue. Turn right and drive 0.4 miles to the vehicle-restricted bridge at 62nd Avenue. Park along the road where a space is available.

From the 405 (San Diego) Freeway in Culver City, take the Culver Boulevard exit and head 2.25 miles southwest (towards the ocean) to Lincoln Boulevard. Proceed with the directions above.

**Hiking directions:** Walk into Del Rey Lagoon Park, and stroll through the grassy park along the lagoon. Return to Pacific Avenue and head north. Cross the vehicle-restricted bridge over Ballona Creek to the walking and biking path on the levee separating Ballona Creek from the Marina Del Rey Harbor Channel. The left fork follows the paved, built-on-boulders path between the two waterways. The path leads beyond the shoreline to the end of the harbor channel, a great spot for observing boats coming in and out of the harbor. Use caution and good judgment if venturing west across the cemented boulders along the last 100 yards.

Return and follow the levee inland. At a half mile past the bridge, the harbor channel curves north, away from Ballona Creek and the hiking/biking path. Continue along the paved path, or take the dirt trail to the north of the paved trail. A short distance ahead, a path curves left to Fisherman's Village, a tourist area resembling a New England seaport town with shops, galleries, and boat docks. This is the turn-around spot.

To hike farther, continue on the main trail along Ballona Creek, reaching the Lincoln Boulevard underpass 0.8 miles ahead. ∎

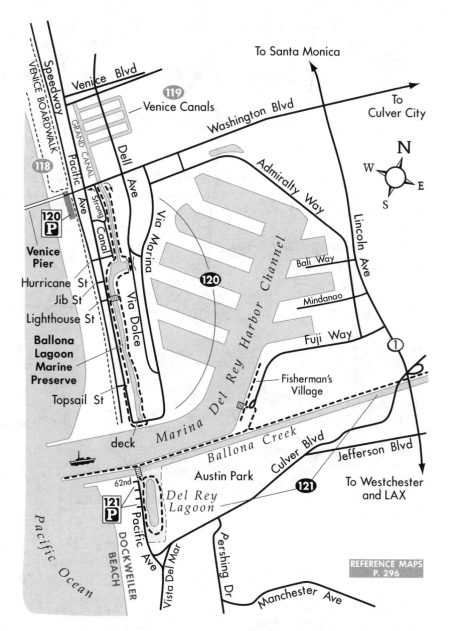

# Marina Del Rey

**120.** Ballona Lagoon Marine Preserve

**121.** Del Rey Lagoon and Ballona Creek

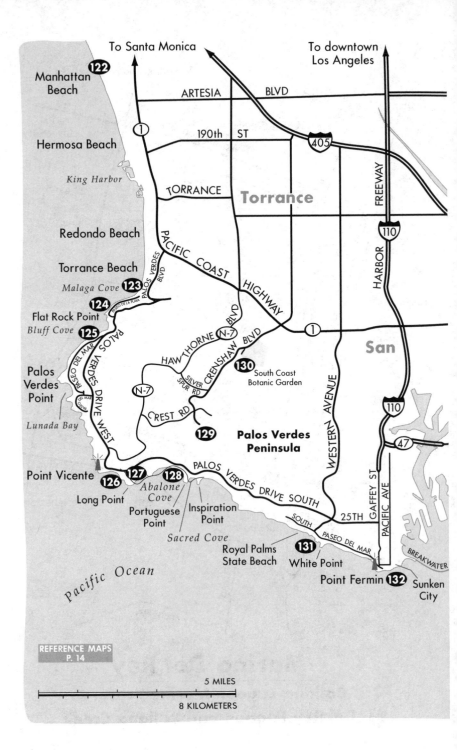

To Santa Monica

To downtown
Los Angeles

**122** Manhattan Beach

ARTESIA BLVD

1

190th ST

405

Hermosa Beach

*King Harbor*

TORRANCE

**Torrance**

FREEWAY

Redondo Beach

PACIFIC COAST HIGHWAY

110

Torrance Beach

*Malaga Cove* **123**

PALOS VERDES BLVD

HARBOR

**124**

PASEO DE LA PLAZA

Flat Rock Point

*Bluff Cove* **125**

N-7

HAWTHORNE BLVD

1

**San**

Palos Verdes Point

PASEO DEL MAR

PALOS VERDES DRIVE WEST

SILVER SPUR RD

CRENSHAW BLVD

**130** South Coast Botanic Garden

*Lunada Bay*

N-7

CREST RD

**129**

**Palos Verdes Peninsula**

WESTERN AVENUE

110

47

Point Vicente **126** **127** **128**

Long Point

*Abalone Cove*

PALOS VERDES DRIVE SOUTH

GAFFEY ST

PACIFIC AVE

Portuguese Point

Inspiration Point

*Sacred Cove*

SOUTH

25TH

PASEO DEL MAR

BREAKWATER

Royal Palms State Beach

**131**

White Point

Point Fermin **132** Sunken City

*Pacific Ocean*

REFERENCE MAPS P. 14

5 MILES

8 KILOMETERS

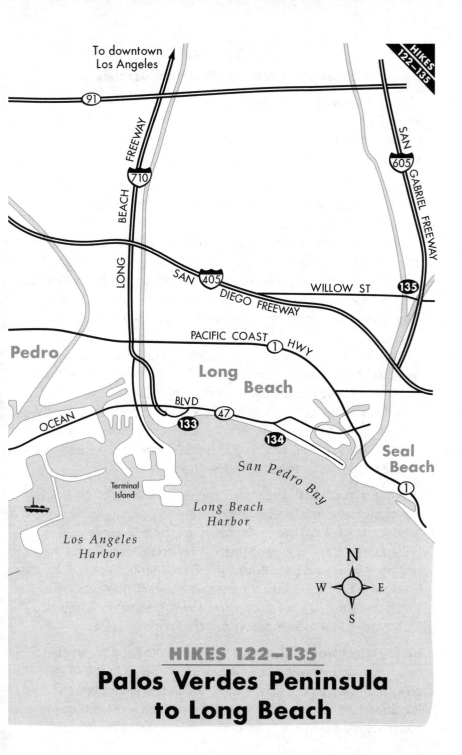

To downtown
Los Angeles

91

FREEWAY

BEACH

710

LONG

SAN GABRIEL FREEWAY

605

SAN

SAN
405
DIEGO FREEWAY

WILLOW ST

135

PACIFIC COAST 1 HWY

**Pedro**

**Long**
**Beach**

BLVD

OCEAN

47

133

134

**Seal**
**Beach**

1

Terminal
Island

*San Pedro Bay*

*Long Beach*
*Harbor*

*Los Angeles*
*Harbor*

N
W E
S

**HIKES 122—135**

# Palos Verdes Peninsula
# to Long Beach

# 122. The Strand
## Manhattan • Hermosa • Redondo Beaches

**Hiking distance:** 6 miles round trip
**Hiking time:** 3 hours
**Elevation gain:** Level
**Maps:** U.S.G.S. Redondo Beach and Venice

**Summary of hike:** Manhattan, Hermosa, and Redondo Beaches are strung together along the southern end of Santa Monica Bay in the area known as South Bay. They are laid-back, quintessential southern California beaches with clean, broad, white sand beaches, popular for surfing, swimming, fishing, volleyball, and hanging out. The three well-maintained beach communities have piers, which are surrounded by quaint shops and outdoor cafes. They have grown together, yet have retained their own distinct characters.

This hike follows The Strand, a paved pedestrian boardwalk lining the back end of the beaches. The boardwalk links the three towns and is used by walkers, joggers, and skaters. The Strand connects to an aquarium, parks, and three beach piers with shops and restaurants. The towns are also linked by the South Bay Bicycle Trail, which stretches 20 miles from Will Rogers State Beach to its terminus at Redondo Beach.

**Driving directions:** The three beaches can be accessed from numerous routes off the San Diego Freeway, including Rosecrans Avenue, Manhattan Beach Boulevard, Artesia Boulevard, and 190th Street. This hike begins by the Manhattan Beach Pier at the end of Manhattan Beach Boulevard. From the 405 (San Diego) Freeway in Lawndale, take the Manhattan Beach Boulevard exit, and drive 2.8 miles west to downtown Manhattan Beach at Ocean Drive. Park in an available metered parking space.

**Hiking directions:** Walk out on the 900-foot Manhattan Beach Pier, and view the coastline from offshore. At the rounded end of the pier is a small marine lab and aquarium. Return to The Strand on the low bluffs atop the seawall and head south, passing numerous pedestrian-only walking streets that connect the residential streets to The Strand. Below are the biking trail, volleyball courts, sandy beach, and the ocean. In less than a half mile, cross into Hermosa Beach. Continue past beachfront homes and apartments to the 900-foot-long Hermosa Beach Pier at the foot of Pier Avenue. Pier Avenue is lined with outdoor restaurants and interesting shops. Continue south to King Harbor at 2.3 miles, where the beach ends. Walk inland to Harbor Drive at Herondo Street. Follow the sidewalk to the right on Harbor Drive, passing King Harbor to the end of the road at a parking structure. Descend to the right to the walking path, and meander through horseshoe-shaped Redondo Beach Pier amid shops and restaurants. At the south end of the pier, the path leads into Veterans Park, our turn-around spot. Return by retracing your steps. ∎

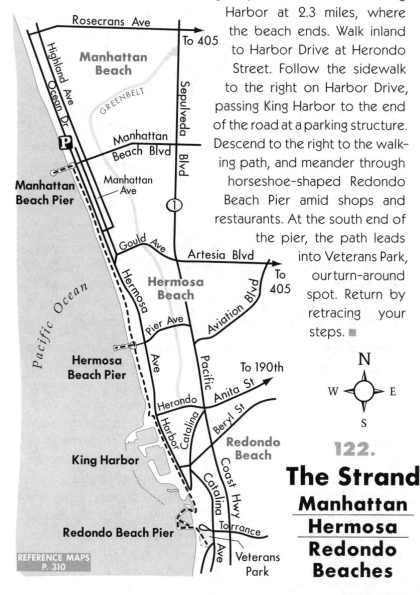

## 122.
# The Strand
## Manhattan
## Hermosa
## Redondo
## Beaches

# 123. Malaga Cove and Flat Rock Point

**Hiking distance:** 4 miles round trip
**Hiking time:** 2 hours
**Elevation gain:** 300 feet
**Maps:** U.S.G.S. Redondo Beach

**Summary of hike:** Malaga Cove and Flat Rock Point are at the north end of the Palos Verdes Peninsula. Malaga Canyon, formed by a major water drainage, slices through the northern slopes of the peninsula and empties into the ocean at Malaga Cove. Flat Rock Point borders the north end of Bluff Cove under soaring 300-foot cliffs. The point has some of the best tide-pools in the area. This hike begins on sandy Torrance County Beach and quickly reaches the rocky tidepools and near-vertical cliffs at Malaga Cove. The trail continues along the rugged, rocky shoreline along the base of the eroded cliffs to Flat Rock Point. For extended hiking, Hikes 123—125 are adjacent to each other with connecting trails.

**Driving directions:** From the Pacific Coast Highway/Highway 1 at the south end of Redondo Beach, turn south on Palos Verdes Boulevard. Drive 1.1 mile to Paseo De La Playa and turn right. Continue 0.7 miles to Torrance County Beach. Park in the lot on the left. A parking fee is required seasonally.

**Hiking directions:** Take the ramp down from the bluffs to the sandy beach. Head south (left), strolling on the sand to-wards the Palos Verdes cliffs. The views extend out to Palos Verdes Point (Hike 124). At 0.7 miles, the sand gives way to rock at the foot of the cliffs. Curve west and follow the wide walking path into Malaga Cove. Just before reaching the Palos Verdes Beach Club, a paved access path—our return route—follows stream-fed Malaga Canyon up an easy grade to the bluffs at Via Corta and Paseo Del Mar. Continue along the shoreline beneath the steep cliffs on the rounded shoreline rocks, passing Malaga Cove and the beach club. The shoreline reaches Flat Rock Point and the tidepools at 1.7 miles. From the point, cross over the rocky ridge into Bluff Cove. Curve into the crescent-shaped cove to an access trail. Hike 124 continues along the shoreline.

To return, ascend the cliffs on the wide, easy path for a quarter mile to the bluffs on Paseo Del Mar. Follow Paseo Del Mar to the left a half mile to Via Arroyo. Walk through the intersection into the parking lot on Via Arroyo, on the ocean side of Malaga Cove School. Pick up the paved Malaga Canyon Trail on the left, and descend through the canyon to the ocean, completing the loop. Return to Torrance Beach on the right. ■

To Redondo Beach

Pacific Coast Hwy

Calle Miramar

Palos Verdes Boulevard

123 P

TORRANCE COUNTY BEACH

Paseo de la Playa

N

W E

S

Pacific Ocean

Malaga Cove

MALAGA

Palos Verdes Drive North

Via Corta

Paseo Del Mar

Via Media

Via Almar

Via Arroyo

CANYON

124 P

Flat Rock Point

Palos Verdes Drive West

PALOS VERDES CLIFFS

Bluff Cove

124

REFERENCE MAPS
P. 310

Paseo Del Mar

125 P

To San Pedro

**123.**
# Malaga Cove
# Flat Rock Cove

# 124. Bluff Cove to Lunada Bay

**Hiking distance:** 6 miles round trip
**Hiking time:** 3 hours
**Elevation gain:** 300 feet
**Maps:** U.S.G.S. Redondo Beach

**Summary of hike:** Bluff Cove and Lunada Bay are both crescent-shaped rocky beach pockets resting beneath sheer, terraced cliffs. They are popular with surfers and tidepoolers. The path begins at Flat Rock Point and leads down to the rocky Bluff Cove. The jagged shore, lined with cliffs, passes numerous smaller coves as it winds to horseshoe-shaped Lunada Bay. This bay is bounded by Palos Verdes Point (also known as Rocky Point) and Resort Point. In 1961, a Greek freighter named *Dominator*, en route from Vancouver, Canada, to the Los Angeles Harbor, ran aground in thick fog just north of Rocky Point. Watch for the rusted remnants of the abandoned ship.

**Driving directions:** From the Pacific Coast Highway/ Highway 1 at the south end of Redondo Beach, turn south on Palos Verdes Boulevard. Drive 1.5 miles and curve to the right onto Palos Verdes Drive West to the first stop sign. Turn right on Via Corta. Drive 0.4 miles and turn right on Via Arroyo. Drive one block to Paseo Del Mar. Turn left and continue 0.5 miles to a distinct path on a left bend in the road. Surfers' vehicles are often parked along this bend.

**Hiking directions:** Take the wide path down the cliffs on an easy, tapered grade overlooking the rock formations at Flat Rock Point. At the north end of Bluff Cove, a steep side path descends to the tidepools at Flat Rock Point. The main trail curves left into the rocky beach at crescent-shaped Bluff Cove. Slowly follow the shoreline southwest, walking over the eroded boulders under the 300-foot bluffs. As you approach Rocky Point, watch for scattered remains of the *Dominator*. Follow the point into Lunada Bay. As you circle the bay, watch for a steep path ascending the cliffs, just before Agua Amarga Canyon. Carefully climb up the eroded cliffs to the grassy open space atop the bluffs. If you prefer to continue hiking along the shoreline, follow Lunada Bay around Resort Point into a small pocket cove. Another precipitous trail ascends the cliffs to the open space on the bluffs. Return along the bluffs following Paseo Del Mar and Palos Verdes Drive northbound. ■

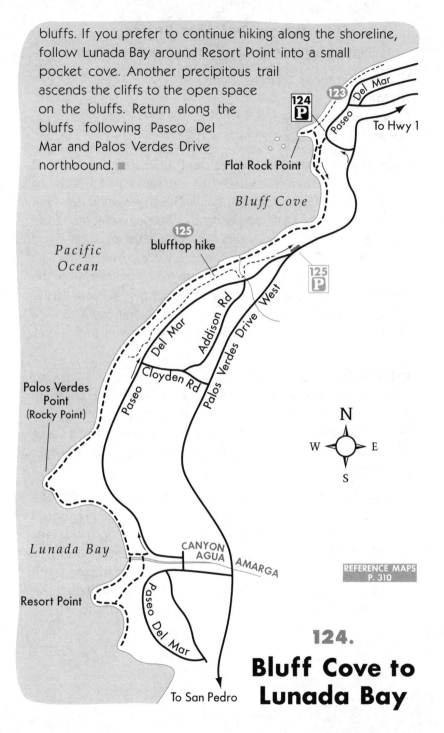

## 124.
# Bluff Cove to Lunada Bay

# 125. Paseo Del Mar Bluffs
## PALOS VERDES ESTATES SHORELINE PRESERVE

**Hiking distance:** 1.3 miles round trip
**Hiking time:** 45 minutes
**Elevation gain:** Level
**Maps:** U.S.G.S. Redondo Beach

**Summary of hike:** The Palos Verdes Estates Shoreline Preserve is a 130-acre undeveloped stretch of land running 4.5 miles along the southwest coast of the peninsula. The city-owned preserve includes scalloped blufftop parklands, footpaths that lead from the overlooks to the rocky shore, plus the adjacent submerged offshore land. This hike follows the grassy oceanfront bluffs high above Bluff Cove (Hike 124), parallel to Paseo Del Mar. From the cliff's edge are incredible views of Bluff Cove, Catalina Island, the Channel Islands, and the beach cities along Santa Monica Bay to Point Dume. It is also a great area to view migrating gray whales.

**Driving directions:** From the Pacific Coast Highway/Highway 1 at the south end of Redondo Beach, turn south on Palos Verdes Boulevard. Drive 1.5 miles and curve to the right onto Palos Verdes Drive West to the first stop sign at Via Corta. Continue straight ahead for 1.7 miles to a parking lot on the right, just before the Paseo Del Mar turnoff.

**Hiking directions:** Take the grassy blufftop path from the south end of Bluff Cove. The parkland parallels the crenelated cliffs bordered by Paseo Del Mar. The level, cliff-top trail leaves the edge of the cliffs and curves inland, looping around a stream-carved gorge before returning to the cliffs. The meandering path ends at a row of palm trees adjacent to an oceanfront residence across from Cloyden Road. Return along the same route. ■

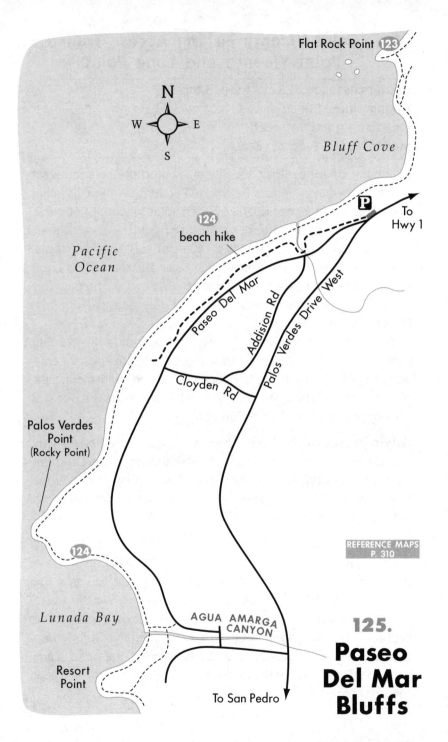

Flat Rock Point 123

Bluff Cove

N
W · E
S

P

To
Hwy 1

124
beach hike

Pacific
Ocean

Paseo Del Mar

Addision Rd

Palos Verdes Drive West

Cloyden Rd

Palos Verdes
Point
(Rocky Point)

124

Lunada Bay

AGUA AMARGA
CANYON

Resort
Point

To San Pedro

REFERENCE MAPS
P. 310

**125.**
# Paseo
# Del Mar
# Bluffs

# 126. Point Vicente Fishing Access Trail to Point Vicente and Long Point

**Hiking distance:** 1.5 miles round trip
**Hiking time:** 1 hour
**Elevation gain:** 140 feet
**Maps:** U.S.G.S. Redondo Beach

**Summary of hike:** Point Vicente is situated on the southwest point of the Palos Verdes Peninsula. Perched on the cliffs high above the shore is the historic 67-foot Point Vicente Lighthouse, built in 1926. The lighthouse warned ships of the rocky shoals in the Catalina Channel. From the 140-foot scalloped bluffs are vistas of the lighthouse, Santa Catalina Island, and Long Point, the former site of Marineland on the southeast end of the bay. This is a premier spot to observe migrating gray whales from mid-December through March.

The Point Vicente Fishing Access Trail descends the eroding cliffs to the rounded cobblestone beach beneath Point Vicente and Long Point, where the tidepools are teeming with marine life. The crescent-shaped bay with large offshore rocks is a popular site for scuba divers, surfers, and anglers.

**Driving directions:** From the Pacific Coast Highway (Highway 1) at the south end of Torrance, take Hawthorne Boulevard south 7.3 miles to its terminus at the coast. Turn left on Palos Verdes Drive South, and drive 0.8 miles to the posted fishing access. Park in the lot on the right.

**Hiking directions:** Walk to the west (upper) end of the parking lot. Take the well-defined dirt path, just beyond the restrooms. Descend the cliffs on an easy grade towards the prominent Point Vicente Lighthouse. Halfway down the slope, switchback left, dropping down to the rocky cobblestone shoreline. The beach pocket is bordered on the west by steep cliffs and a natural rock jetty. On the south end, the beach ends near Long Point, where the cliffs drop 100 feet into the sea near the offshore rock outcroppings. ■

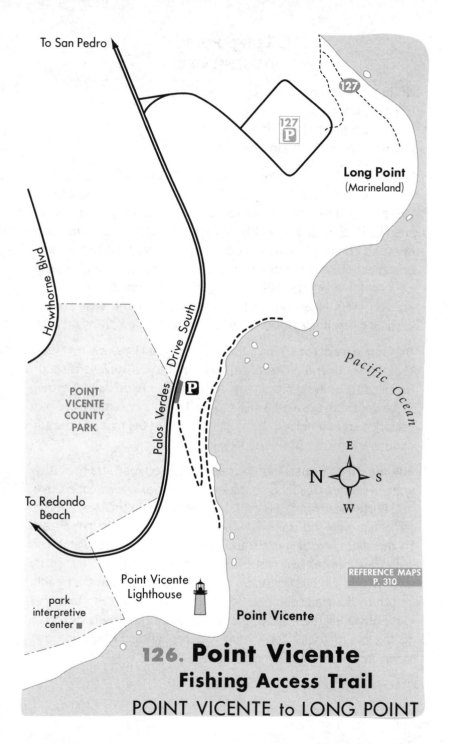

To San Pedro

127
P

127

**Long Point**
(Marineland)

Hawthorne Blvd

Palos Verdes Drive South

P

POINT
VICENTE
COUNTY
PARK

*Pacific Ocean*

To Redondo
Beach

E
N — S
W

REFERENCE MAPS
P. 310

Point Vicente
Lighthouse

park
interpretive
center ■

**Point Vicente**

**126. Point Vicente**
**Fishing Access Trail**
POINT VICENTE to LONG POINT

# 127. Long Point
## (MARINELAND)

**Hiking distance:** 1 mile round trip
**Hiking time:** 45 minutes
**Elevation gain:** 100 feet
**Maps:** U.S.G.S. Redondo Beach

**Summary of hike:** Long Point extends seaward at the southwest point of the Palos Verdes Peninsula. Marineland, a defunct 108-acre marine amusement park, was situated on the bluffs atop Long Point from 1954 to 1987. It closed due to its remoteness and competition from modern aquatic parks and aquariums. Beach access is still permitted from the enormous Marineland parking lot atop the 100-foot bluffs. The trail descends the eroded cliffs to an isolated beach pocket at the base of the vertical cliffs. It is a popular snorkeling and scuba diving area.

**Driving directions:** From the Pacific Coast Highway (Highway 1) at the south end of Torrance, take Hawthorne Boulevard south 7.3 miles to its terminus at the coast. Turn left on Palos Verdes Drive South, and drive 1.3 miles to the Long Point turnoff, the old entrance to Marineland. Turn right and drive 0.4 miles to the far southwest corner of the parking lot.

**Hiking directions:** Take the partially paved road/trail past the vehicle barrier. Descend to the east, overlooking Abalone Cove and Portuguese Point (Hike 128). Halfway down the descent is a large flat area and trail split. The road continues straight ahead to the sheer, eroding cliffs and rocky beach pocket. Watch for a narrow, intermittent waterfall dropping 60 feet off the cliffs. After exploring the tidepools and rock formations at the beach, return to the trail split. Bear left, leaving the road, and take the dirt path along the edge of the 100-foot bluffs. Slowly descend to the tip of rocky Long Point, where pelicans often line the ridge. Return along the same route. ∎

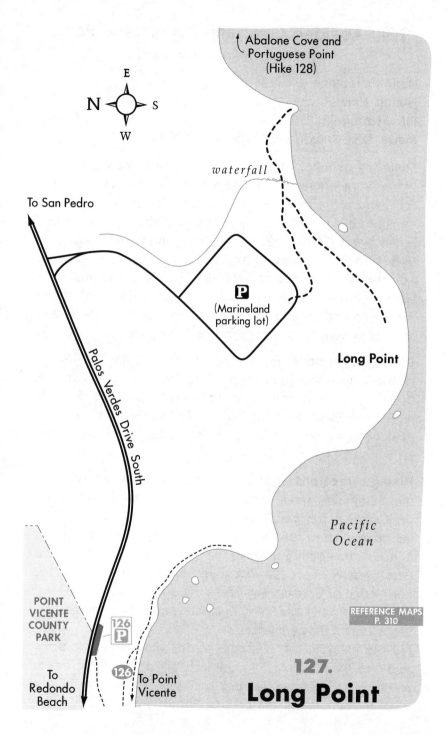

↑ Abalone Cove and
Portuguese Point
(Hike 128)

*waterfall*

**P**
(Marineland
parking lot)

**Long Point**

To San Pedro

Palos Verdes Drive South

*Pacific
Ocean*

REFERENCE MAPS
P. 310

POINT
VICENTE
COUNTY
PARK

126
**P**

126

To Point
Vicente

To
Redondo
Beach

**127.**
**Long Point**

# 128. Abalone Cove and Portuguese Point

## 5970 Palos Verdes Drive South

**Hiking distance:** 2 miles round trip
**Hiking time:** 1 hour
**Elevation gain:** 150 feet
**Maps:** U.S.G.S. Redondo Beach and San Pedro

**Summary of hike:** Abalone Cove Shoreline Park and Ecological Preserve is a federal reserve where grassy 180-foot bluffs easily access the rocky shoreline. The 80-acre preserve extends from Abalone Cove to Portuguese Point and Sacred Cove (also known as Smugglers Cove). Sacred Cove is bordered by tidepools at both points. From Portuguese Point are magnificent views of Abalone Cove, Long Point (Hike 127), Sacred Cove, Inspiration Point, White Point (Hike 131), Point Fermin (Hike 132), and Catalina Island. The oceanfront park sits at the foot of the unstable and actively slipping Portuguese Bend landslide area.

**Driving directions:** From the Pacific Coast Highway/ Highway 1 at the south end of Torrance, take Hawthorne Boulevard south 7.3 miles to its terminus at the coast. Turn left on Palos Verdes Drive South, and drive 2.2 miles to the posted Abalone Cove Shoreline Park entrance. Turn right and park in the lot. A parking fee is required.

**Hiking directions:** From the east end of the parking lot, cross the grassy picnic area onto a wide gravel path. Continue to a vehicle-restricted road. Bear left and wind up the hillside on the vehicle-restricted road to Palos Verdes Drive. Bear to the left on the narrow path, parallel to the highway, for 0.2 miles to the Portuguese Point access. Walk up the curving, gated road to the north edge of the peninsula and a trail split. First, take the left fork out to Portuguese Point, which stays atop the peninsula and loops around the perimeter.

After enjoying the awesome coastal views from the point, return to the trail split Take the left fork down to the beach and tidepools near an old rock enclosure. The trail to the left leads to the base of the cliffs at Portuguese Point. To return, follow the shoreline trail back along Abalone Cove for 0.4 miles to Upper Beach, a raised, man-made sandy beach and lifeguard station just above the rocky shore. Curve right and take the old paved road to a trail junction. The footpath to the left ascends the cliffs through the dense brush, back to the parking lot. ■

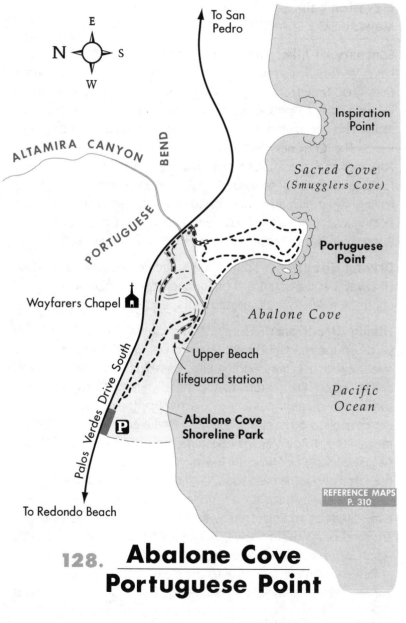

E
N ◇ S
W

To San Pedro

ALTAMIRA CANYON

BEND

Inspiration Point

Sacred Cove
(Smugglers Cove)

PORTUGUESE

Portuguese Point

Wayfarers Chapel

Abalone Cove

Upper Beach

lifeguard station

Pacific Ocean

Palos Verdes Drive South

P

Abalone Cove Shoreline Park

REFERENCE MAPS
P. 310

To Redondo Beach

128. **Abalone Cove Portuguese Point**

# 129. Crenshaw Extension Trail and Portuguese Bend Overlook

**Hiking distance:** 2.8 miles round trip
**Hiking time:** 1.5 hours
**Elevation gain:** 500 feet
**Maps:** U.S.G.S. Torrance

**Summary of hike:** This hike begins in Del Cerro Park in Rancho Palos Verdes, which sits atop the Palos Verdes Peninsula at more than 1,100 feet. From the park overlook are spectacular southern views of the 13 distinct marine terraces that make up the peninsula and the massive 270-acre landslide area of Portuguese Bend. The Crenshaw Extension Trail descends from Del Cerro Park into the precarious bowl-shaped canyon, still active with faults and shifting ground. A trail system winds through the rolling green hills and ancient wave-cut terraces to the shady Portuguese Bend Overlook, perched high above Portuguese Bend, Portuguese Point, and Inspiration Point (Hike 128).

**Driving directions:** From the Pacific Coast Highway/Highway 1 at the south end of Torrance, take Crenshaw Boulevard south 3.9 miles to the trailhead at the end of the road.

**Hiking directions:** Before starting down the trail, walk 30 yards up the road, and bear left into Del Cerro Park for a bird's-eye view of the surrounding hills, coastline, and the trails you are about to hike. Return to the metal trailhead gate, and take the unpaved road, passing a few hilltop homes. Descend into the unspoiled open space overlooking layers of rolling hills, the magnificent Palos Verdes coastline, and the island of Catalina. At just under a half mile is a 3-way trail split by a water tank on the left. Follow the main road, curving to the right a quarter mile to an unsigned footpath on the left. Detour left to the distinctive 950-foot knoll dotted with pine trees. From the overlook are sweeping coastal views, including Point Vicente, Portuguese Point, Inspiration Point, and Catalina Island.

Return from the overlook to the main trail. Continue downhill, curving left on a wide horseshoe bend. Just beyond the bend, a road veers off to the right, leading to Narcissa Drive. Twelve yards past this road split is a distinct footpath on the left. Leave the road and take this path through a forest of feathery sweet fennel plants. The path curves left, overlooking Portuguese Canyon. A switchback cuts back to the west and climbs the hillside to a ridge at a T-junction. The right fork follows the ridge uphill to the summit again, completing a loop on the pine covered knoll. Descend from the knoll to the main trail on the same route hiked earlier. Bear right, returning to the trailhead. ■

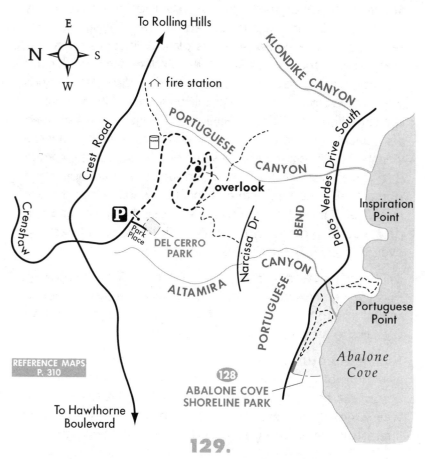

## 129.
# Crenshaw Extension Trail
# Portuguese Bend Overlook

# 130. South Coast Botanic Garden

26300 Crenshaw Boulevard · Palos Verdes Peninsula
Open daily 9 a.m.—5 p.m.

**Hiking distance:** 1—2 miles round trip
**Hiking time:** 2 hours
**Elevation gain:** 100 feet
**Maps:** U.S.G.S. Torrance
South Coast Botanic Garden map

**Summary of hike:** The South Coast Botanic Garden, owned by Los Angeles County, was developed on a sanitary landfill site in 1959. The 87-acre garden includes plant collections representing southern Africa, Australia, and the Mediterranean. Within this impressive garden is a rose garden with more than 1,600 hybrids that circle a large fountain, a children's garden with a miniature enchanted house, a gazebo, an arched bridge over a fish pond, a succulent and cactus garden, herb and vegetable gardens, a volunteers' garden, a water-wise garden, and a fuchsia garden. A large man-made lake with an island supports an abundant bird population. A canyon with a channel of water winds through riparian and marshland habitats, a woodland of pines and junipers, coastal redwoods, flowering fruit trees, palm trees, and over 50 species of eucalyptus trees.

**Driving directions:** From the Pacific Coast Highway/ Highway 1 at the south end of Torrance, take Crenshaw Boulevard south 1 mile to the posted turnoff on the left. Turn left and drive 0.2 miles to the parking lot. An entrance fee is required.

**Hiking directions:** Walk past the gift shop to a hub of trails at the top of the garden. A paved road/trail circles the perimeter of the botanic garden. Numerous unpaved roads and trails weave through the tiered landscape leading to the lake. Let your interests lead you through the gardens along your own route. ■

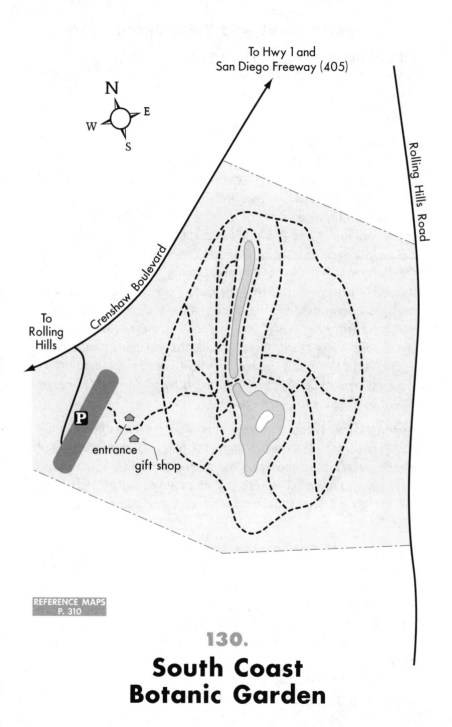

To Hwy 1 and
San Diego Freeway (405)

N
W E
S

Rolling Hills Road

Crenshaw Boulevard

To
Rolling
Hills

**P**

entrance

gift shop

REFERENCE MAPS
P. 310

**130.**

# South Coast
# Botanic Garden

# 131. White Point and Point Fermin Park

**Hiking distance:** 4 miles round trip
**Hiking time:** 2 hours
**Elevation gain:** 100 feet
**Maps:** U.S.G.S. San Pedro

**Summary of hike:** White Point in San Pedro was home to the Royal Palms Hotel, a booming spa resort with hot sulphur pools predating the 1920s. Falling victim to storms, pounding surf, and an earthquake in 1933, all that remain are majestic palms, garden terraces, and remnants of the concrete foundation. To the east of the point is White Point Beach, a rocky cove with tidepools below the sedimentary cliffs. Point Fermin Park, located at the southernmost point in Los Angeles County, sits atop grassy tree-shaded bluffs jutting prominently out to sea. The scenic 37-acre park has flower gardens, mature fig trees, and curving pathways that lead from the bluffs to the rocky shoreline. Point Fermin Lighthouse is an historic Victorian structure that sits on the edge of the vertical cliffs. It was built in 1874 with lumber and bricks shipped around Cape Horn. The lighthouse was in use for nearly a century (illustration on page 333).

**Driving directions:** From the intersection of Western Avenue and 25th Street in San Pedro, drive 0.5 miles south to the end of Western Avenue at the coastline. Curve left onto South Paseo Del Mar, and drive 0.1 mile to the White Point Bluff Park parking lot on the right. Park in the lot for a fee or alongside the road for free.

**Hiking directions:** Descend the cliffs on the dirt path or walk west down the paved road to Royal Palms Beach Park. Head east and follow the coastline around White Point, crossing over small boulders and slabs of rock. Stroll along the rocky shore of White Point Beach below the ruins of the Royal Palms Hotel. Continue following the shoreline past a group of old homes at the base of the sheer 120-foot cliffs. At 1.2 miles, take the distinct path on the left, and head up the cliffs to the west. Half way up, the path becomes paved. Wind through a palm tree grove and to the top of the bluffs across from Barbara Street, at the west end of Point Fermin Park. Continue east for one mile through the narrow tree-shaded park along the edge of the grassy bluffs to Point Fermin and the lighthouse. This is our turn-around spot. Return along the same path, or follow South Paseo Del Mar back to the trailhead. To extend the hike, continue through Sunken City (Hike 132). ■

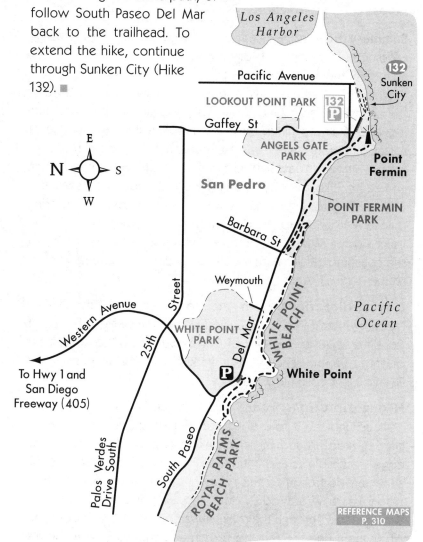

## 131. **White Point Point Fermin Park**

# 132. Sunken City

**Hiking distance:** 0.8 miles round trip
**Hiking time:** 1 hour
**Elevation gain:** 100
**Maps:** U.S.G.S. San Pedro

**Summary of hike:** Sunken City sits on six acres of slipping, eroding, and sinking land adjacent to Point Fermin Park. The "city," at the southernmost point in Los Angeles County, was once a neighborhood of exclusive homes. Waves undercut the base of the sandstone and shale cliffs, which began slumping and sliding in 1929 and again in the early 1940s. It is now a jumble of rolling land with palm trees, isolated slabs of the old road, tilting sidewalks, streetcar tracks, remnants of house foundations, and sentry-like chimneys along the surf-swept rocky seashore. Several meandering paths weave through the bluffs. Exploring this surreal landscape is like entering the "twilight zone." The Point Fermin Marine Life Refuge follows a half-mile stretch of the coastline below. A few trails drop down the dramatic cliffs to the rocky shoreline and tidepools.

**Driving directions:** From the south end of the Harbor Freeway/Interstate 110 in San Pedro, take the Gaffey Street exit. Continue south to the end of Gaffey Street on the oceanfront bluffs at South Paseo Del Mar. Park straight ahead in the Point Fermin Park parking lot.

**Hiking directions:** At the east (left) end of the parking area, walk around the 3-foot concrete boundary used as a warning barrier. Step around the chainlink fence, and bear left to the edge of the bluffs and a junction. The right fork descends the sheer eroded cliffs to the rocky shoreline and bountiful tidepools. For now, stay to the left, choosing one of several paths that meander through the rolling maze of the old neighborhood. After exploring the tangled terrain and shoreline, visit the historic Point Fermin Lighthouse, built in 1874. ■

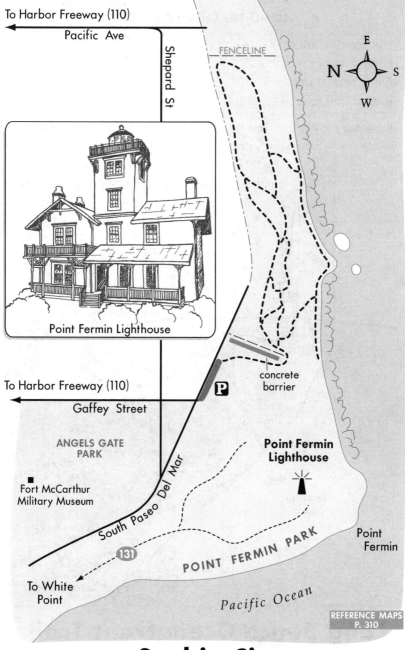

To Harbor Freeway (110)

Pacific Ave

Shepard St

FENCELINE

E
N ◈ S
W

Point Fermin Lighthouse

concrete
barrier

To Harbor Freeway (110)

**P**

Gaffey Street

ANGELS GATE
PARK

Point Fermin
Lighthouse

☀

■ Fort McCarthur
Military Museum

South Paseo Del Mar

131

POINT FERMIN PARK

Point
Fermin

To White
Point

Pacific Ocean

REFERENCE MAPS
P. 310

132. **Sunkin City**

# 133. Long Beach Oceanfront Trail
## LONG BEACH CITY BEACH

**Hiking distance:** 7 miles round trip
**Hiking time:** 3.5 hours
**Elevation gain:** Level
**Maps:** U.S.G.S. Long Beach

**Summary of hike:** The Long Beach Oceanfront Trail is a paved walking and biking path along the San Pedro Bay coastline in Long Beach. Long Beach is the southernmost coastal city in Los Angeles County. Long Beach City

# 133.
# Long Beach Oceanfront Trail
## LONG BEACH CITY BEACH

Beach, which fronts the path, extends four miles from the Long Beach Harbor to the Alamitos Peninsula and San Gabriel River on the Orange County line. This hike begins at the mouth of the Los Angeles River in Queensway Bay by Shoreline Village, a tourist attraction with shops and restaurants. The path follows the coastline along Long Beach City Beach to Belmont Pier. En route is Bluff Park, an elevated grassy park above the wide, sandy beach overlooking San Pedro Bay. Bluff Park backs the beach and runs parallel to Ocean Boulevard. Offshore from the beach and path are four artificial tropical islands with postcard-perfect fronts. They are actually landscaped oil drilling platforms.

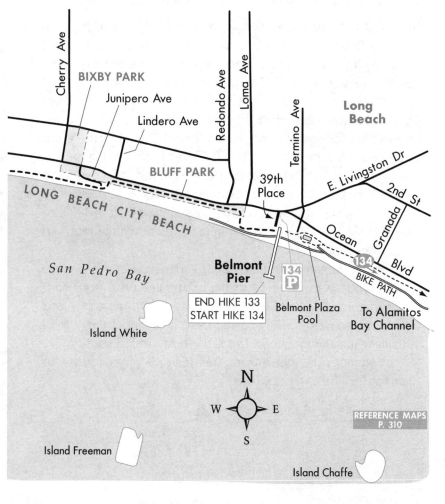

Belmont Pier—the destination for the hike—is a 1,600-foot T-shaped pier that bisects Long Beach City Beach. The pier was built in 1968 at the foot of 39th Place in Belmont Shore, a charming seaside community filled with shops and eateries. After Belmont Pier, the coastal path continues to Alamitos Bay—Hike 134.

**Driving directions:** From the 405 (San Diego) Freeway in Long Beach, take 710 (Long Beach Freeway) south to its end. Follow the Downtown Long Beach/Aquarium signs onto Shoreline Drive. Turn right and curve into the huge Long Beach Marina parking lot and park near Shoreline Village. A parking fee is required.

**Hiking directions:** Follow the paved walking and biking path along the Downtown Shoreline Marina to Shoreline Village. Curve left along the narrow, palm-lined breakwater in Queensway Bay. Pass the *Queen Mary*, an 81,000-ton luxury liner built in 1934 and retired after more than a thousand transatlantic voyages. Continue past several short fishing and overlook piers for a half mile to the breakwater's end, across from Island Grissom. Return to Shoreline Village and continue 0.5 miles east, passing the marina boat slips. The path curves away from the small marina to the back end of wide, sandy Long Beach City Beach. Continue east, curving past the historic lifeguard station built in 1938, to a parking lot where Junipero Avenue winds down the bluffs to the shoreline parking lot.

Climb up the stairs to grassy Bluff Park, just west of Lindero Avenue. Follow the tree-filled park 0.8 miles on the 40-foot bluffs to Loma Avenue. Descend the stairway to the beach and follow the coastline, rising to the base of Belmont Pier off of 39th Place in Belmont Shore. This is the turn-around spot.

To continue, the oceanfront trail leads 2 miles farther to Alamitos Peninsula—Hike 134. ■

# 134. Belmont Pier to Alamitos Bay Channel
## LONG BEACH CITY BEACH

**Hiking distance:** 4 miles round trip
**Hiking time:** 2 hours
**Elevation gain:** Level
**Maps:** U.S.G.S. Long Beach and Seal Beach

map
page 338

**Summary of hike:** Long Beach City Beach stretches over 4 miles, from Long Beach and the Alamitos Peninsula in Belmont Shore to the Alamitos Bay entrance channel at the Orange County border. This hike begins at Belmont Pier, a 1,620-foot-long T-shaped pier extending from the foot of 39th Place. The hike explores both shores of the narrow Alamitos Peninsula to the mouth of Alamitos Bay. The route follows the Seaside Walk, a wooden boardwalk, and Bay Shore Walk, a paved walkway, along the San Pedro Bay coastline. From Belmont Pier, the hike can be extended west on the Long Beach Oceanfront Trail—Hike 133.

**Driving directions:** From the Pacific Coast Highway (Highway 1) in Seal Beach, head north to 2nd Street in Long Beach. Turn left and drive 1.7 miles to Livingston Drive. Veer left and continue 0.4 miles to Termino Avenue. Turn left and drive 2 blocks into the beachfront parking lot on the east side of Belmont Pier, adjacent to the Belmont Plaza Olympic Pool.

**Hiking directions:** From Belmont Pier, head east on the paved boardwalk along either side of the Belmont Plaza Olympic Pool. Both routes merge a short distance ahead. A bike path also winds east through the wide sandy beach. At just over a half mile, pass a row of palm trees by Granada Avenue. Offshore, the scenic, tropical-looking islands with palm trees are actually disguised oil platforms.

At one mile, the paved bike path joins the walking path at the head of Alamitos Peninsula by 54th Place. Walk on the sandy strand to the Seaside Walk, a wooden boardwalk that begins at 55th Place. Continue 0.7 miles to the end of the oceanfront boardwalk at 69th Place. Return to the sand, reaching Alamitos Park and the Alamitos Bay Channel by 72nd Place. Walk to the right, passing the lifeguard station to the jetty. Atop the jetty, a rock-lined path, frequented by fisherman, extends out to sea. Return to the small grassy park. A paved path follows the edge of Alamitos Bay, ending at the marina. Return to Ocean Boulevard

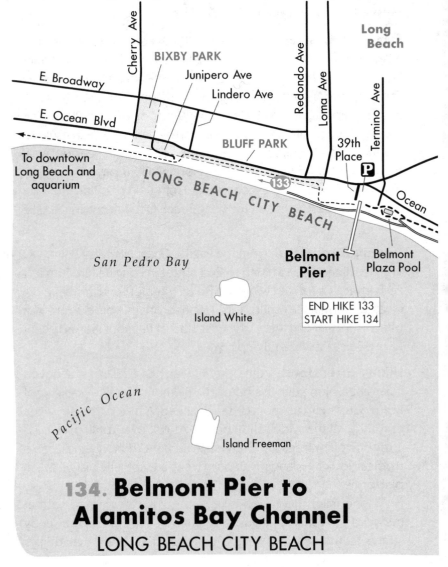

## 134. Belmont Pier to Alamitos Bay Channel
### LONG BEACH CITY BEACH

and walk west to 65th Place. At the north end of the street, pick up the Bay Shore Walk, a paved public walkway. Follow the path 0.4 miles along the bay to the end at 55th Place. Cross Ocean Boulevard, completing the loop. Retrace your steps to Belmont Pier. To extend your hike along the oceanfront, continue west to Bluff Park and the Long Beach Oceanfront Trail—Hike 133. ■

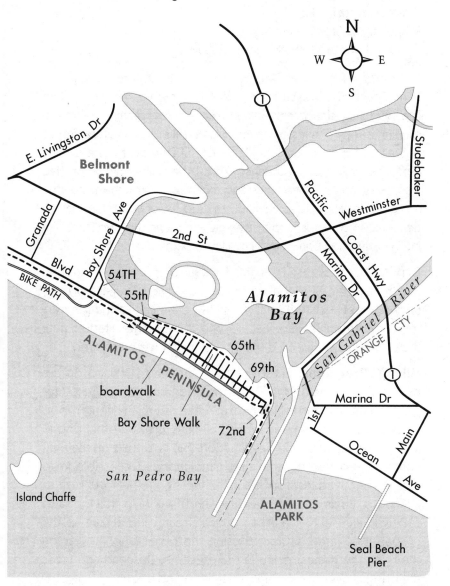

# 135. El Dorado Nature Center
## EL DORADO PARK
7550 E. Spring Street · Long Beach · Open Tues.–Sun.

**Hiking distance:** 2-mile loop
**Hiking time:** 1 hour
**Elevation gain:** Level
**Maps:** U.S.G.S. Los Alamitos
El Dorado Nature Center Trail Map

**Summary of hike:** El Dorado Park is a 450-acre parkland in Long Beach just west of the Los Angeles–Orange County line. The park includes fishing lakes, tree groves, picnic shelters, a petting zoo, 4.5 miles of paved biking trails, and a nature center. This hike loops through the 105-acre El Dorado Nature Center, a pastoral w on the southeast end of the park. An interpretive trail loops around two lakes and meanders through the sanctuary along rolling hills, tree-lined meadows, chaparral communities, oak woodlands, and a stream connecting the two lakes. An interpretive trail pamphlet is available at the museum.

**Driving directions:** From the 405 (San Diego) Freeway in Long Beach, take the Studebaker Road exit. Drive 1.4 miles north to Spring Street and turn right. Continue 0.8 miles to the park entrance on the right. Park just beyond the entrance station, near the posted trailhead on the right. A parking fee is required.

**Hiking directions:** Enter the lush, forested parkland on the paved path to the bridge. Cross the bridge to the nature center, perched on an island in North Lake. After visiting the center, loop clockwise to the backside of the buildings. Cross another bridge, leaving the island to a 3-way junction. The two trails on the right comprise a paved quarter-mile, handicapped-accessible loop. Take the unpaved left fork along the west edge of North Lake to a junction. Begin the One-Mile Trail and Two-Mile Trail loops to the right. Parallel North Lake's outlet stream, and zigzag up the chaparral-covered hillside, passing the observation tower on the right, the highest point in the preserve. Descend and cross the bridges over the stream two times. Wind through eucalyptus and oak groves, and cross another bridge over the stream to a junction. The One-Mile Trail continues to the left. Stay to the right on the Two-Mile Trail, and descend to the north shore of South Lake. Follow the west edge of the lake to the inlet stream. Cross a bridge and return to the south end of the lake. The meandering path returns to the north, completing the loop at North Lake. Return to the right. ■

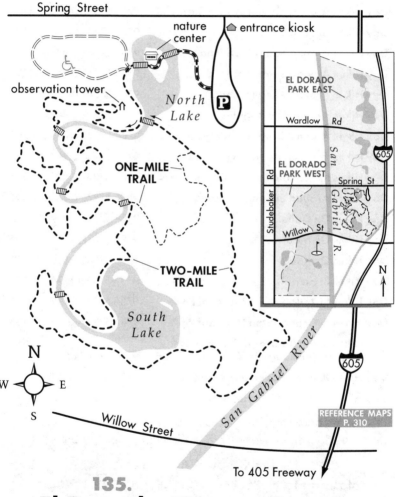

## 135.
# El Dorado Nature Center
## EL DORADO PARK

# DAY HIKE BOOKS

| | | |
|---|---|---|
| Day Hikes On the California Central Coast | 978-1-57342-058-7 | 17.95 |
| Day Hikes On the California Southern Coast | 978-1-57342-045-7 | 14.95 |
| Day Hikes Around Sonoma County | 978-1-57342-053-2 | 16.95 |
| Day Hikes Around Napa Valley | 978-1-57342-057-0 | 16.95 |
| Day Hikes Around Monterey and Carmel | 978-1-57342-036-5 | 14.95 |
| Day Hikes Around Big Sur | 978-1-57342-041-9 | 14.95 |
| Day Hikes Around San Luis Obispo | 978-1-57342-051-8 | 16.95 |
| Day Hikes Around Santa Barbara | 978-1-57342-060-0 | 17.95 |
| Day Hikes Around Ventura County | 978-1-57342-043-3 | 14.95 |
| Day Hikes Around Los Angeles | 978-1-57342-061-7 | 17.95 |
| Day Hikes Around Orange County | 978-1-57342-047-1 | 15.95 |
| Day Hikes In Yosemite National Park | 978-1-57342-059-4 | 13.95 |
| Day Hikes In Sequoia and Kings Canyon N.P. | 978-1-57342-030-3 | 12.95 |
| Day Hikes Around Sedona, Arizona | 978-1-57342-049-5 | 14.95 |
| Day Hikes On Oahu | 978-1-57342-038-9 | 11.95 |
| Day Hikes On Maui | 978-1-57342-039-6 | 11.95 |
| Day Hikes On Kauai | 978-1-57342-040-2 | 11.95 |
| Day Hikes In Hawaii | 978-1-57342-050-1 | 16.95 |
| Day Hikes In Yellowstone National Park | 978-1-57342-048-8 | 12.95 |
| Day Hikes In Grand Teton National Park | 978-1-57342-046-4 | 11.95 |
| Day Hikes In the Beartooth Mountains Billings to Red Lodge to Yellowstone N.P. | 978-1-57342-052-5 | 13.95 |
| Day Hikes Around Bozeman, Montana | 978-1-57342-054-9 | 13.95 |
| Day Hikes Around Missoula, Montana | 978-1-57342-032-7 | 13.95 |

# ay Hikes Around Orange County

Residents and travelers alike will find this book an essential guide to exploring Orange County. This southern California county is framed by the Pacific Coast on one side while the Santa Ana Mountains run along its backside, offering diverse landscape and scenery.

Despite the presence of the Orange County metropolis, nearly 30% of the county's acreage is parklands, wildlife sanctuaries, national forests, and wilderness preserves. These 106 day hikes provide access to the natural, undeveloped areas, offering hundreds of miles of hiking trails. Highlights include magnificent rock formations, bay-side coves, tidal estuaries, peninsulas, waterfalls, mountain-peak ridge walks, sculpted canyons, and sweeping views from the ocean to the cities.

256 pages • 106 hikes • 1st Edition 2005 • ISBN 978-1-57342-047-1

## Day Hikes Around Ventura County

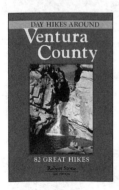

This guide includes 82 day hikes in this scenic coastal county just north of Los Angeles. Ventura County's unique topography spans from the Pacific Coast to the mountainous interior and the vast tracts of national forest land. The many communities that lie throughout the area have been thoughtfully integrated within the green space and undeveloped land. A network of hiking trails weaves throughout the countryside, across the open space, parks, forests, and mountain ranges that together form an ecological corridor. Included is an excellent cross-section of hikes, from relaxing beach strolls along the Pacific Ocean to mountain-top hikes with expansive views.

184 pages • 82 hikes • 2nd Edition 2003 • ISBN 978-1-57342-043-3

# Day Hikes On the California Southern Coast

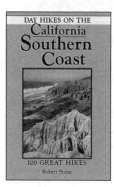

This guide is a collection of 100 great day hikes along 238 miles of southern California coastline, from Ventura County to the U.S.—Mexico border. The area has some of the most varied geography in the state...a blend of verdant canyons, arid bluffs, and sandy coastline.

Discover hundreds of miles of trails in scenic and undeveloped land, despite the expansive urban areas. Highlights include wide sand beaches, marine terraces, rocky headlands, tidal estuaries with coves and caves, sandstone cliffs, lighthouses, great locations for viewing wildlife, expansive dunes, forested canyons, waterfalls, thousands of acres of undeveloped public lands, and panoramic ocean-front overlooks.

224 pages • 100 hikes • 1st Edition 2004 • ISBN 978-1-57342-045-7

# Day Hikes On the California Central Coast

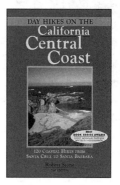

The Central California coast has some of the most spectacular scenery in the state. Rugged coastal terraces are backdropped by mountain ranges that run parallel to the Pacific coastline. Picturesque communities dot a landscape abundant with valleys, white sand beaches, cool forests, and natural preserves. The surf crashes onto craggy headlands and carved canyons along the Big Sur stretch of coast.

This guide includes 400 miles of coastline between San Francisco and Los Angeles. The hikes describe how and where to access the best trails and features from Highway 1, offering many opportunities to explore the beautiful landscape.

320 pages • 120 hikes • 2nd Edition 2009 • ISBN 978-1-57342-058-7

# INDEX

## A

Abalone Cove 324
Adventure Pass 11
Alamitos Peninsula/Bay 337
Amarillo Beach 108
Amir's Garden 214
architectural landmarks. *See historic sites*
Arroyo Seco 258, 264
Arroyo Sequit 33, 46, 52
Arroyo Sequit Park 52
astronomical observing site 52

## B

Backbone Trail 12, 32, 36, 66, 68, 157, 159
Baleen Wall 75, 76
Ballona Creek 307
Ballona Lagoon Marine Preserve 306
Bay Shore Walk 337
beach access 46, 56, 59, 108, 110, 298, 300, 312, 314, 316, 320, 322, 324, 330, 335, 337
Beacon Hill 208
Bee Rock 212
Belmont Pier 335, 337
Belmont Shore 336, 337
Berlin Forest 204
Big Sycamore Canyon 25, 30
Big Tujunga Canyon 250
Bird Sanctuary Nature Trail 206
bird watching 110, 112, 175, 206, 306, 322
Black Hill 248
Blinderman Trail 176
Bluff Cove 316, 318

Bluff Park 335
Boney Mountain 20, 27, 35
Boney Mountain State Wilderness 27
botanical sites/gardens 96, 100, 180, 202, 204, 210, 214, 220, 281, 298, 328
Bronson Caves 198
Brush Canyon 200
Buckhorn Canyon 254
Burkhart Trail 254

## C

Caballero Canyon 142
Calabasas Motorway 128, 129
Calabasas Peak 128
Canyon View Trail 35
Castro Crest corridor 68
Castro Peak Fire Lookout 282
Century Lake 120
Cerro Negro 248
Chantry Flat 288
Charlton Flat 252
Charmlee County Park 54
Cheeseboro Canyon 74, 78, 80
Cheeseboro/Palo Comado Canyons 72, 74, 76, 78, 80
Cheeseboro Ridge 80
Chicken Ridge 160
China Flat 72
Chumash Trail 20, 82
Circle X Ranch 33, 35, 36
Cold Creek Canyon 134
Cold Creek Canyon Preserve 134, 136
Cold Creek Preserve 128, 129
Cold Creek Valley Preserve 132

Coldwater Canyon Park 180
Cooks Canyon 241
Cooks Canyon Lookout 245
Coolidge Trail 208
Cooper Canyon Falls 254
Corral Canyon Park 106
Corral Sunshine Motorway 220
Corriganville Park 88
Crenshaw Extension Trail 326
Cross Mountain Park System 184

**D**

Dan Blocker State Beach 106
Danielson Ranch 32
Dante's View 204
Dawn Mine 274
Dead Horse Trail 144
Dearing Mountain Trail 183
Deer Valley Loop 102
Del Cerro Park 326
Del Rey Lagoon 307
Delta Flats 237
Deukmejian Wilderness Park 241, 245
Devil's Slide 92
Dirt Mulholland 140, 142, 162, 166
Dixie Canyon Park 170
Dockweiler Beach 307
dog parks 140, 190
Dry Canyon 104
Dume Cove 59
Dunsmore Canyon 245

**E**

Eagle Rock 145
East Canyon 218
East Topanga Fire Road 148
Eaton Canyon County Park 278, 281

Eaton Canyon Falls 278
Echo Mountain 261, 267
Edmund D. Edelman Park 138
El Dorado Park 340
El Matador State Beach 56
El Pescador State Beach 56
Escondido Canyon Natural Area 98
Escondido Falls 98

**F**

Fall Creek Falls 250
Fern Canyon Nature Trail 210
Fern Canyon Trail 208
Ferndell Park 202
filming sites 88, 116, 120, 175, 198
Fisherman's Village 308
Flat Rock Point 314, 316
Flynn, Errol 190
fossils 28, 129
Franklin Canyon Lake 175
Franklin Canyon Park 172, 175, 176
Fryman Canyon Overlook 183
Fryman Canyon Park 183, 184

**G**

Gabrielino National Recreation Trail 258, 264, 284, 288, 291
Getty View Trail 168
gold discovery sites/mines 221, 274
Gould Mesa Campground 264
Grand Canal 305, 306
gray whale observation 59, 318, 320
Griffith Park 12, 194, 196, 198, 200, 202, 204, 206, 208, 210, 212, 214
Griffith Park Observatory 202, 204
The Grotto 33
Grotto Trail 33

# H

Hahamongna Watershed Park 264
Haines Canyon 240
Henninger Flats 281
Hermit Falls 291
Hermosa Beach 312
historic sites 88, 91, 96, 102, 118, 157,
    166, 202, 221, 261, 267, 270, 281,
    284, 332
Hoegees Camp 288
Hollyridge Trail 196
Hollywood Hills 12
Hollywood Reservoir 192
Hollywood sign 196
Hope, Bob 106
Hummingbird Trail 84

# I

Inspiration Point 157
Iron Mountain 238

# K

Kinney, Abbott 303

# L

Laguna Peak 20, 23
La Jolla Peak 20, 23
La Jolla Valley 20, 23
La Piedra State Beach 56
Las Virgenes Canyon 80, 124
La Tuna Canyon Park 235
Le Mesnager Trail 245
Leo Carrillo State Park 44, 46, 48,
    50
Liberty Canyon 122, 124
lighthouses 320, 330, 332
Long Beach City Beach 334, 337
Long Beach Oceanfront Trail 334
Long Point 322

lookout towers 136, 248, 252, 281
Los Angeles Zoo (old) 212
Los Pinetos Trail 226
Los Robles Trail System 40, 41
Lower Beacon Trail 208
Lower Franklin Canyon Park 172
Lower Zuma Canyon 62, 64
Lunada Bay 316

# M

Malaga Cove 314
Malibu bluffs 56
Malibu Bluffs Recreation Area 108
Malibu Colony 110
Malibu Creek State Park 118, 120,
    122, 124
Malibu Lagoon State Beach 110
Malibu Pier 110
Malibu Point 110
Manhattan Beach 312
Marina Del Rey 306, 307
marinas 306, 334, 337
Marineland 322
Marvin Braude Mulholland
    Gateway Park 142
Mash set 120
Meyer Memorial State Beach 56
military outposts 166
Millard Canyon 270, 271, 276
Millard Falls 271, 276
Mineral Wells Picnic Area 214
Mishe Mokwa Trail 36
Monrovia Canyon Falls 293
Monrovia Canyon Park 293
Mountains Restoration Trust 134
Mount Bell 200
Mount Disappointment 261
Mount Hollywood 204

Mount Lee 196
Mount Lowe 261, 267, 270
Mount Lowe Railway 261, 267, 270
Mount Lukens 240, 241
Mount Markham 261
Mount Wilson 281, 284, 290
Mount Wilson Toll Road 281
Mugu Peak 20, 23
Mulholland Dam 192
Mulholland Scenic Overlook 166
Musch Trail 145
Muscle Beach 300, 303

## N

Newton Canyon 66, 68
Newton Canyon Falls 66
Nicholas Flat 48, 50
North Beach 46

## O

Ocean Front Walk 302
Ocean Vista 48
Old Boney Trail 27
Old Stagecoach Trail 91
Old Zoo Trail 212
Orcutt Ranch Horticulture Center 96
overlooks 25, 36, 48, 50, 54, 59, 86,
    102, 136, 145, 148, 150, 157, 159,
    166, 168, 202, 204, 208, 233, 245,
    248, 252, 261, 268, 281, 326

## P

Pacific Crest Trail 254
Palisades Park 298
Palo Comado Canyon 74
Palos Verdes Estates Shoreline
    Preserve 318
Palos Verdes Peninsula 13, 311
Palos Verdes Point 316
Paramount Ranch 116

Parker Mesa Overlook 148, 150
Paseo Del Mar Bluffs 318
Pepperdine University 108
Peter Strauss Ranch 112
petting zoo 340
Pine Mountain. *See Vetter Mountain*
Pirates Cove. *See Dume Cove*
Placerita Canyon State Park 221,
    222, 226
Placerita Falls 222
Pohl Overlook 183
Point Dume 59
Point Dume Natural Preserve 59
Point Dume State Beach 59
Point Fermin Lighthouse 330, 332
Point Fermin Marine Life Refuge 332
Point Fermin Park 330, 332
Point Mugu State Park 20, 23, 25,
    27, 30
Point Vicente 320
Point Vicente Lighthouse 320
Portuguese Bend 324, 326
Portuguese Bend Overlook 326
Portuguese Point 324
The Promenade 300
Puerco Beach 108

## Q

Queen Mary 336
Queensway Bay 335

## R

Reagan Ranch 118
Reagan, Ronald 118
Red Box Gap 264
Redondo Beach 312
Red Rock Canyon 129
Resort Point 316
Rice Canyon 218

Ridge Motorway 248
Rim of the Valley Trail 241
Rising Sun Trail 100
Robert H. Meyer Memorial State
    Beach 56
Roberts Camp 284
rock formations/caves 33, 36, 46,
    57, 76, 82, 84, 86, 91, 94, 120, 128,
    129, 132, 134, 148
Rock Pool 120
Rocky Oaks Park 70
Rocky Peak 86
Rocky Peak Park 82, 84, 86
Runyan Canyon Park 190
Rustic Canyon 159

**S**

Sacred Cove 324
Sage Ranch Park 94
Sam Merrill Trail 267
Sandstone Peak 36
San Gabriel Mountains 13, 216
San Pedro Bay 334, 337
San Rafael Hills 248
Santa Anita Canyon 284, 288, 291
Santa Clarita Woodlands Park 218
Santa Monica Bay 13
Santa Monica Beach Promenade
    300
Santa Monica Mountains 12
Santa Monica Pier 298, 300
Santa Monica State Beach 298,
    300
Santa Susana Stage Road 91
Santa Ynez Canyon 152
Santa Ynez Fire Road 145
Santa Ynez Waterfall 152

San Vicente Mountain Park 162, 166
Satwiwa Native American Indian
    Cultural Center 27, 32
Seaside Walk 337
Sepulveda Pass Open Space 168
Sequit Point 46
Sequit Ridge 44
Serrania Park 140
Shepherds' Flat 75, 76
Smugglers Cove. *See Sacred Cove*
Solstice Canyon 100, 102
Solstice Canyon Falls 100
Sostomo Trail 102
South Bay Bicycle Trail 300, 302,
    312
South Beach 46
South Coast Botanic Garden 328
Split Rock 36
Stough Canyon 230
Stough Canyon Motorway 230
The Strand 312
Sturtevant Falls 284
Sugarloaf Peak 116
Sullivan Canyon 160
Sullivan Ridge 162
Summit Valley 138
Sunken City 332
Sunset Ridge 274
Sunset Ridge Trail 270
surfing beaches 110, 312, 316, 320
Surfrider Beach 110
Switzer Falls 258
Sycamore Canyon 27
Sycamore Canyon Campground
    26, 30
Sycamore Canyon Falls 27

## T

Talepop Trail 124
Temescal Canyon 154
Temescal Gateway Park 154
Thomas Guide 11
tidepools 59, 314, 316, 320, 322, 324, 330
Topanga Fire Lookout 136
Topanga Overlook. *See Parker Mesa Overlook*
Topanga State Park 142, 144, 145, 148, 150, 152, 154
Torrance Beach 315
Trail Canyon Falls 237
TreePeople Park 180, 183
trees (unique) 96, 122
trekkies 198
Trippet Ranch 144, 145, 148
Triunfo Canyon Trail 41
Tropical Terrace 100, 102

## U

Upper Franklin Canyon Park 175, 176
Upper Zuma Canyon 66

## V

Venice Beach 302
Venice Beach Boardwalk 302
Venice Canals 303
Venice Pier 302
Verdugo Motorway 230, 235
Verdugo Mountains 13, 230, 232, 235, 248
Verdugo Peak 233
Vetter Lookout 252
Vetter Mountain 252
vista points. *See overlooks*

## W

Walker Ranch Campground 221, 222, 226
Wardens Grove 232
waterfalls 23, 27, 33, 52, 66, 98, 100, 104, 152, 222, 237, 250, 254, 258, 271, 276, 278, 284, 291, 293
Waterman Mountain 254
Weldon Canyon Motorway 218
Western Town 116
Westridge Fire Road 162
White City 267
White Horse Canyon Trail 40
White Point 330
White Point Beach 330
Wilacre Park 180
wildlife sanctuary 340
Wildwood Canyon Park 232
Willow Creek 48
Will Rogers State Historic Park 157, 159
Wilson Canyon Saddle 226
Winter Creek 288
Woodland Hills 140

## Y

Yellow Hill Trail 44

## Z

Zuma/Trancas Canyons 62, 64, 66, 68

LINDA STONE

## About the Author

Since 1991, Robert Stone has been writer, photographer, and publisher of Day Hike Books. He is a Los Angeles Times Best Selling Author and an award-winning journalist of Rocky Mountain Outdoor Writers and Photographers, the Outdoor Writers Association of California, and the Northwest Outdoor Writers Association. He is also an active member of the Bay Area Travel Writers.

Robert has hiked every trail in the Day Hike Book series. With 23 hiking guides in the series, many in their fourth and fifth editions, he has hiked thousands of miles of trails throughout the western United States and Hawaii. When Robert is not hiking, he researches, writes, and maps the hikes before returning to the trails. He spends summers in the Rocky Mountains of Montana and winters on the California Central Coast.